Besalú

MARTÍ GIRONELL ✤ JORDI PUIG

TRIANGLE ▼ POSTALS

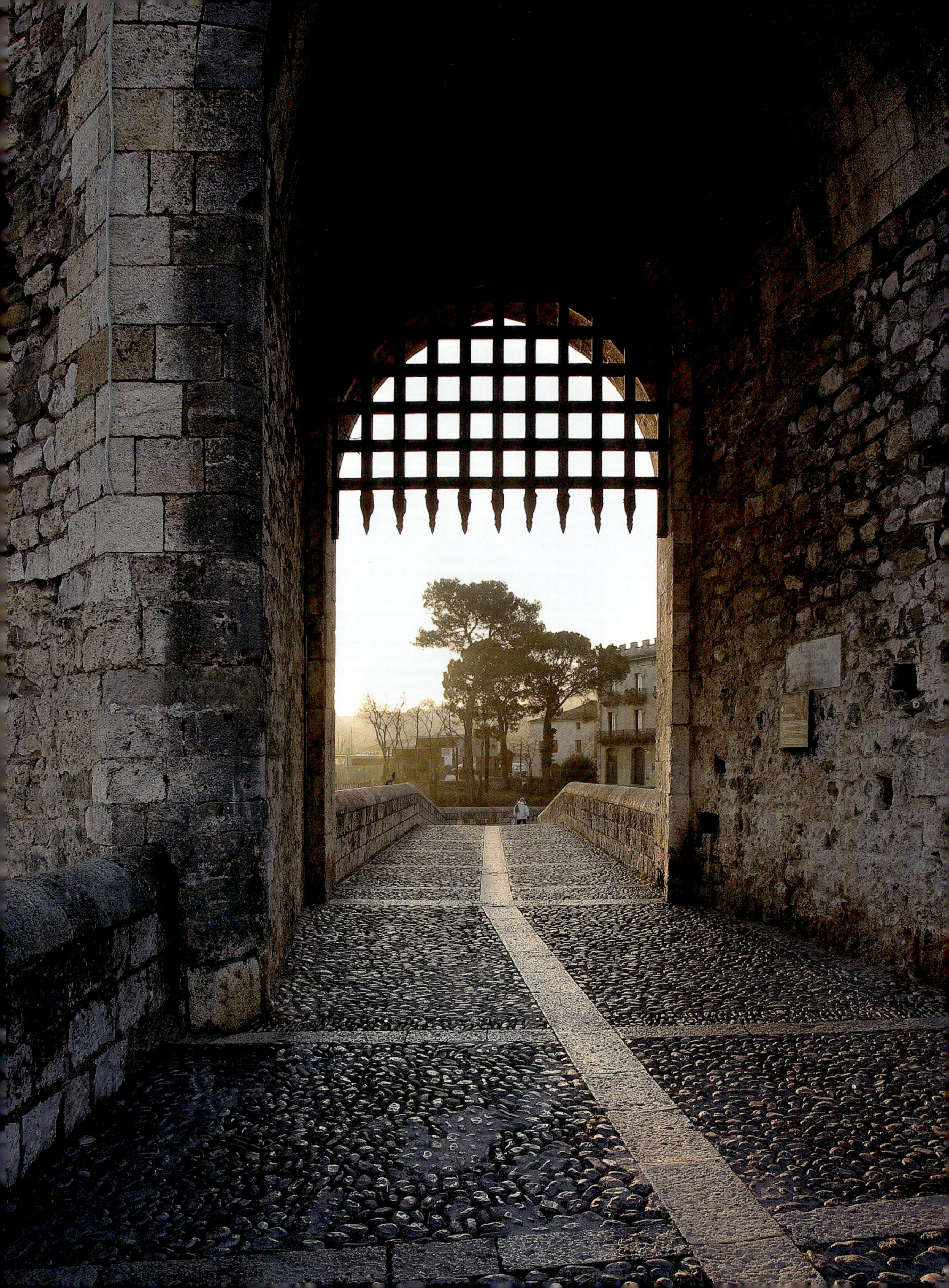

Besalú

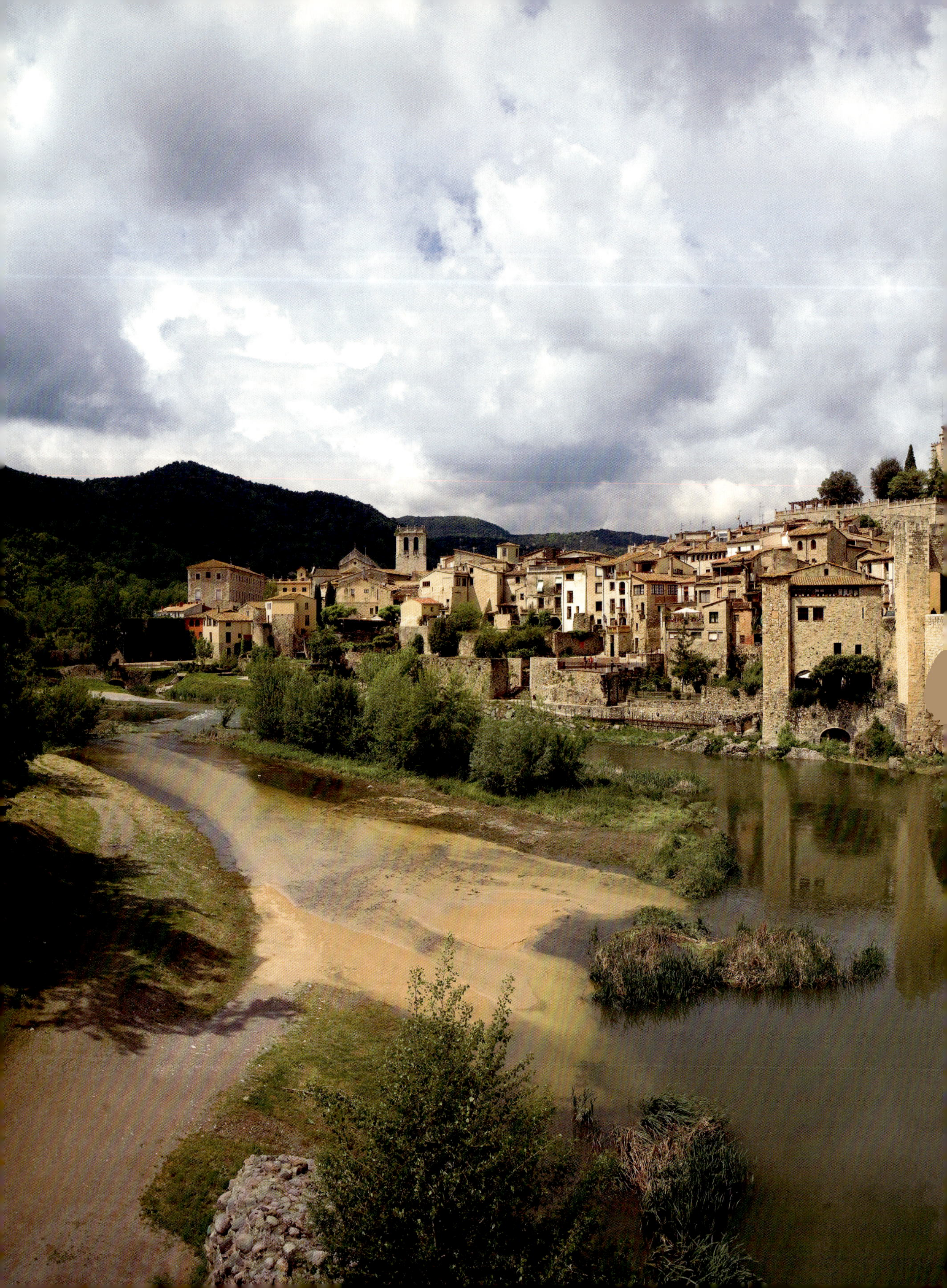

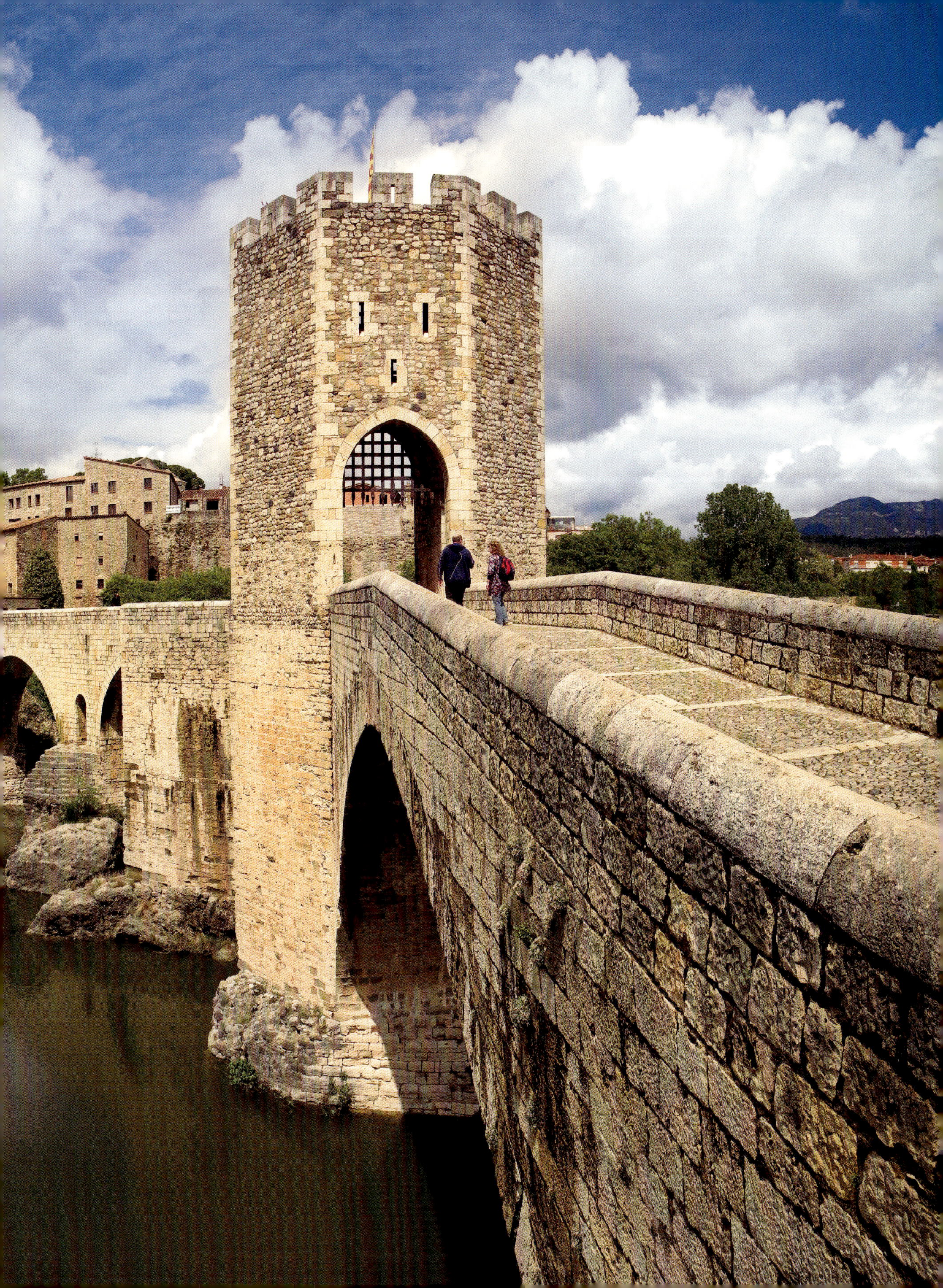

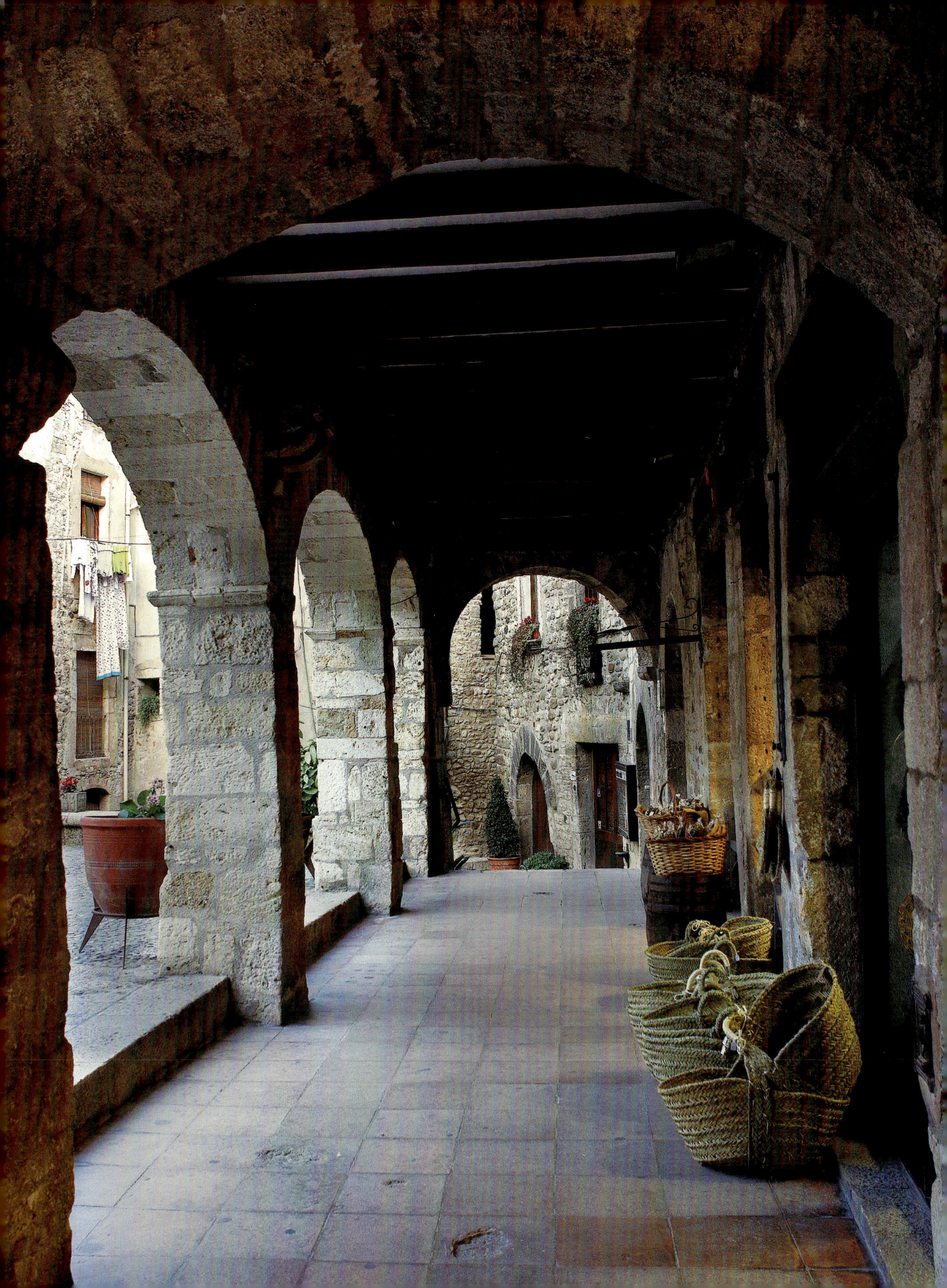

Experience the history and heritage

MARTÍ GIRONELL GAMERO

Besalú is my home, and speaking about one's home is always difficult, because apart from the sentimental value that it already has in itself, one feels really comfortable at home. The only way of making someone understand why one is so much in love with the place they live, is to invite them there and show them all the corners so that they can get a first-hand idea for themselves. I often say —because I believe it to be true— that the best way for someone to understand some specific events and circumstances is to tell them in a way that, to our speaker, they have the same effect on them as experiencing them and seeing them in the first person, out on the street. You have to experience it from the front line of life, in other words, you must apply yourselves so that you are soaked with daily life. You must submerge it into the nervous fabric that makes this town vibrate. I wish that, taking a walk through a year in the life of this Besalú, will be enough for you to capture the charm of a community with thousands of years of history.

What characterises a region, a land, is the harmonious conjunction between the landscape and the people who inhabit it. That the setting determines the character is the gospel truth. If this equation works, then the integrity of this land is guaranteed, and it will also be sufficiently prepared to integrate everything that reaches it, for good and for bad. A setting that shapes the way of being of people who work for their land, to make their towns big and place them on the map. People who, despite the shortages with which they can coexist, know how to make the most of what is around them. People deeply-rooted in the land, who go out of their way to explain why you should not skip a single one of the corners that conceal its Iberian, Jewish and earl-ruled past. An amalgam of cultures that has seasoned a land so that it was fertile. A fertility that has been reflected in many spheres and which has had a bearing on the expansion of the town beyond the banks of the River Fluvià. In its origin, the town was situated at the foot of the hill where the castle was raised, from which emerged the streets that would later forge its personality. They say that the origins of Besalú are even more ancient. The remains of the Iberian settlement which were found in Can Ring testify to this. Moreover, perhaps the origins, the roots of this Besalú, began to be created on this point between La Garrotxa, Empordà and the Pla de l'Estany, by the inhabitants of a group of Neanderthal settlement who had settled in the spot of Can Racó.

I have always lived in the district of Can Camps and, due to its situation. I have always felt rather privileged because I have been able to look ahead and have a face-to-face dialogue with the noble and earl-ruled part, that which provided the founding of Besalú: the castle. Can Camps, also known as the group of houses of Mare de Déu del Mont, is situated just on the other side of the Capellades stream, the waters of which run in front of the count's castle of which, today, only the ruins of the old collegiate of Santa María remain. From Can Camps, there is a visual contact that makes direct dialogue possible with everything that represented the nucleus of power of the old county capital. Not only the *castrum* —the precinct where the count's castle was erected—, but also the old canonry, the Palau de la Moneda and other buildings. It does not require a great deal of imagination to transport yourself to the most outstanding times of its long history. Besalú began to forge its name when it acquired importance as the capital of an independent county after the death of Wilfred the Hairy. Years later, with the death without heir of Bernat III, it lost this status that it had been awarded since 920. Around 1000, towards the end of the Carolingian domination, Besalú

Plaça de la Llibertat

was one of the most important Catalan counties and embraced a territory that went from the valleys of Camprodon to the lands of Banyoles and Figueres; from the high basin of the River Ter, almost touching at the southeast the city of Girona, extending as far as the plain of Empordà. The boundaries reached as far as the limits of Vallespir and Fenollet. Today, however, that is now history and as someone said, "History only serves to understand the present and to face up to the future with guarantees". In any case, between you and me, the best way of knowing, understanding and enjoying Besalú, the historic and the contemporary, is to come and discover its idiosyncrasy, the peculiarities that make it unique.

Below, you will be witnesses to these traits that mark the pace of a town that, aware and proud of its past, looks ahead to carve out its future.

Besalú is one of the best-conserved Romanesque towns of Catalonia and one of the most attractive in the Spanish state. Not in vain, in 1966 it was declared a National Historic-Artistic Monument for its great architectural value. A stroll around its medieval streets enables one, among other things, to discover the secrets that the old county capital conceals. Walking around Besalú means experiencing a medieval adventure first hand, starting off on a journey through history and going back to a time full of splendour. In order to delve into this period, it will be enough to visit the key spots, unique spaces that will allow you to understand what the character of this city and its inhabitants was like at the beginning of the 11th century. The Plaça Major, the main square, with arcades that was and still is the nerve centre of Besalú, and which in former times housed the comings and goings of the market; the Jewish quarter, of narrow, winding streets, full of mystery and superstitions, which will lead you in a winding way towards the synagogue to be able to then go down to the baths of purification, the miqveh. And from here there is now a brief view of the originality of the bridge. The monastery of Sant Pere, the old hospital of Sant Julià, Can Llaudes, also known as Casa Cornellà, the castle of the count and the collegiate of Santa Maria, the church of Sant Vicenç...

It is a journey to a place that will not leave you indifferent. You do not need to be told, check for yourselves delving into any corner of the old centre. At the end of the route you will have walked, you will have more than enough elements to interpret and discover the secrets of the charm and heritage of Besalú. Depending on the path you choose, you will be able to experience one adventure or another, but you will always be within the domain of medieval Besalú, the most authentic. Now I will be able dig up the talk I gave when I worked as a tourist guide and, with the desire to earn a bit of cash, let's lose ourselves in the corners of the old quarter, from Carrer Rocafort, gateway to the Jewish quarter, to Carrer del Portalet, which comes out at the river. This is beside the orchards that were once kept by the Bemedictine monks of the monastery of Sant Pere, previously situated outside the city walls, something that contributed to the isolation and spiritual downturn. The only thing remaining of the monastery today is the cloister and the church, founded in 977 by the count-bishop Miró Bonfill and consecrated in 1003 by Count Tallaferro. After the sale of Church lands by Mendizábal, in 1835, the large Benedictine community abandoned the monastic site. Its majesty contrasts with the austerity that the travertine stone temple gives off. Despite this sobriety and simplicity, it has several attractions. Behind the main altar, and separated by eight columns, there is an apse aisle or ambulatory —of the few that are conserved—, which was the place where pilgrims passed in medieval times to venerate the relics of Saint Prim and Saint Felicia. Walking around the spot, it is well worth looking up towards the capitals where there are sculpted images from the Bible, such as the slaughter of the innocents ordered by King Herod, or the Three Kings of the Orient. Inside the church —in both the side and central naves— we also find the tombs of abbots and monks. Visitors, as well as the local people of Besalú, are always attracted by the skull and crossbones that preside over all the tombs as if it was the pirate flag. It could not be further from the truth. The head of the skeleton means that, faced with death, we are all equal, even the self-denying servants of God. For symbols, however, we must look at the large window of the façade: two lions, which represent the power and protection of the church. Beneath the lions is a monkey that would be the image of the man seeking the refuge of the church before an attack by the snake, the face of evil, crushed by the lion's paw. The message: if man wishes to be protected from evil, he must bow before the church.

The pilgrimage to the monastery of Sant Pere became so important in that time that the old hospital of Sant Julià in fact became the board and lodging of the pilgrim. Originally, it was a hostelry that was run by the monks of Sant Pere, and as it was the capital and a crossroads, became the resting spot of many globetrotters who stayed there, where they found the charity and hospitality that they were denied in other places. It did not have a healthcare function and neither did it administer actual cures, although it did have a hospital activity, in the strictest sense of the word. The hospital, under the protection of the monastery, sheltered and fed not only the devout pilgrims, but also poor men and women, vagabonds, abandoned children and other sick people and those who led an impoverished life. The clerics of the monastery of Sant Pere took it over and ran it. The centre was maintained, in part, thanks to the donations of many of the deceased who, in order to get to heaven quicker, had recorded it in their wills. We could imagine that, as the years passed, the charitable and generous soul of Sant Julià led to the space becoming a type of cultural container, in other words, it would also house all types of cultural occasions, whether the venue for a photographic or painting exhibition, or the stage for a theatrical work.

Just in front of Sant Pere, beside the small church of Santa Fe, now reconverted into a restaurant, in a corner of El Prat, is Casa Cornellà or Can Llaudes. It has two names because the first owners were the influential Cornellà family, in the medieval era, until in 1476, the Llaudes became the owners. It is one of the best-conserved civil Romanesque buildings —because normally all that is Romanesque is religious— in Catalonia. It was built at the end of the 12th century and the house is structured around a charming courtyard, which provides light to the whole space, worthy of the best Roman *domus*. To reach the noble part of the house there is a stone staircase that connects with an extraordinary gallery of semicircular arches. The granary, in the high part, and the stables, on the ground floor, complete a house that offers a curiosity that many people do not notice. When they enter, on the right, beside the dining rooms, they will see some authentic stone ledges, with some stone benches situated inside the window where the young maid and her mother or grandmother sat, who made sure through the grille nothing more than fine words passed between the couple in love. Leaving Can Llaudes, on the left, take Carrer del Forn and link up with Carrer Ganganell. Halfway along, on the right, you climb the street that leads you to the parish church of Sant Vicenç. You will be welcomed by its impos-

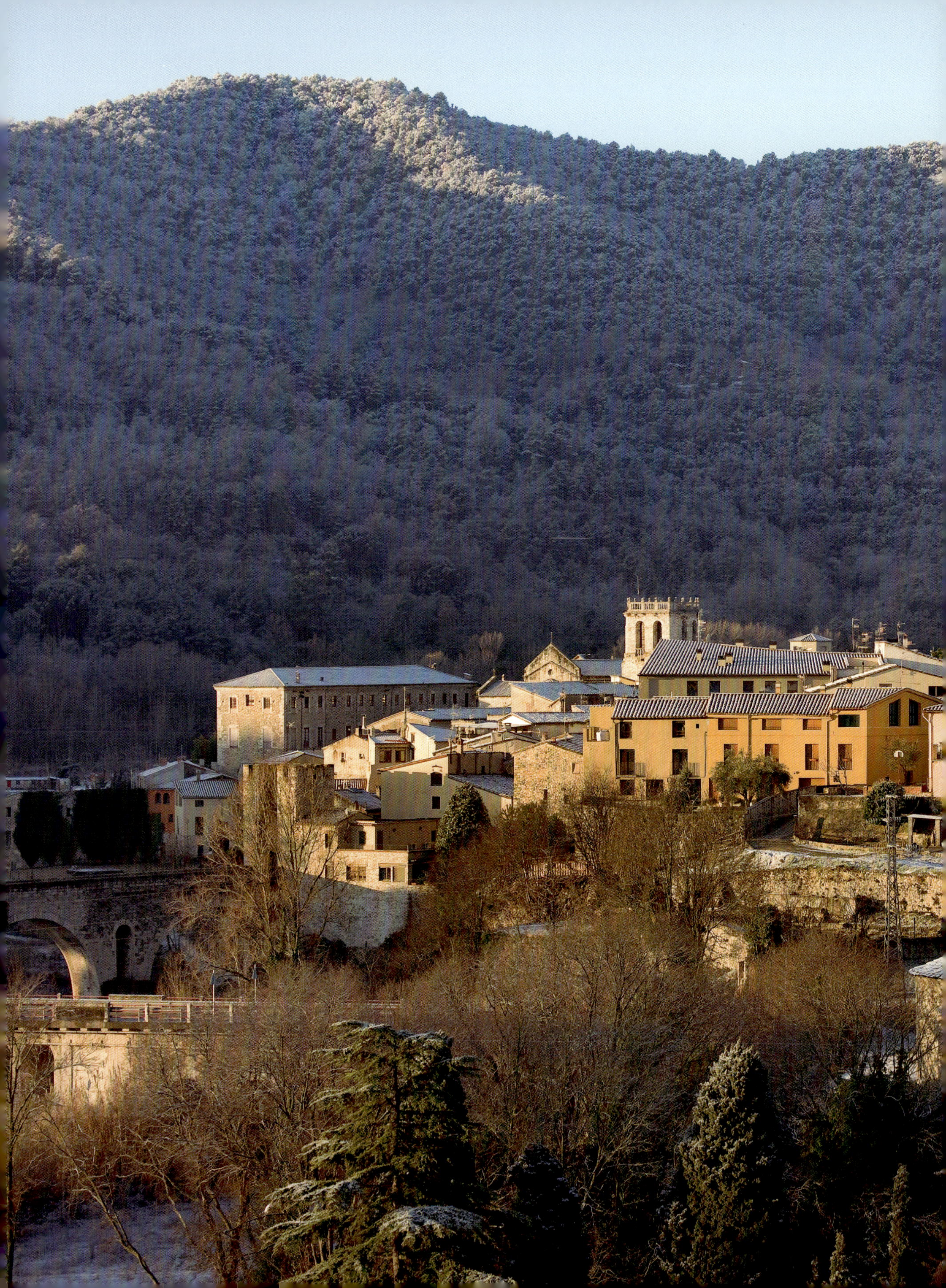

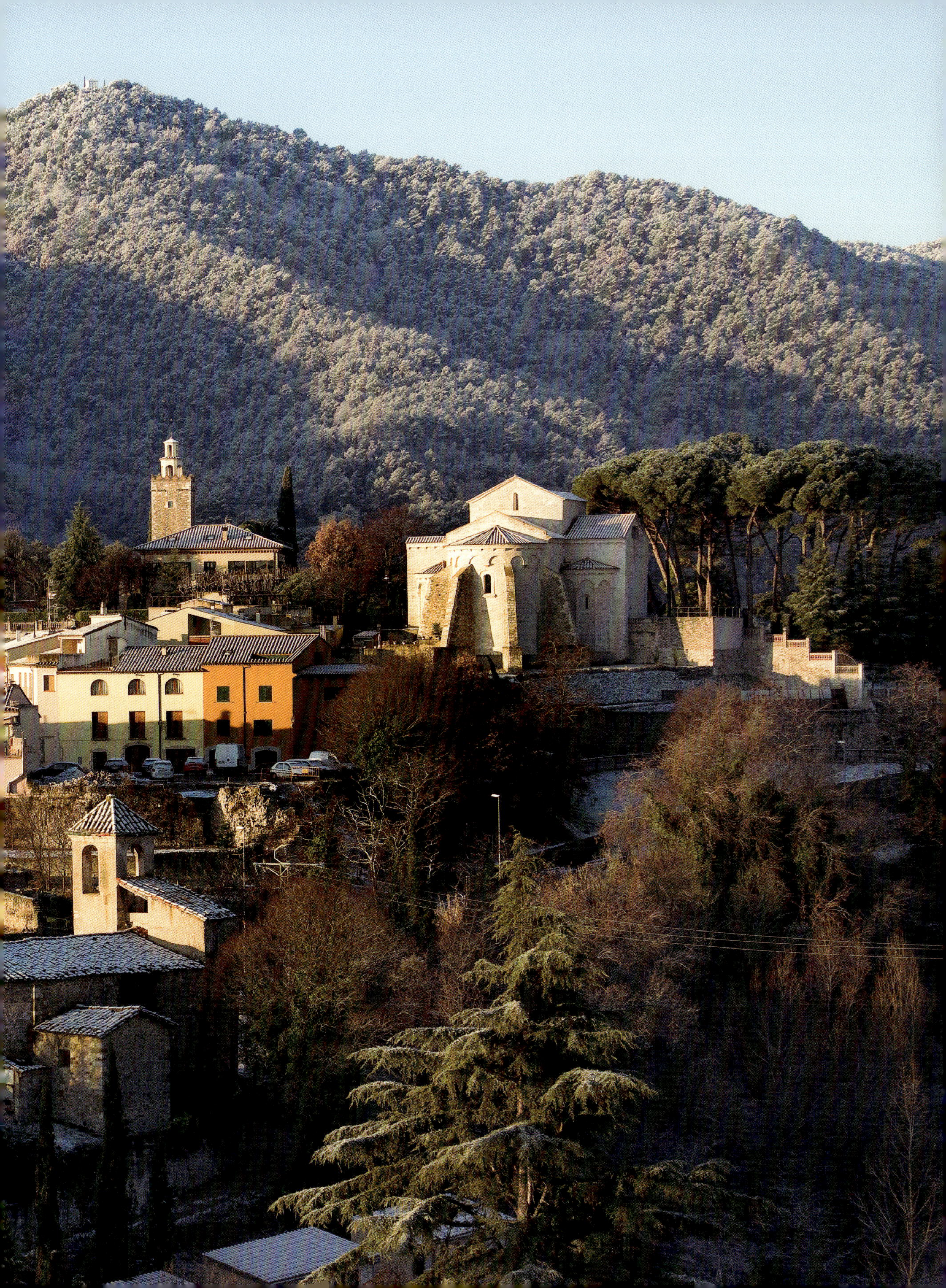

ing façade with an exceptional large window and rose window. We could consider it as the little sister of the monastery of Sant Pere because it was also built in 977, under the auspices of Bishop Miró Bonfill. It is Romanesque but has some elements of transition to Gothic, such as the abovementioned large window and rose window. Inside, the Gothic aesthetics are also appreciated in the chapel where the relic of the True Cross is kept. The one that is there today was loaned by Francesc Cambó, in 1923, and replaced the first one that had been stolen in 1899. The original, of which all trace has been lost, has been brought from Rome by Bernat Tallaferro, in 1017. Also in Gothic style is the tomb of Pere de Rovira, a judge who brought the relics of Saint Vincent to Besalú in 1413. The image of the Virgin of the Dolors is placed there where formerly it was the origin of the Venerable Congregation of this virgin. Personally, I think that the most original details are the exterior capitals of the Sant Rafel doorway: a door with an archivolt and some remarkable capitals. Lions and winged monsters, gryphons and human heads, monstrous heads that bite the ends of the wings; as if they were creatures that had escaped from Hell and brandished their tail scattering their evil spectre across the Earth and pursuing mortal sinners. They are really terrifying. In fact, over two of these capitals, there had been two horned figures that seem to watch over these beasts. The diabolical expressions of these figures carved centuries ago could even terrify the bandit Boquica. Some images, then, that welcomed the lords of the castle when they went mass in Sant Vicenç; they came down from the castle and entered the church by this door so as not to mix with the common people, who entered via the main door. And talking of the lords of the castle, let me tell you superficially of Santa Maria de Besalú, the only church within the walled precinct of the *castrum*, of which only some ruins remain. Despite everything, it does not take much to imagine the majesty the temple must have had in the middle of the period of earls.

The Jewish heritage and legacy was extended with the discovery and later restoration of the synagogue. Until the end of the excavations, which between 2002 and 2005 revealed the foundations of this providential spiritual and social meeting place of the Jewish community of Besalú, the Miqveh or purification baths were the only reference —along with the alleyways of the Jewish quarter— of the children of Israel in the county. In 1264, Jaume I the Conqueror awarded royal privilege to the Jewish community of Besalú to build the synagogue or *schola judeorum*. The word synagogue comes from the Greek *synagon* and means to meet. Because, in fact, this is what it was: a meeting place and shelter that allowed them to feel at one with themselves and to feel closer to God. It was the heart of the district, the centre of life of the Jewish quarter.

All synagogues had a small tabernacle with a permanently-lit candle: the *ner tamid*, meaning eternal flame, which added the previous day's light to the light of the day ahead. They kept vigil so that this flame of the Aron Ha-Kodesh was eternal; an oil candle venerated by all the members of the community in a single room that was probably divided into two floors. Upstairs there was a sort of gallery, a type of raised balcony and separated from lower floor by wooden trellises. The space upstairs was reserved for the women, who followed the prayers from there, and had to be visually separated from the lower section, exclusively for the men.

The central space of the synagogue was simply furnished, nothing luxurious, but it must have transmitted a great sensation of peace and calm. A large wooden cabinet, closed and surrounded by wooden benches, stood in the centre of the room and presided over the room with authority. In a chest was kept the Torah, the sacred book that recounts the will of God revealed to Moses. Strict obedience to its rules was the central point around which the life of the Jews took place. Every day, during the morning religious services, passages were recited from the scriptures, the Mishnah and the Talmud. However, on Monday and Thursday mornings, the sacred book was taken out of this chest and the rabbi read chanting before the faithful. After these liturgies, they were now ready to go down to the mikveh. The first Jews who settled in Besalú discovered a thermal water spring, following the course of the Fluvià, a few metres higher than where we are standing now. During the winter months they purified themselves with hot water... According to tradition, all the water in the world comes from the river that sprang from the garden of Eden, and it is necessary that the water of the mikveh comes from a natural source: the sea, a river, a spring, the rain, snow or melted ice, but water must never be allowed to remain stagnant, in order to avoid impurities. These purifying baths were discovered by coincidence in 1964 and two rabbinic authorities certified their authenticity: they are the only baths found in the Spanish state and the third best conserved in Europe. It is no surprise, then, that Jews from around the world travel to this corner and go down the ten steps to the sacred space, where they recall the spiritual cleaning of the bodies of their ancestors to be reborn, to renew themselves. They submerged themselves in these waters to clean their soul of impurities. The ritual bath by immersion purified the body from contact with dead bodies, certain illnesses or prepared them to attend the services in the temple. And in the case of the women, the bath was compulsory every month, after giving birth and before marrying. This space, along with the synagogue, enables a connection —full of symbolism— between the past and present of Hebrew culture.

Many people from Besalú who had been to the school run by the nuns in the building of the Curia Real could not have imagined that, years later, they would enter there to have a beer, have lunch or supper.

The stones of the walls of this noble building from between the 13th and 15th centuries have been witness to the passing through of several prestigious and distinguished families, both Christian and Jewish. Today it is a building where, in the upper part, we can admire the Gothic hall that conserves a wooden coffered ceiling from the 14th century and some extraordinary ogival arches. On the ground floor is a cultural space that enables visitors to complete the information about Besalú by means of an audiovisual show. And the adjoining rooms are occupied by a restaurant that has the same name as the building. Following the same section of city wall, you will go towards the orchards and El Molí d'en Subirós. This space has been one of the last to be recovered and has been undertaken respecting its original structure.

According to the oldest documents conserved, the earliest mention of the mill is the same year as the founding of the monastery of Sant Pere. It was in 977 and Count Miró Bonfill provided the monastery with properties, rights and rents, among which had been a section of the River Fluvià with its irrigation channels, mills and mill areas. However, it was not until many years later that a description of the mill was found. In the disaster of 1732 the flour mill was located at the foot of the Abbey house. We find another time reference in the inscription "1755", on the front door of the mill. The flood of 1746 must have caused damage and imperfections that resulted in, necessarily, reconstruction work as well as an extension of the mill. It seems that it was then when the house where the miller lived was incorporated. In this period, the building had two owners: the abbot and as public property. They rented it for 800 pounds per year and shared the benefits. With the arrival of industrialisation, at the end of the 19th century, as well as maintaining the flour production, one of the millstones was replaced by a turbine that produced electricity. The activity continued until 1963, when it was abandoned. Progressive deterioration caused the collapse of the upper floors in the nineteen-eighties, and the mill was left demolished. Until now, that is, since they have made a museum of this space in order to show how it worked, beside the Jardí de la Ratafia, between the cloisters and the orchards.

With the permission of the architectural heritage we have just seen, the bridge is, without doubt, the image of the town. The old bridge, the Romanesque bridge, the fortified bridge, is for me —if I may be allowed— *the bridge of the Jews*, but, above all, what characterises this bridge and determines its personality is its particular —and in no way whimsical— form, which makes it even more original and attractive.

The impressiveness of the bridge is only perceived from below, level with the river, close to the Fluvià. Its angular form, respecting the current, and the large stones at the foundations of each pillar constitute the best base over which stands a construction that was key for the defence of the earldom of Besalú. Until a few years ago, the only reference we had was that of document dated 1075, which mentioned that to enter Besalú one had to cross a bridge. Today, through the notary deeds of Besalú that are kept in the Olot County Archive, it is recorded that on the 17th of December 1316, *Bernat de Prat, Ramon de Gesio, Ramon Porter and Guillem Guerau Pauci, jurors of the town of Besalú for one party, and, for the other party, Pere Baró of the town of Perpignan, who due to the works on the bridge of Besalú will come to the town for eight days, as master builder to assess and supervise the construction of the bridge.* He was notified by a letter from the jurors of the town and is informed that he will have continuous residence in Besalú and will obtain all he will need for the construction of the bridge. It is a contract to rebuild the original bridge. Floods and earthquakes made this remodelling necessary. The bridge was erected —the style reveals this— by a master of Lombardy works in the early 11th century, over the rocks of the river, authentic gifts from Mother Nature. Each arch rests over these unmovable tiny mountains. From the seventh pillar, its direction turns to the right for three reasons. Firstly, because otherwise it would have been constantly exposed to the pushes of the water and that would have weakened the structure with the first flood. Secondly, if it had turned in the other direction, it would have broken the current of the water and would have flooded the houses that had spread, at that time, along the river bank. And thirdly, it would have meant an enormous waste, unimaginable costs that the earldom could not afford. The last arches —where the bridge drops— gives it a characteristic air, caused by the wear and tear that the pillar foundations have experienced at the hand of man and which the force of the water has slowly eroded.

During the mandate of King Pere III the Ceremonious the two towers were built, the central one was where the *pagus*, a toll to enter Besalú, had previously been established; a halfpenny to enter on foot and another halfpenny for a loaded donkey, apart from the taxes that were applied to some goods.

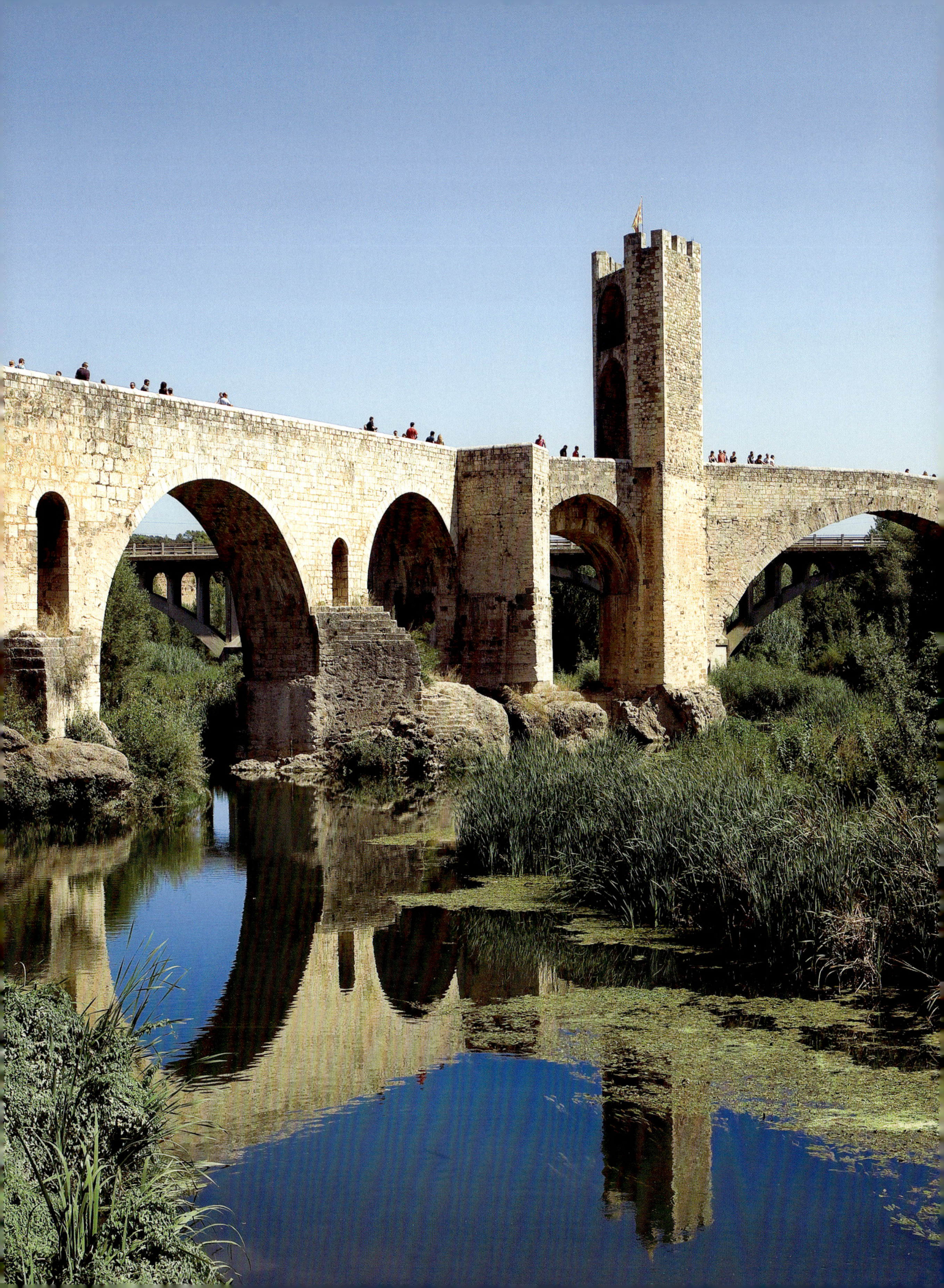

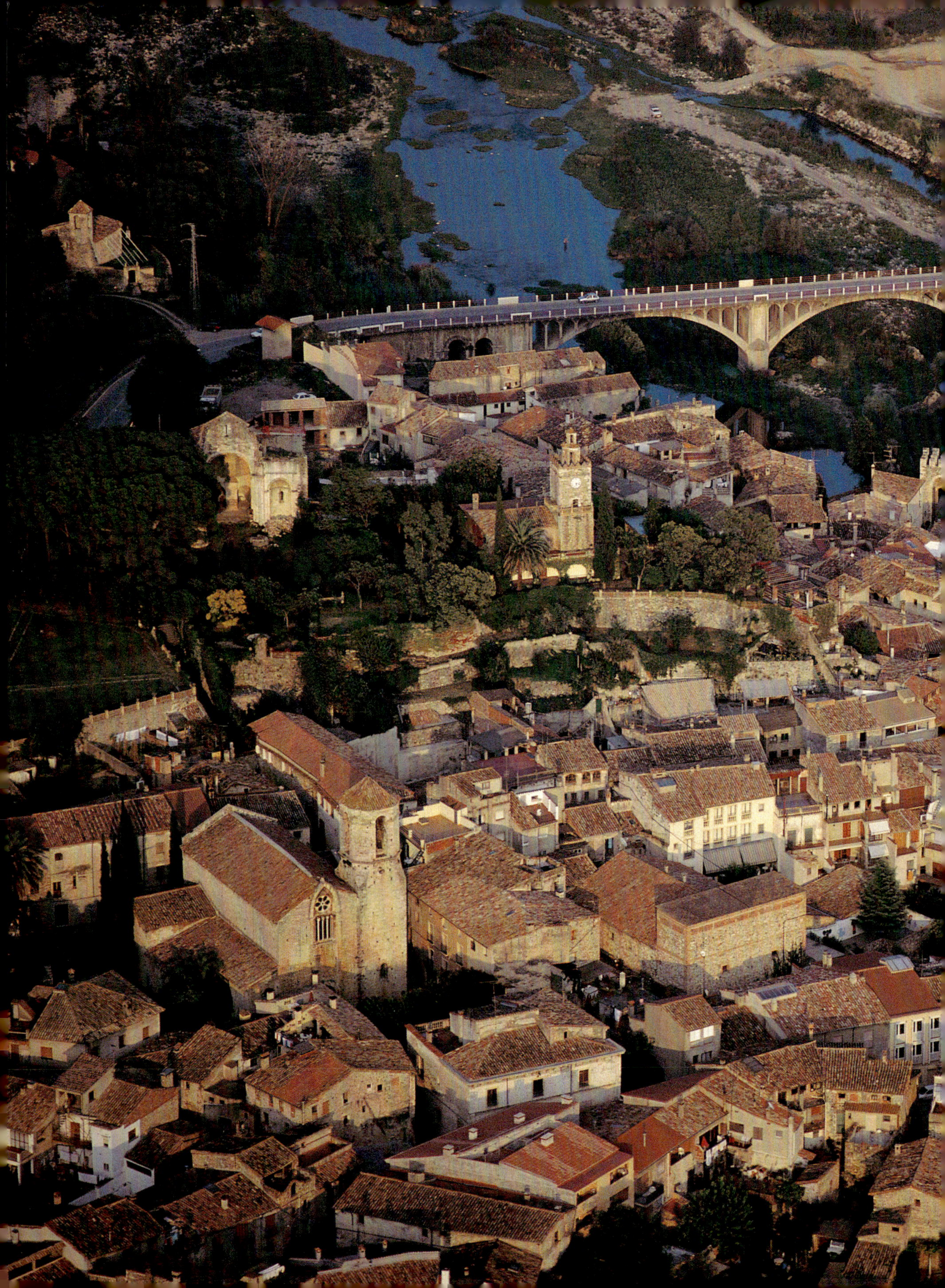

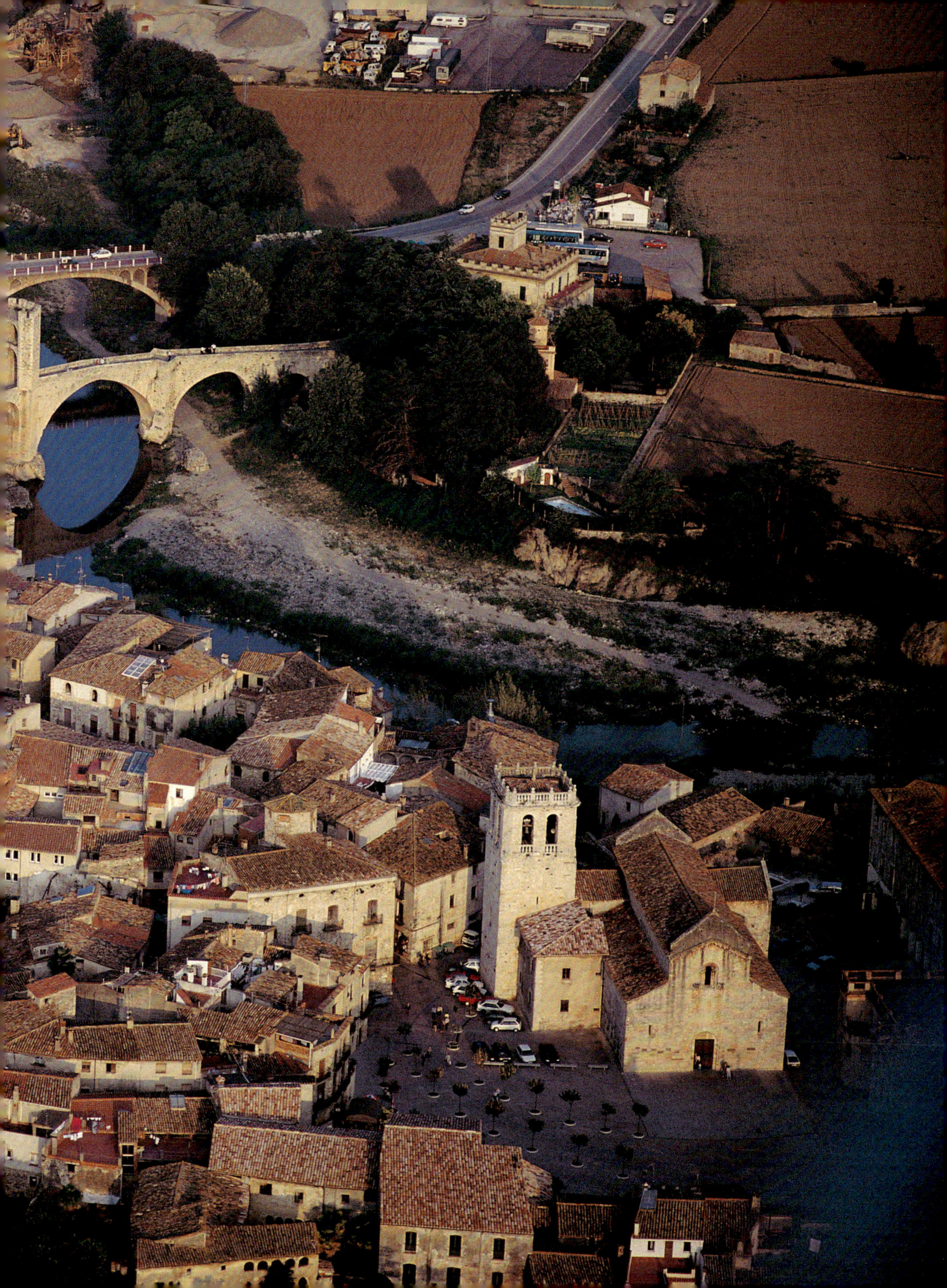

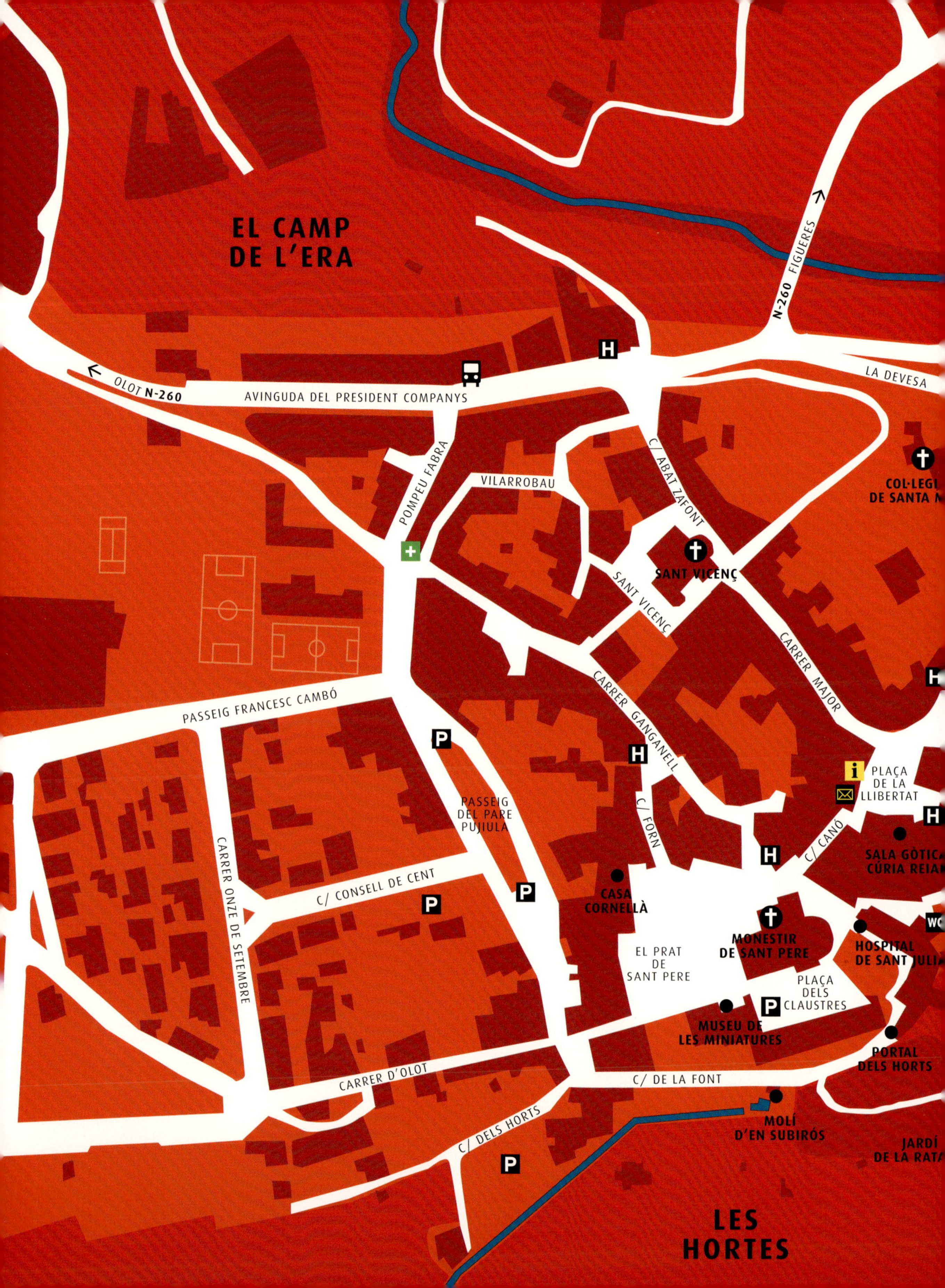

EL CAMP
DE L'ERA
N-260 FIGUERES
OLOT N-260
AVINGUDA DEL PRESIDENT COMPANYS
LA DEVESA
POMPEU FABRA
VILARROBAU
C/ ABAT ZAFONT
SANT VICENÇ
COL·LEGI
DE SANTA M
SANT VICENÇ
CARRER MAJOR
CARRER GANGANELL
PASSEIG FRANCESC CAMBÓ
PASSEIG
DEL PARE
PUJIULA
C/ FORN
PLAÇA
DE LA
LLIBERTAT
C/ CANÓ
SALA GÒTICA
CÚRIA REIAL
CARRER ONZE DE SETEMBRE
C/ CONSELL DE CENT
CASA
CORNELLÀ
MONESTIR
DE SANT PERE
EL PRAT
DE
SANT PERE
HOSPITAL
DE SANT JULIÀ
PLAÇA
DELS
CLAUSTRES
MUSEU DE
LES MINIATURES
PORTAL
DELS HORTS
CARRER D'OLOT
C/ DE LA FONT
C/ DELS HORTS
MOLÍ
D'EN SUBIRÓS
JARDÍ
DE LA RATA
LES
HORTES

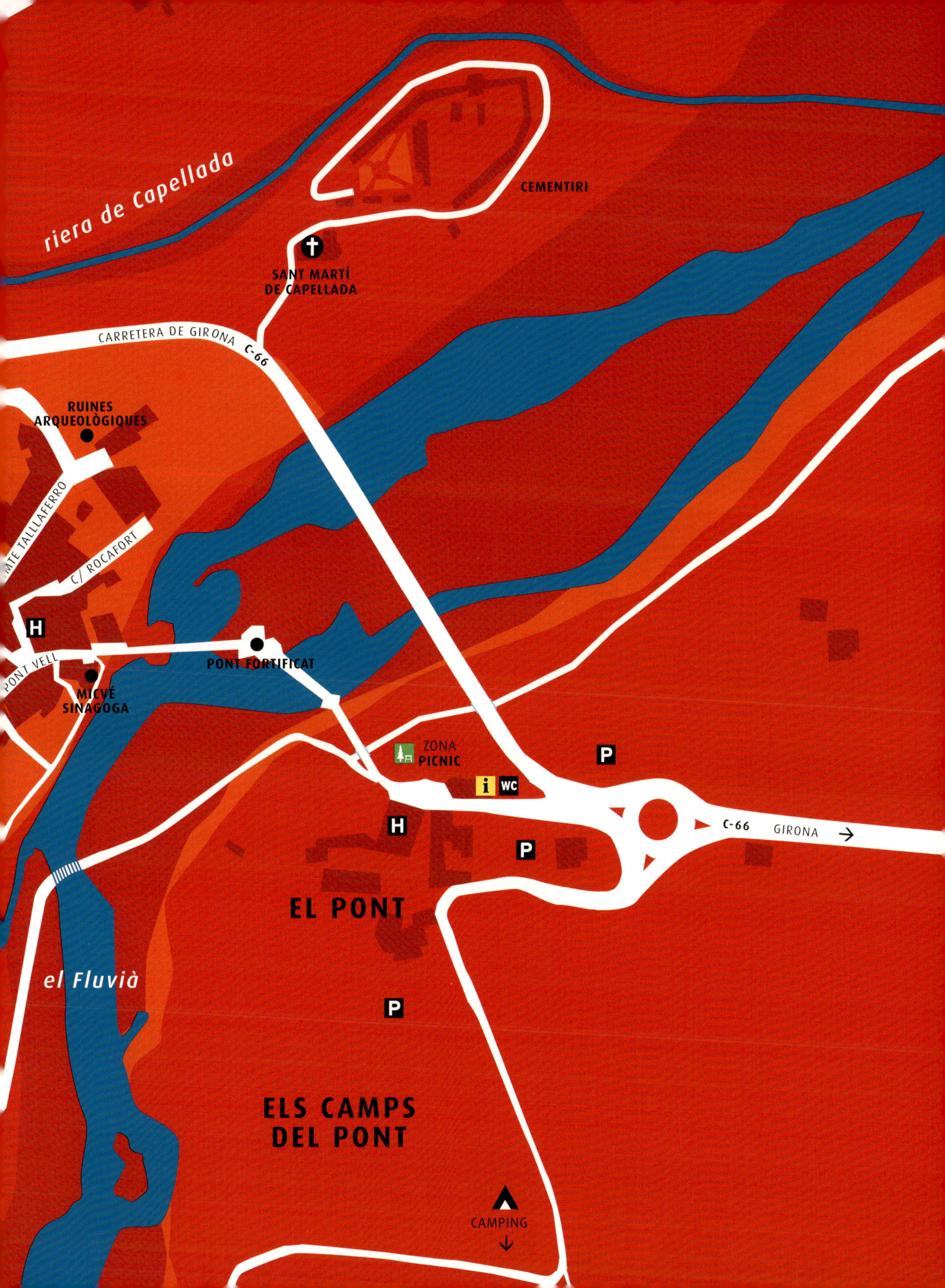

riera de Capellada
CEMENTIRI
SANT MARTÍ
DE CAPELLADA
CARRETERA DE GIRONA
C-66
RUINES
ARQUEOLÒGIQUES
C/ ROCAFORT
H
PONT VELL
PONT FORTIFICAT
MICVÉ
SINAGOGA
ZONA
PICNIC
i
WC
P
H
P
C-66
GIRONA →
EL PONT
el Fluvià
P
ELS CAMPS
DEL PONT
CAMPING

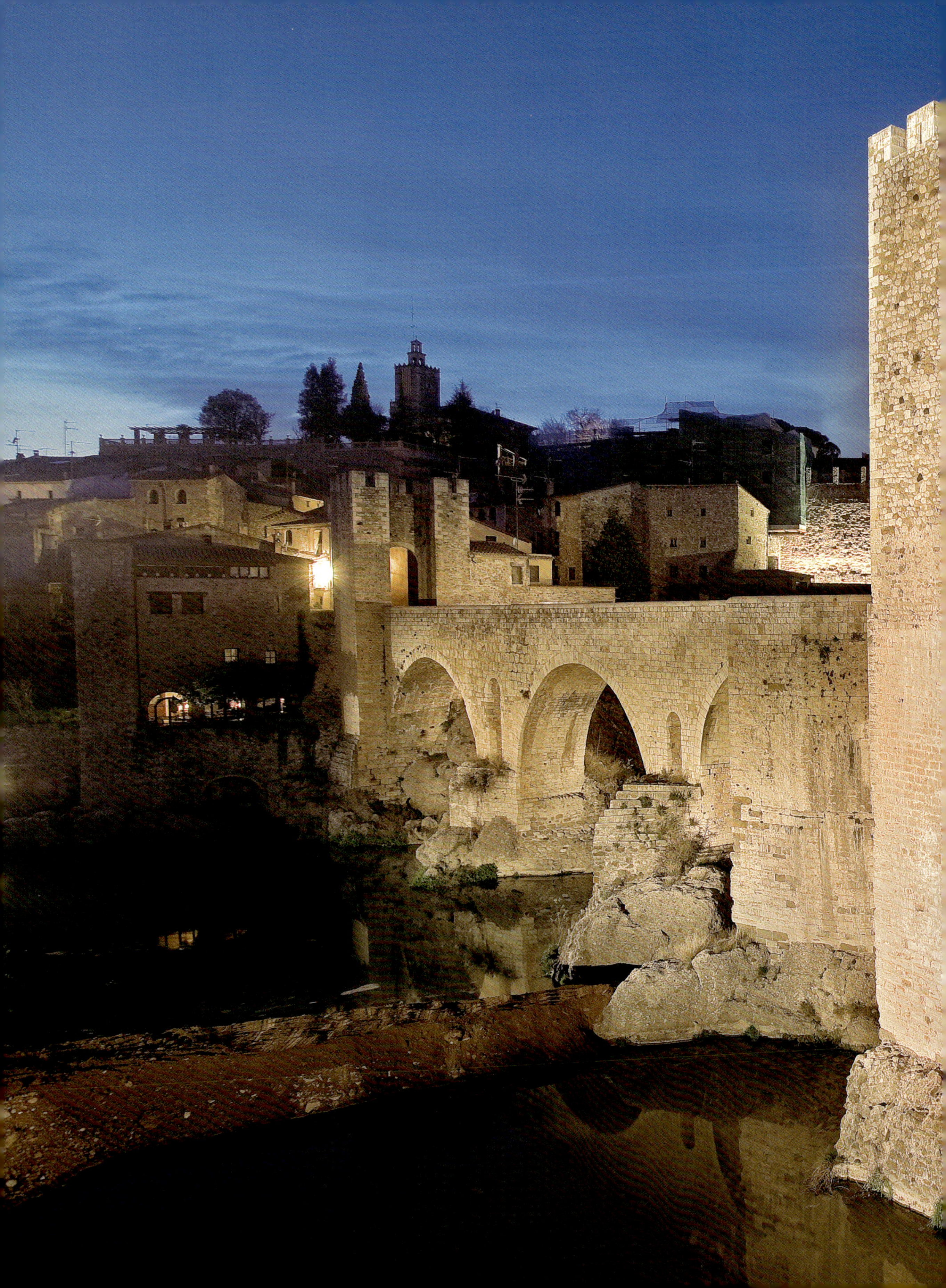

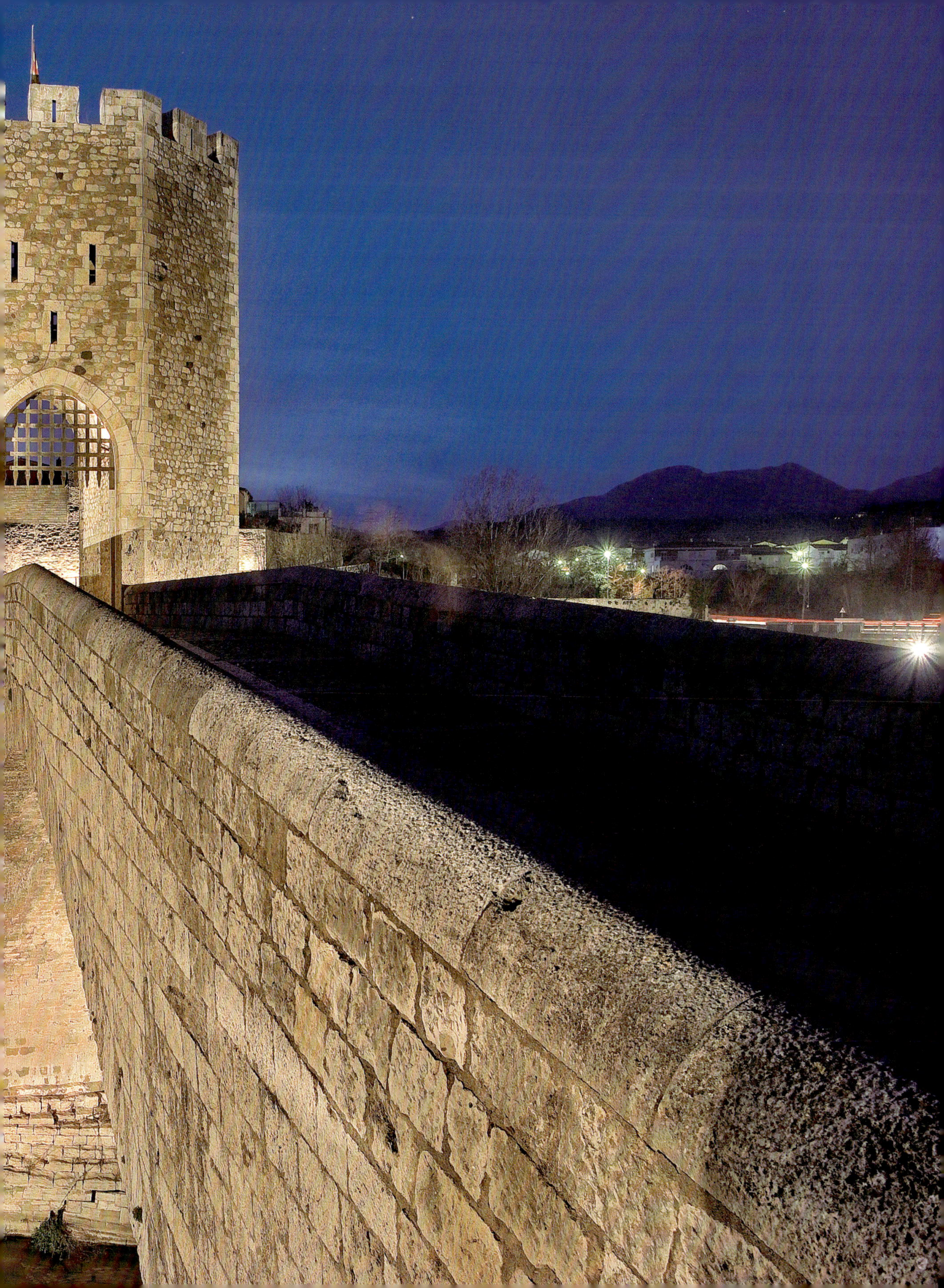

The fortified bridge

Was built in the 11th century and rebuilt on several occasions over the years. It is a bridge with seven arches and is characterised by its angular form, a result of the placing of the pillars over the natural stones of the river. It is 105 metres long and some 30 metres high including the defence tower. In the medieval period, a county *pagus* was installed in the fortified tower, an obligatory toll paid to enter the town.

The bridge was dynamited during the Civil War and later rebuilt by the architect Pons Sorolla, under the criteria of the State Architecture Office. Today it is the symbol of Besalú and the most suitable passing place to enter the *vila vella*, the old town.

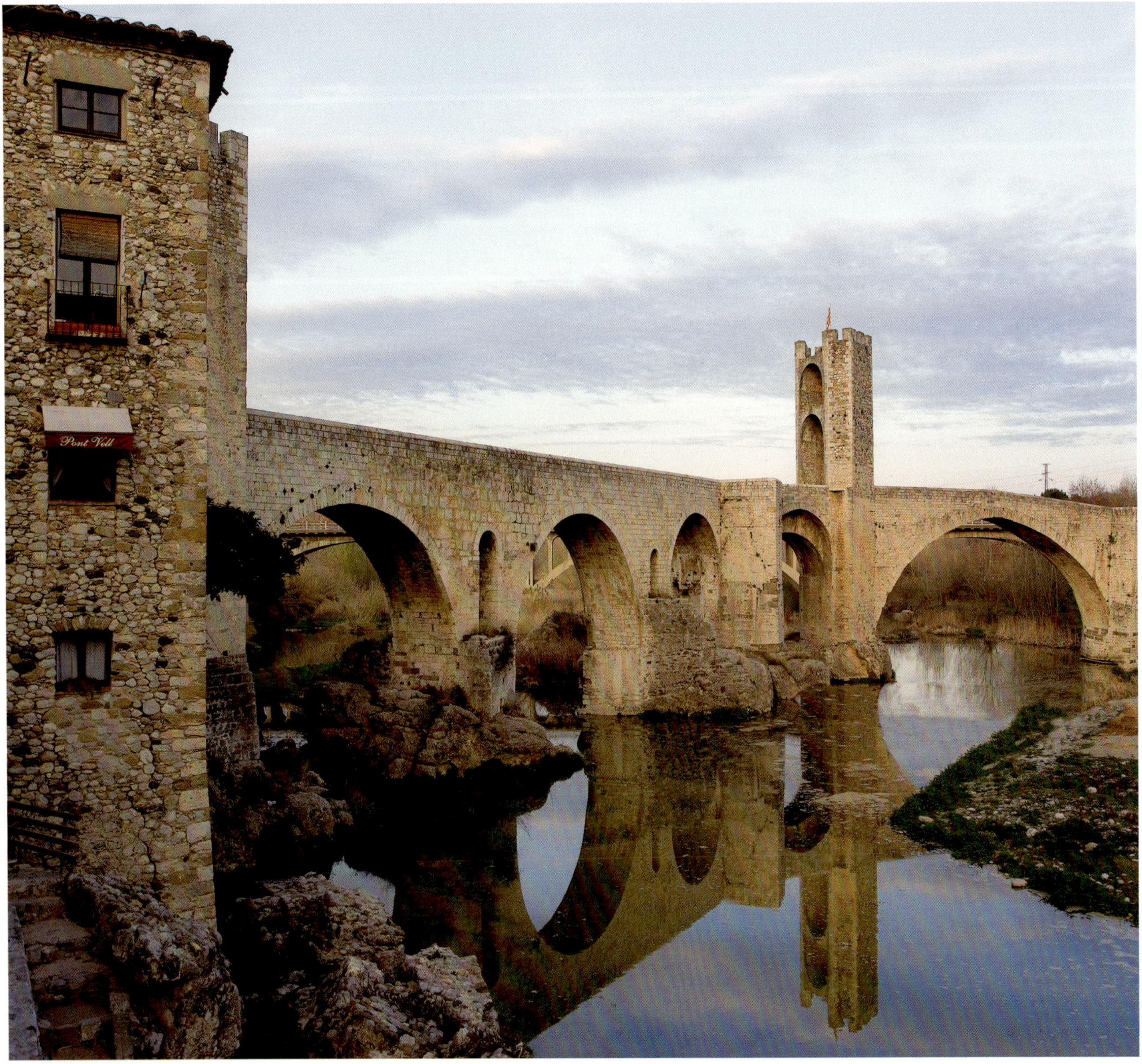

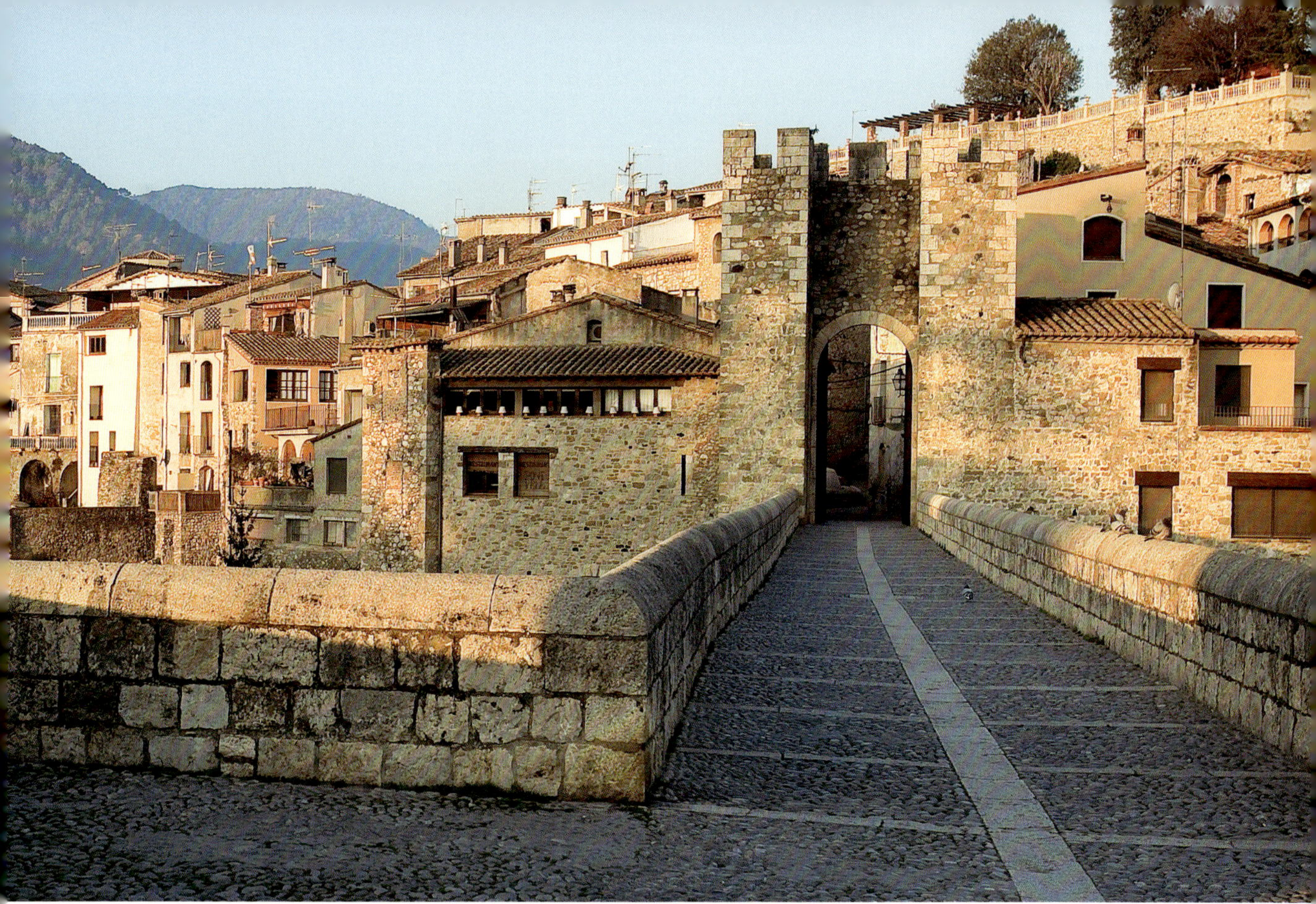

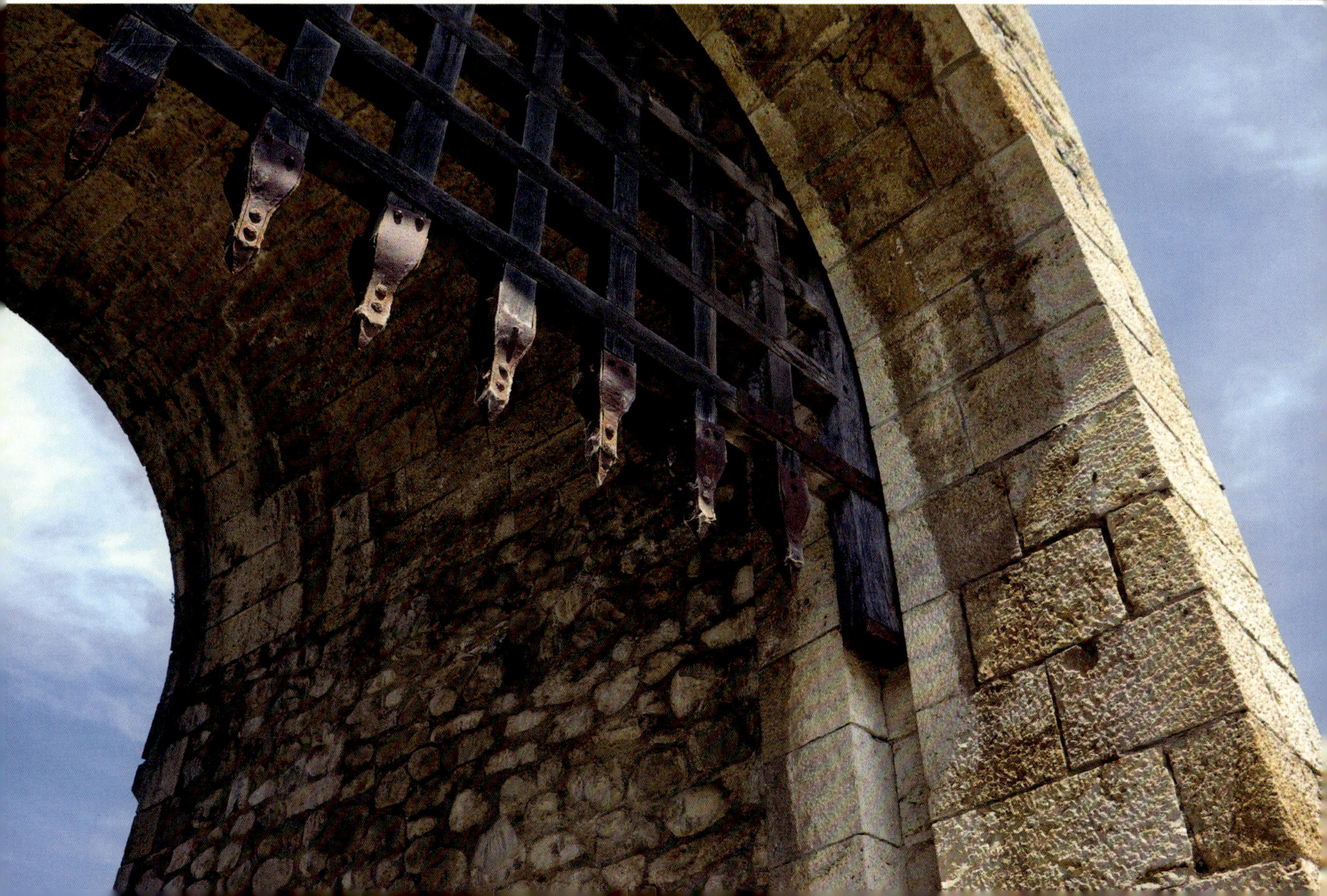

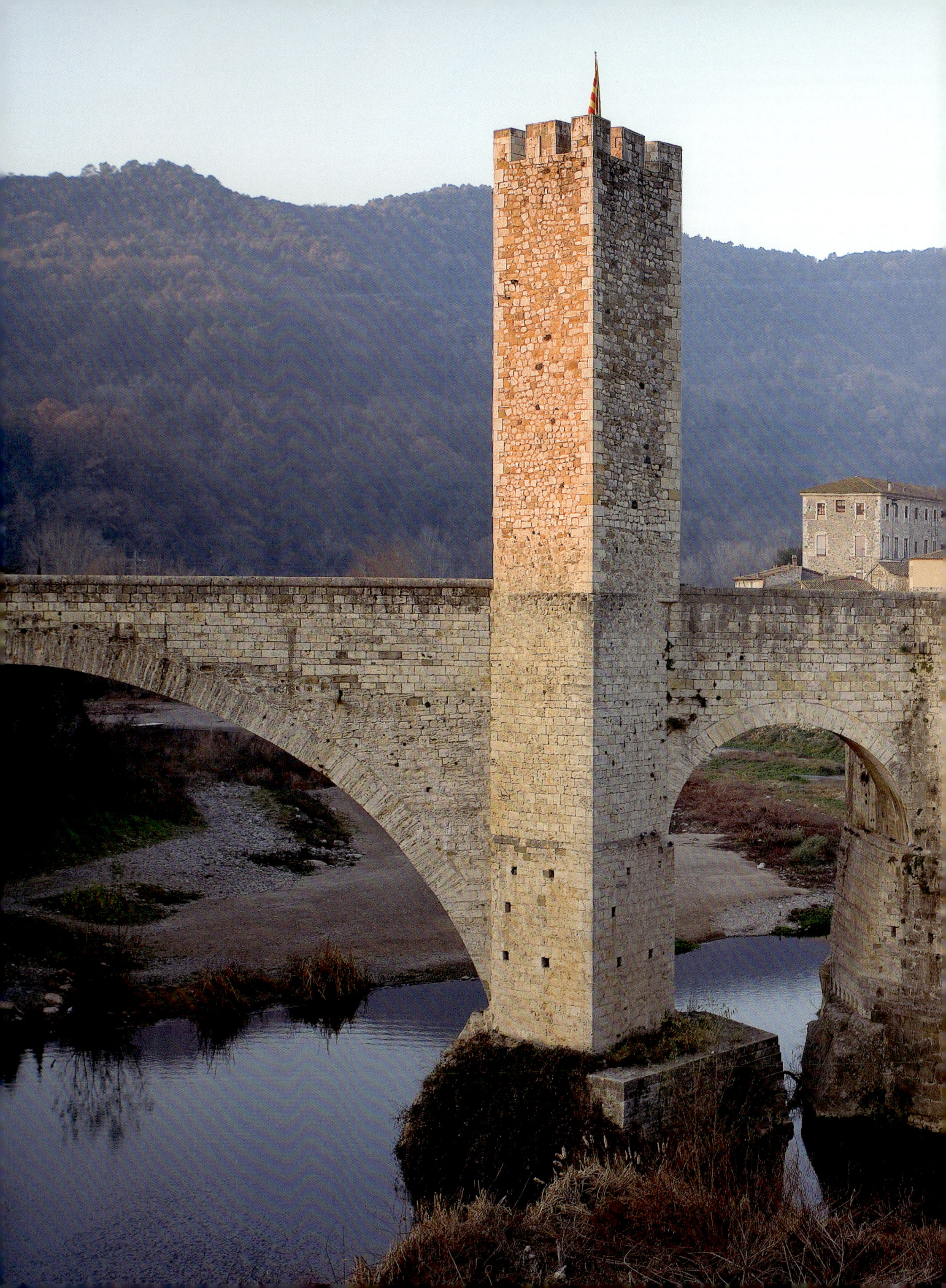

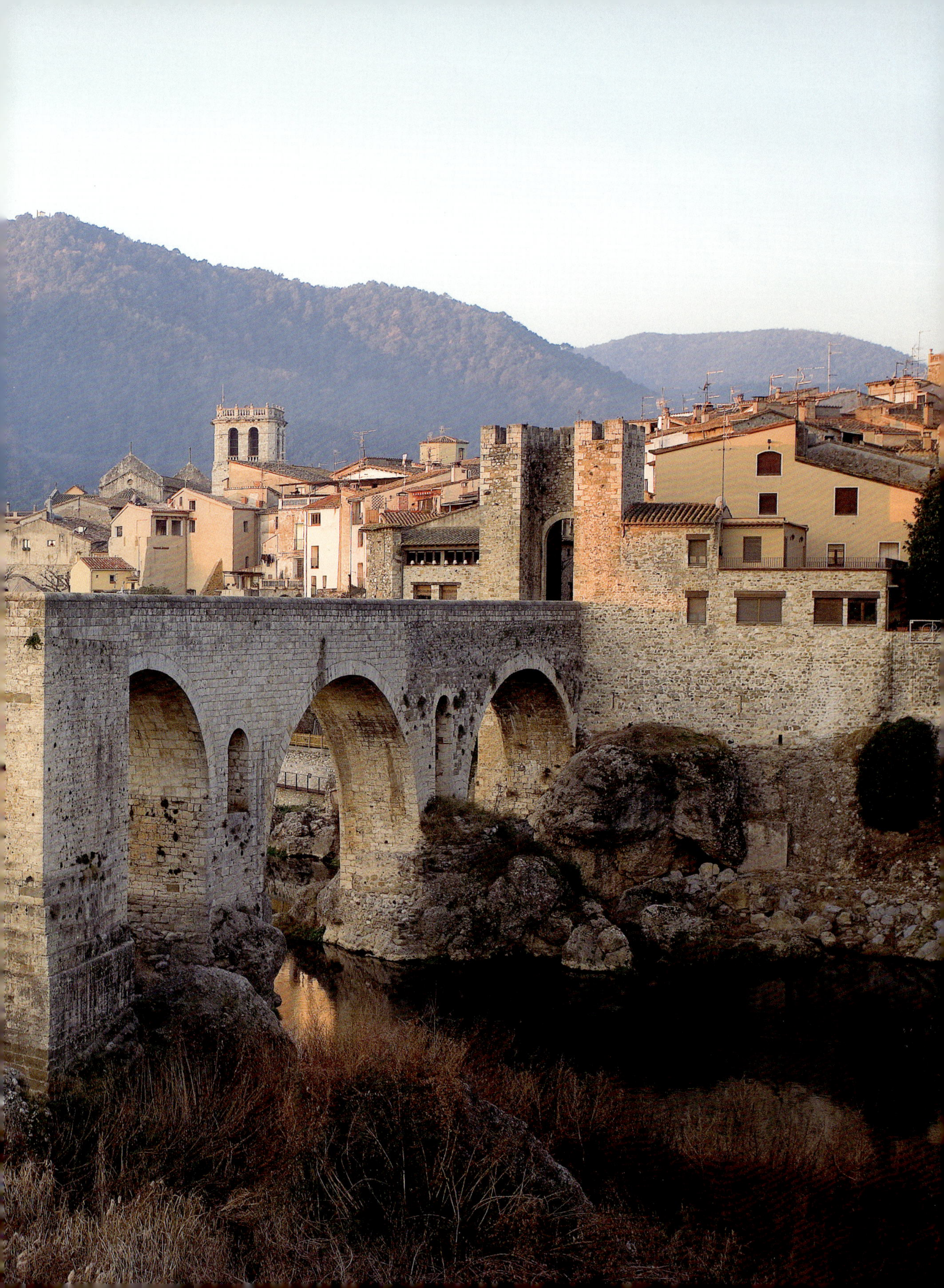

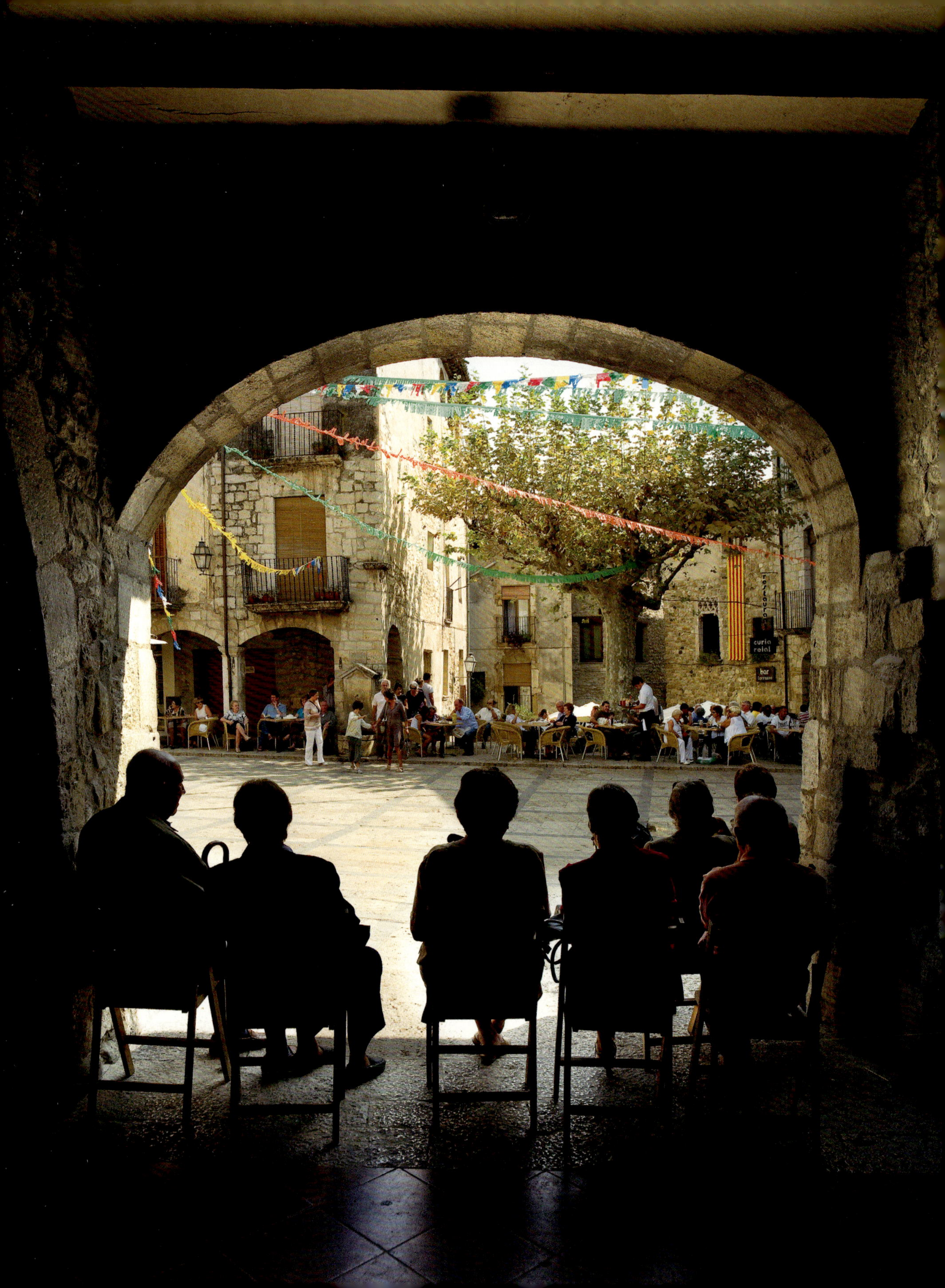
restaurant
curia reial
bar
terrassa

The Plaça de la Llibertat

The main square of Besalú, which with the passing of time and of distinct periods has had its name changed, just like many other towns in Catalonia, according to the powers that be of the time.

It is the town's nerve centre, where the majority of acts and festivals are held, such as the chant of the Salve during the procession of the Dolors.

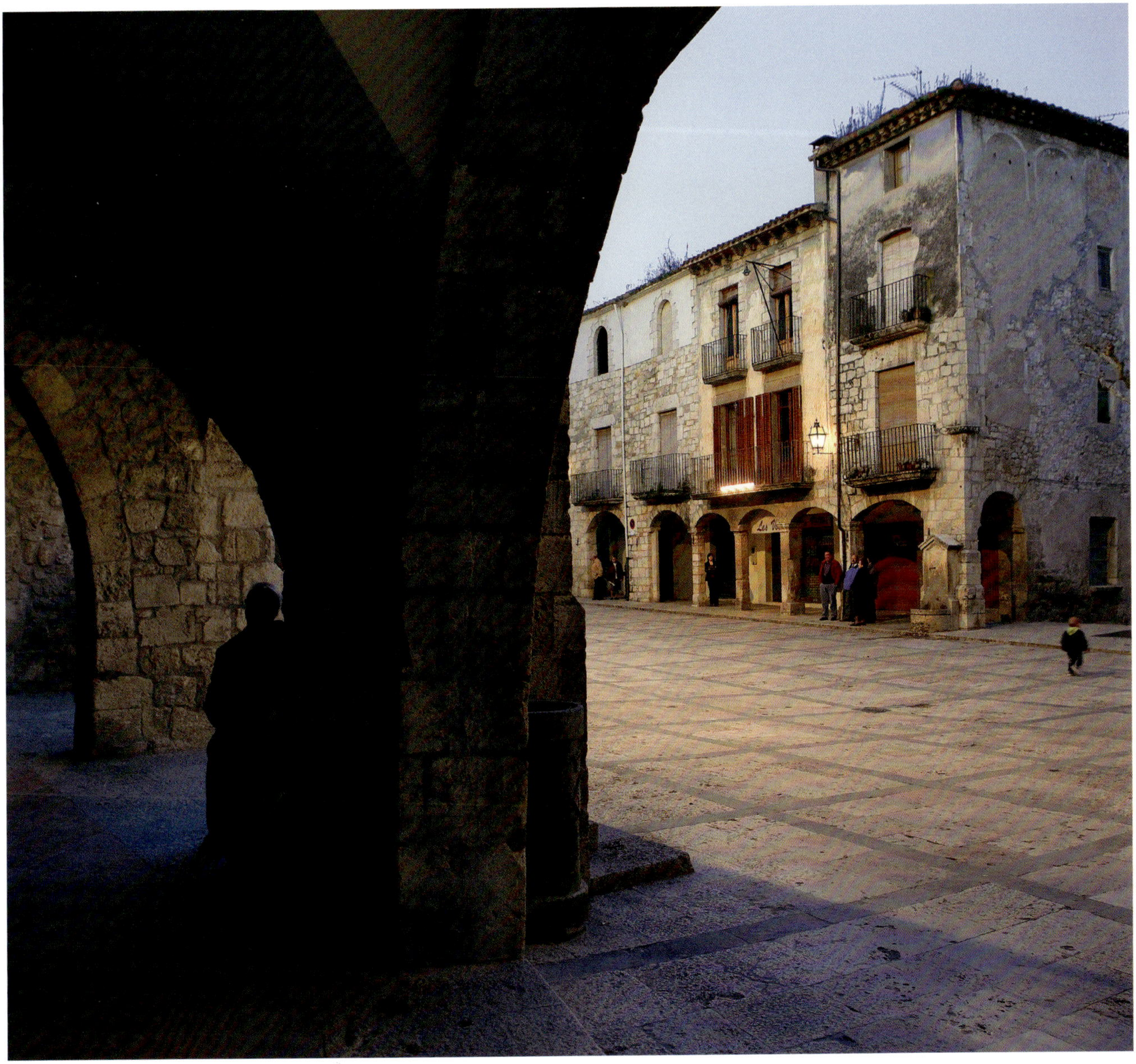

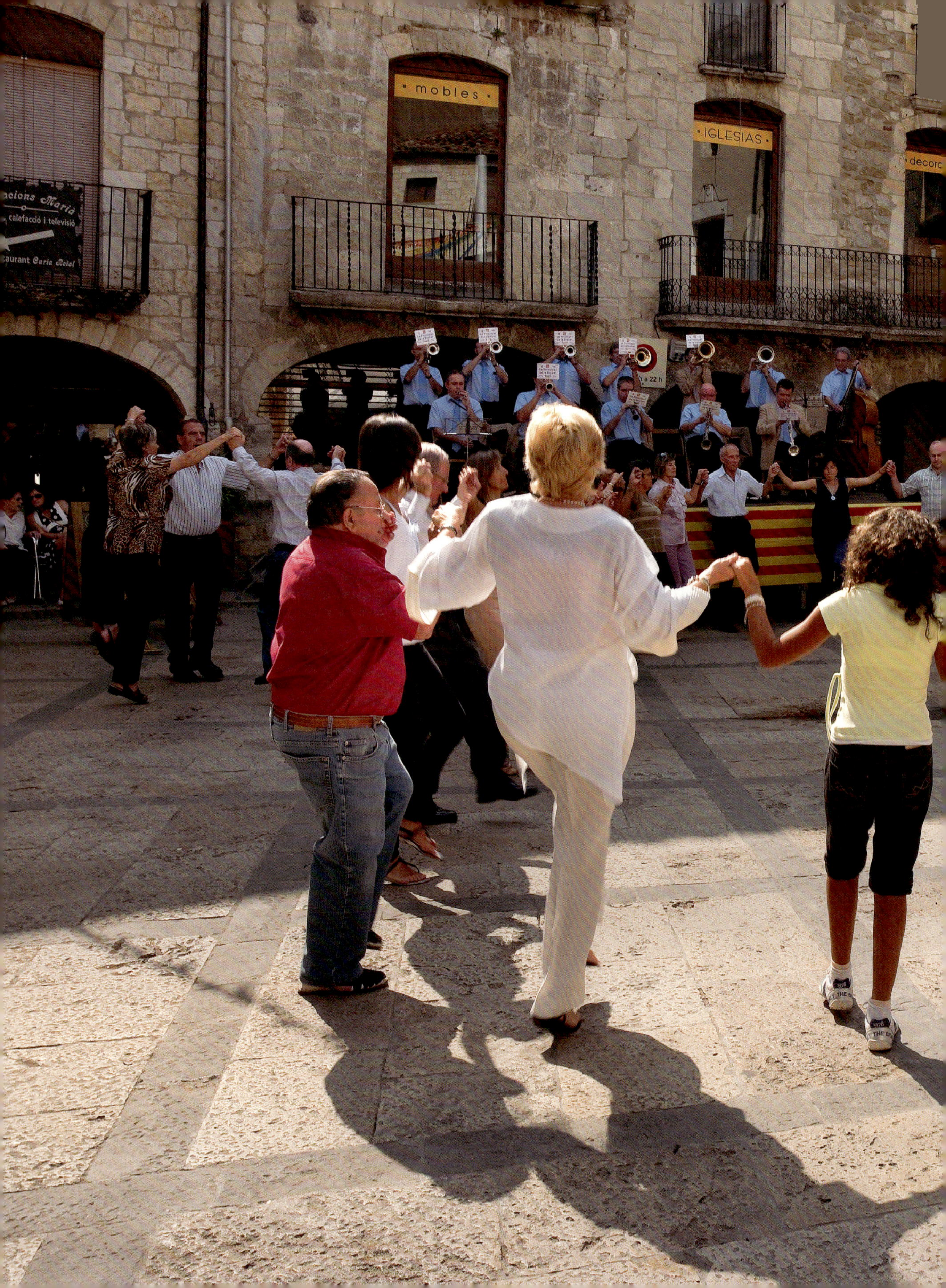
mobles
IGLESIAS
calefacció i televisió

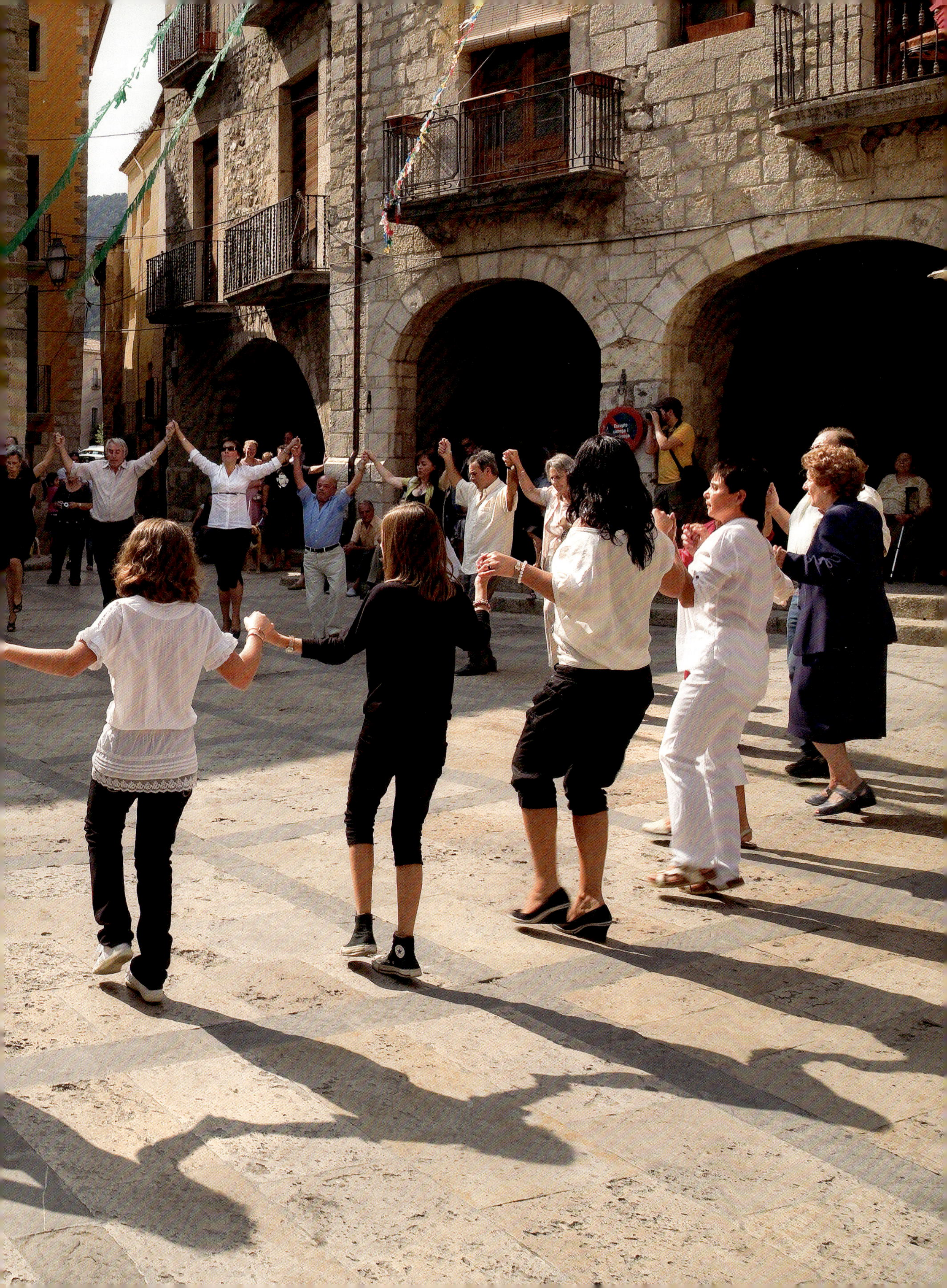

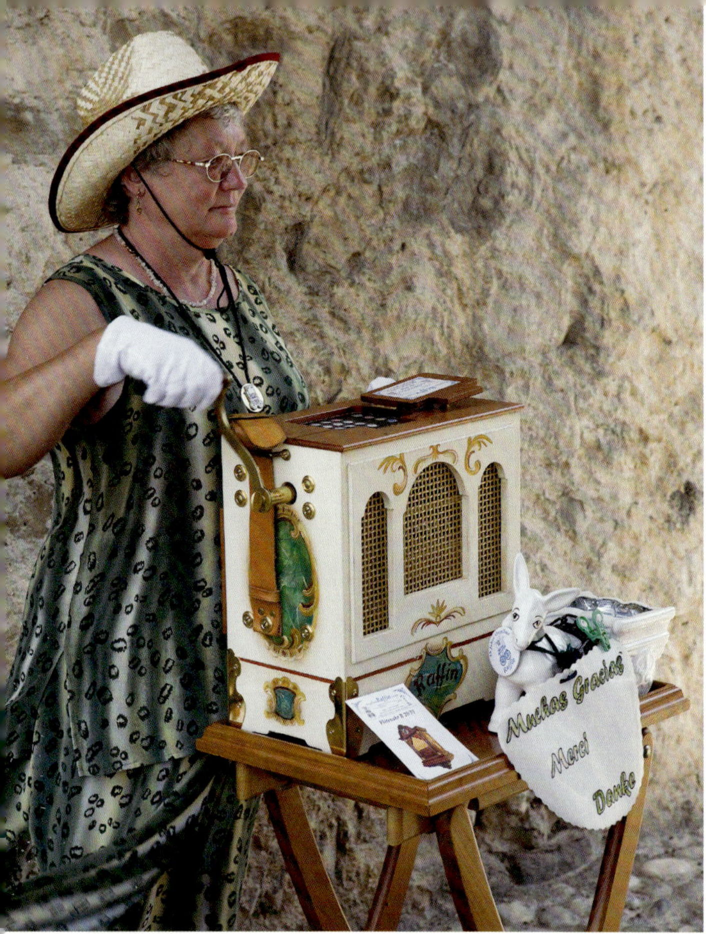
Muchas Gracias
Merci
Danke
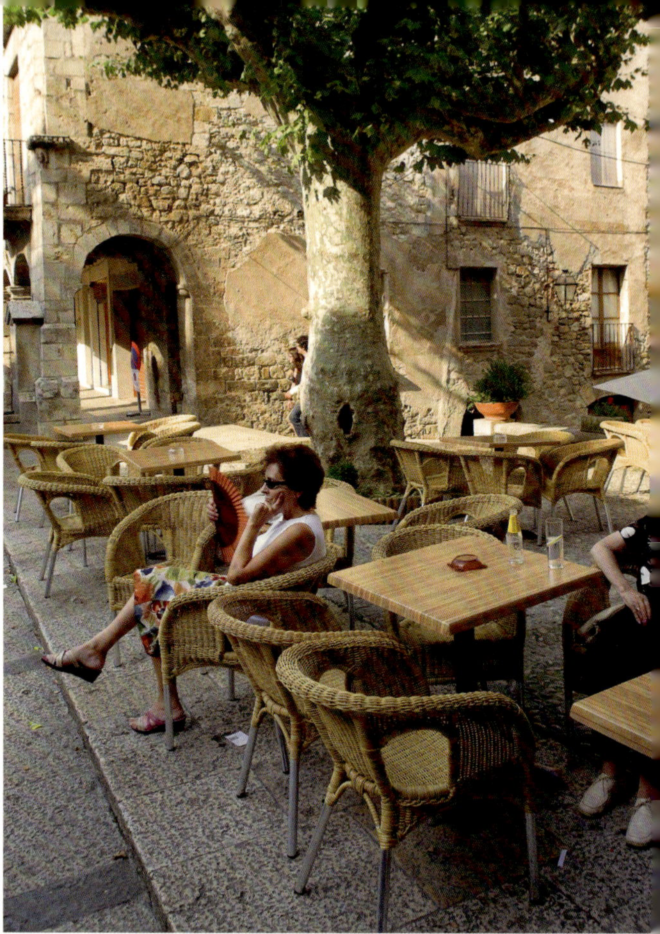
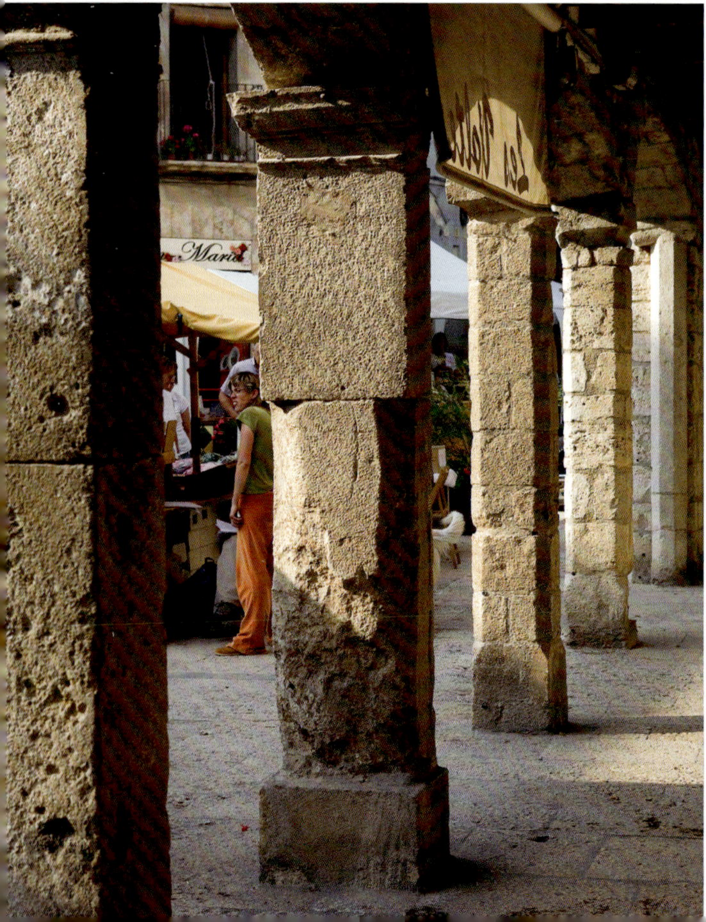
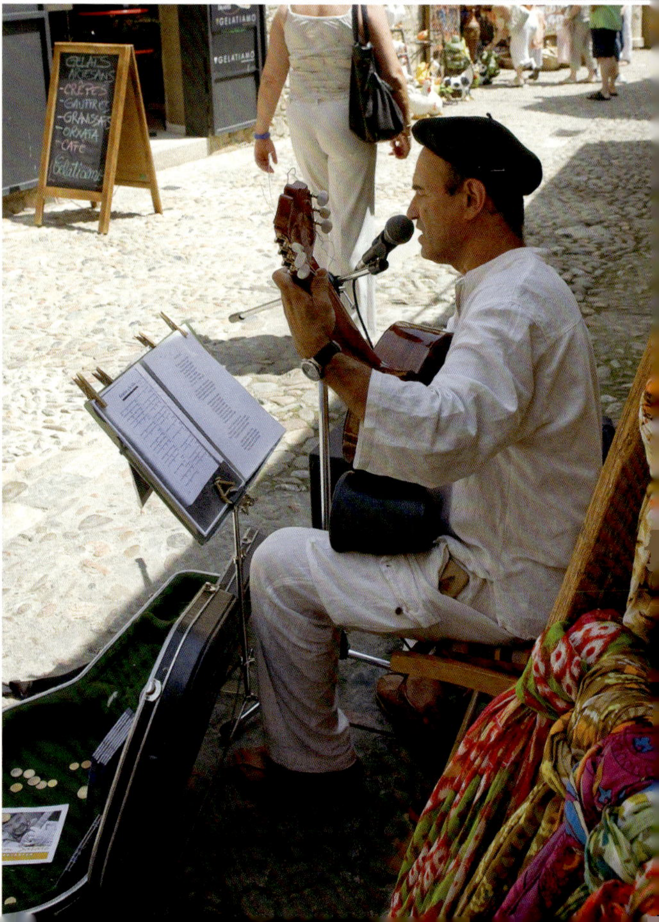

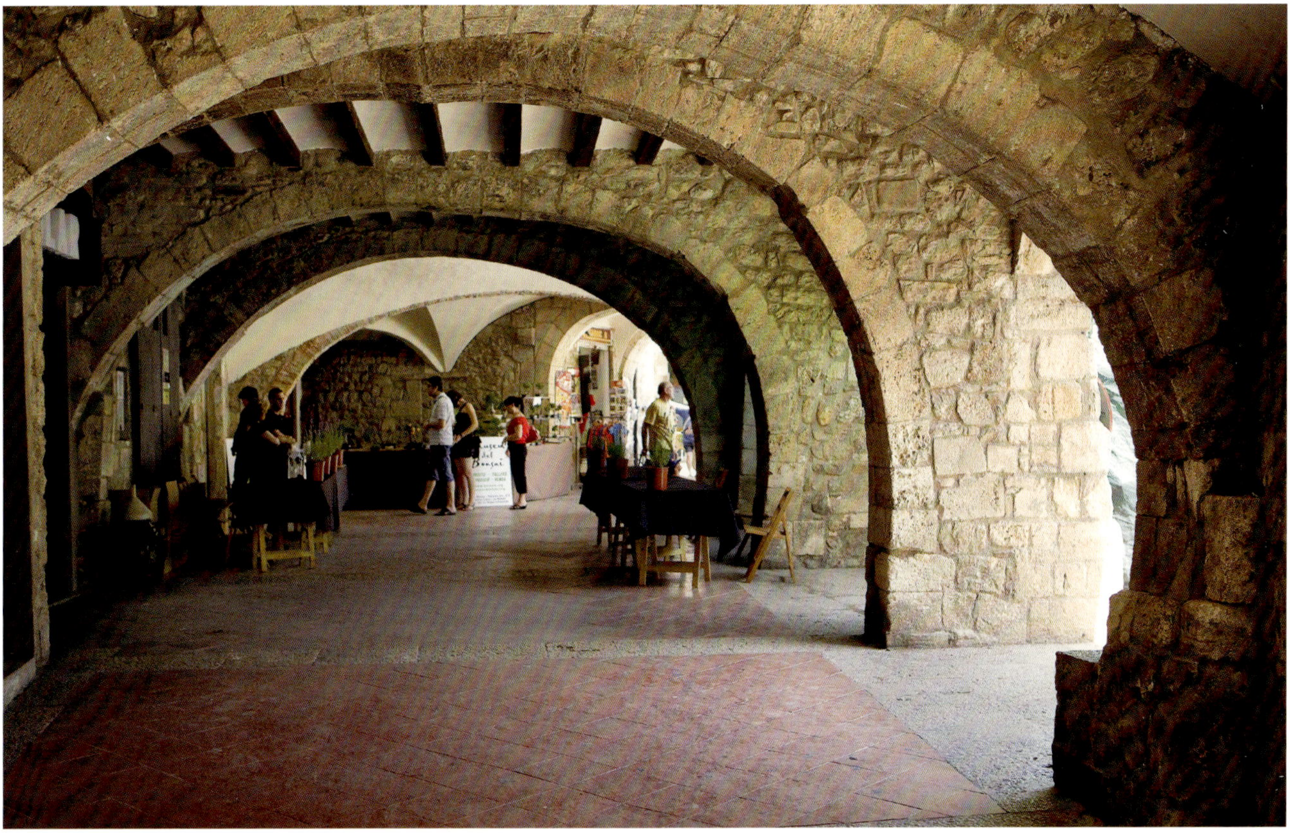

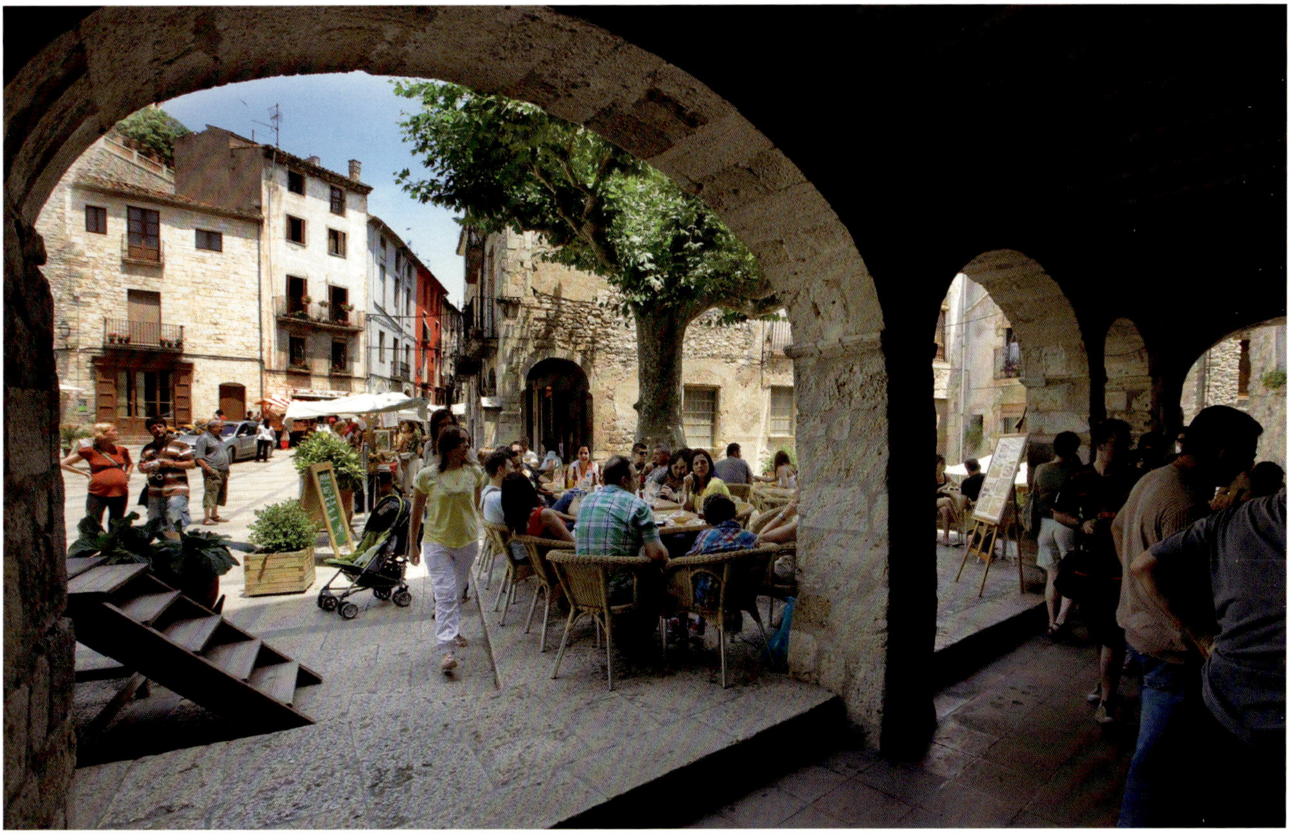

Plaça de la Llibertat

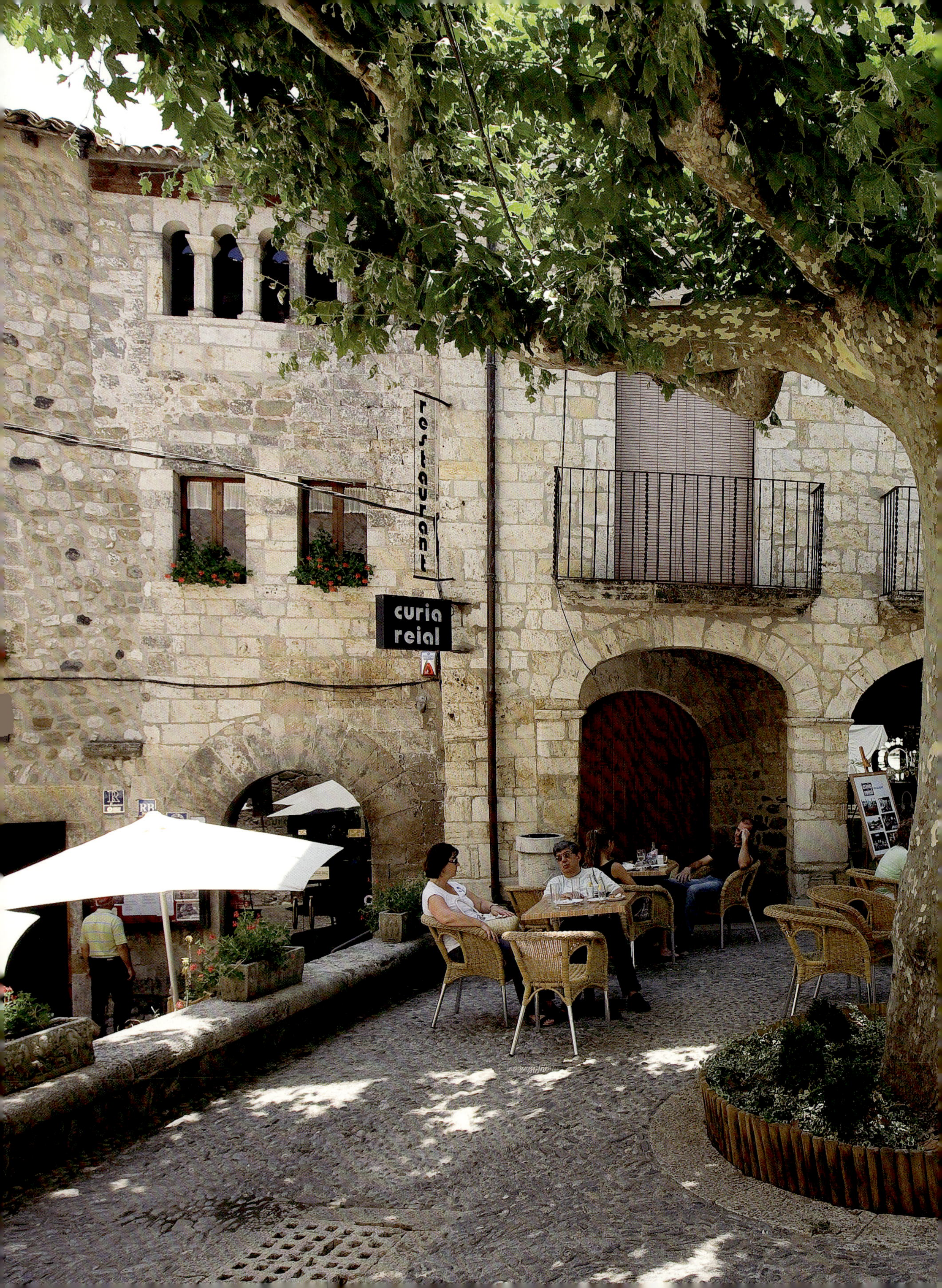
restaurant
curia
reial

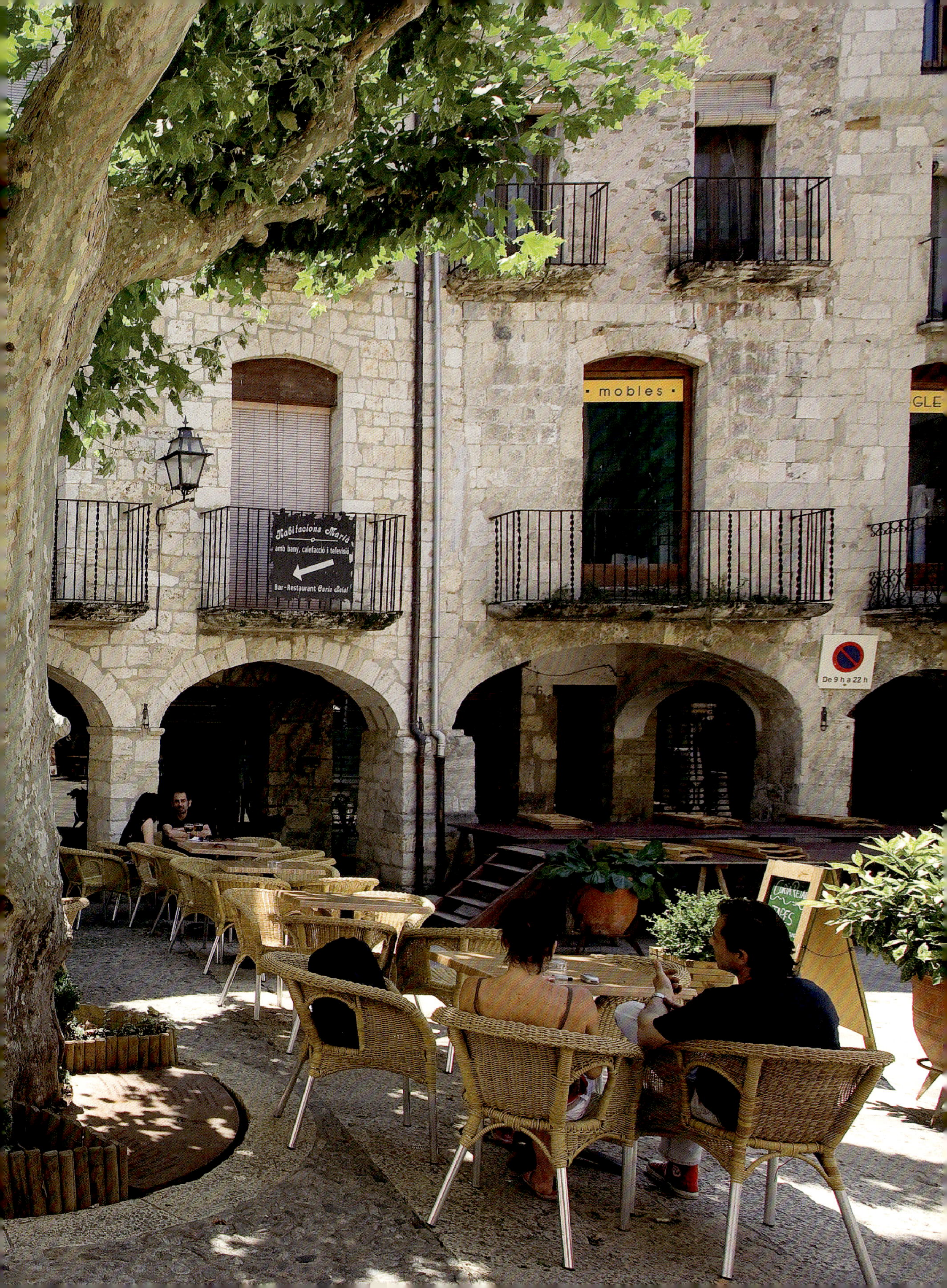
mobles
Habitacions Marià
amb bany, calefacció i televisió
Bar-Restaurant Curia Reial
De 9 h a 22 h

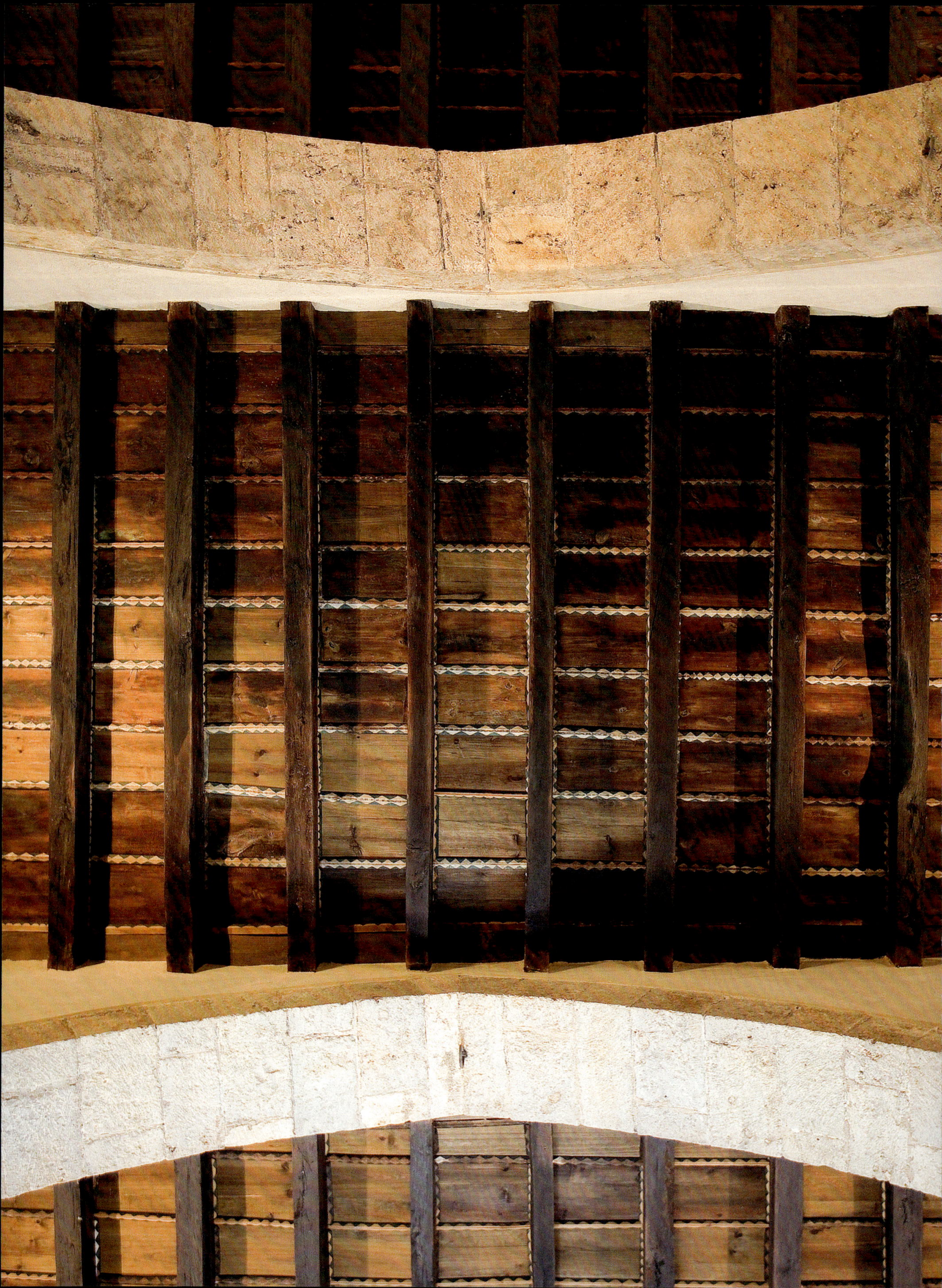

The Cúria Reial

It is a fine ashlar work building with voussoired portal, two windows with columns and simple capitals on the outside. The upper floor is entered through an inner courtyard with arches, where there is a wide staircase, also in masonry stone. The Gothic hall shows the structure of ogival arches and a coffered ceiling from the 14th century. In the same building but below, we also find three rooms that formed the home of the Jewish Astruc David family, who lived there from 1300 until 1362. That was when the house was sold to Bernat Cavaller, attorney of the king, and that was how it took the name of the Palace of Justice.

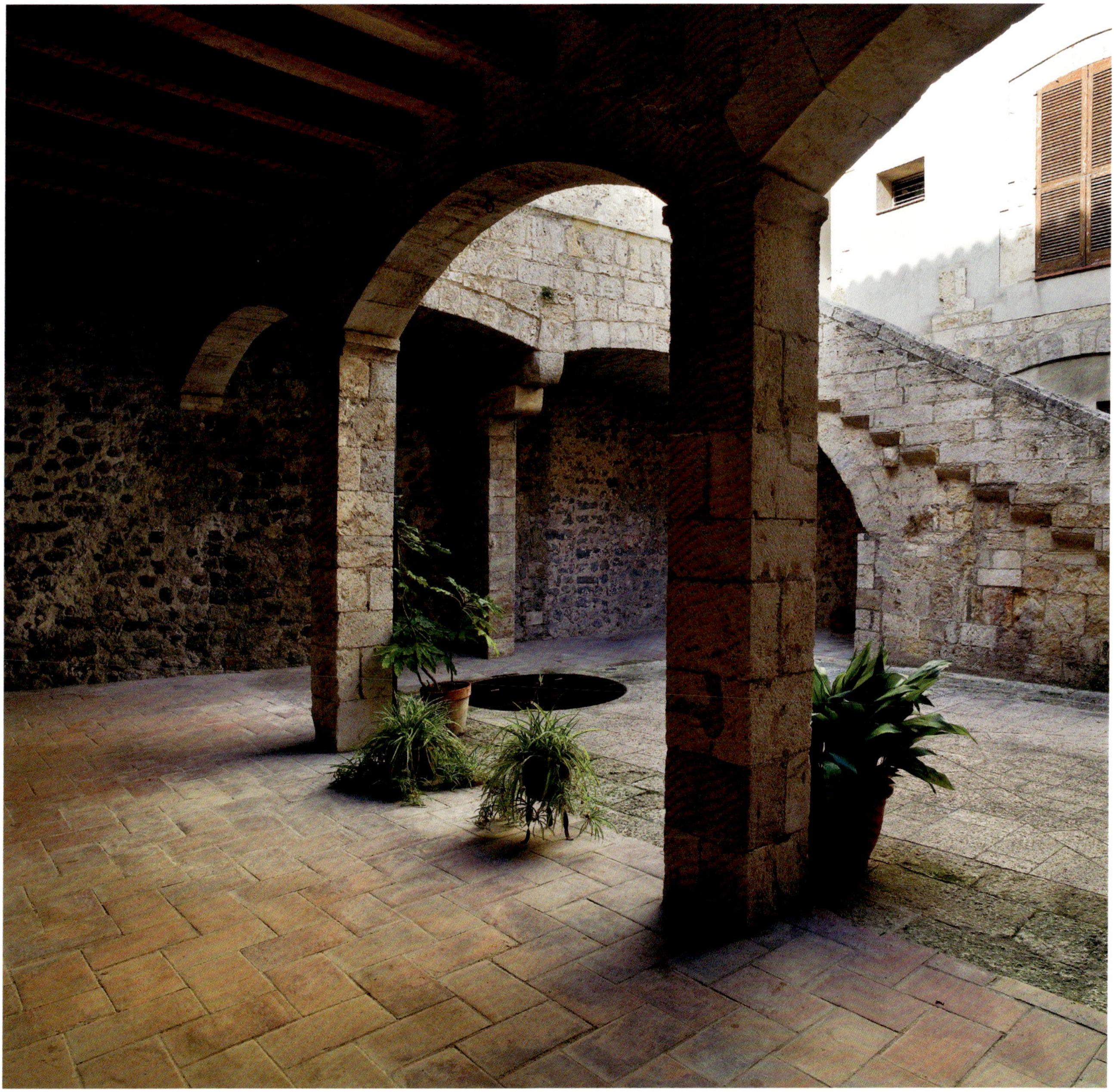

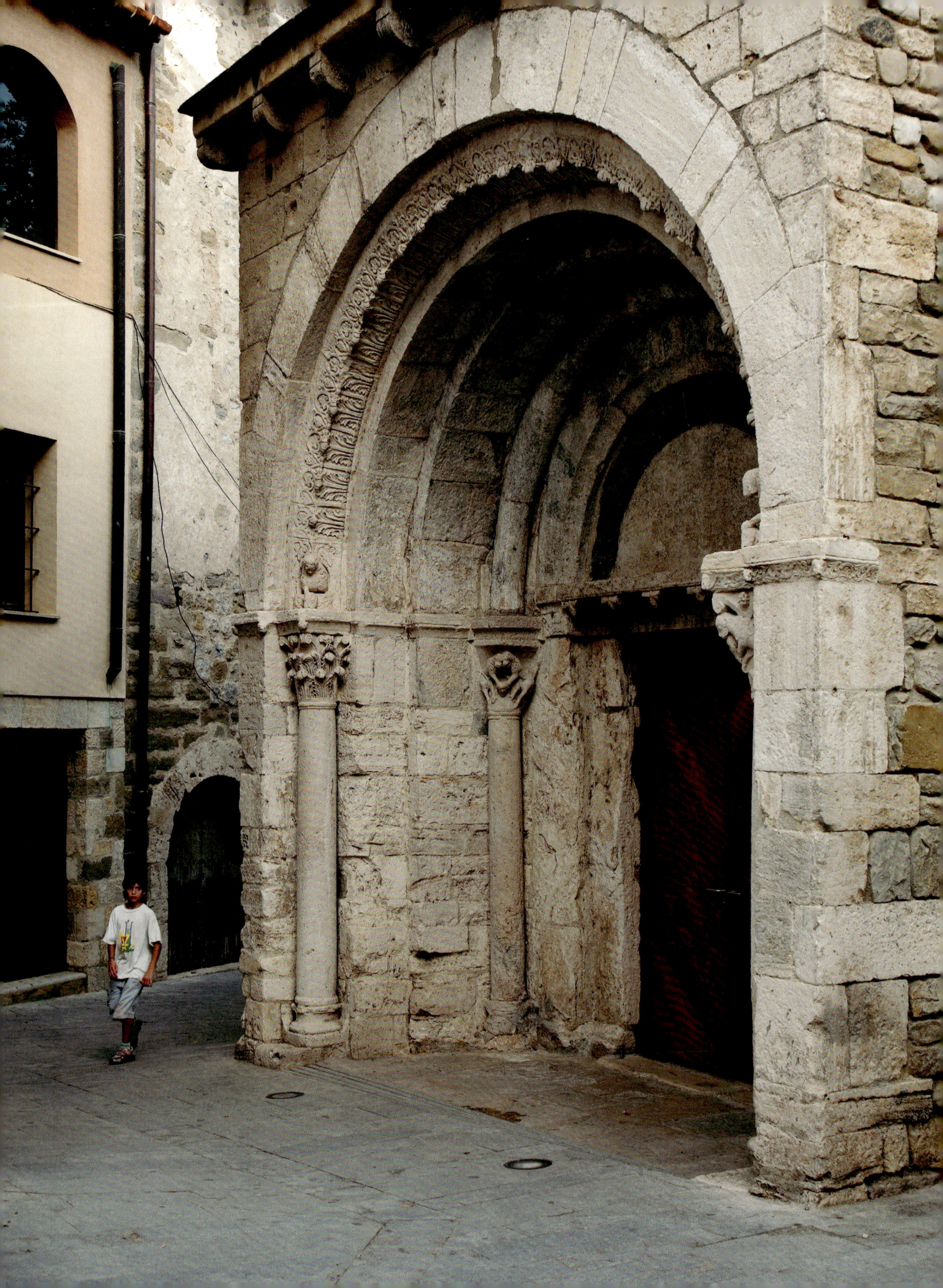

The hospital of Sant Julià

It is situated just behind the apse of the church of Sant Pere. The building forms a rectangular body of a single nave. Of the early temple only the imposing entrance remains, facing west. It is a magnificent, very deep set doorway. Five archivolts outline the entrance arch, and the first and last are supported on two pairs of columns with their corresponding capitals. Of the five arches, only the exterior one is carved with acanthus leaf relief, adorned with plant motifs on the upper part. Of the capitals that crown the four columns, the inner two are identical, while of the outer two, one has a plant decoration and the other includes two lions that share the same head, which placed on the side of the capital, bites the sinful human head. The threshold of the doorway appears adorned with six corbels, decorated with acanthus leaves and flowers, just like the first arch.

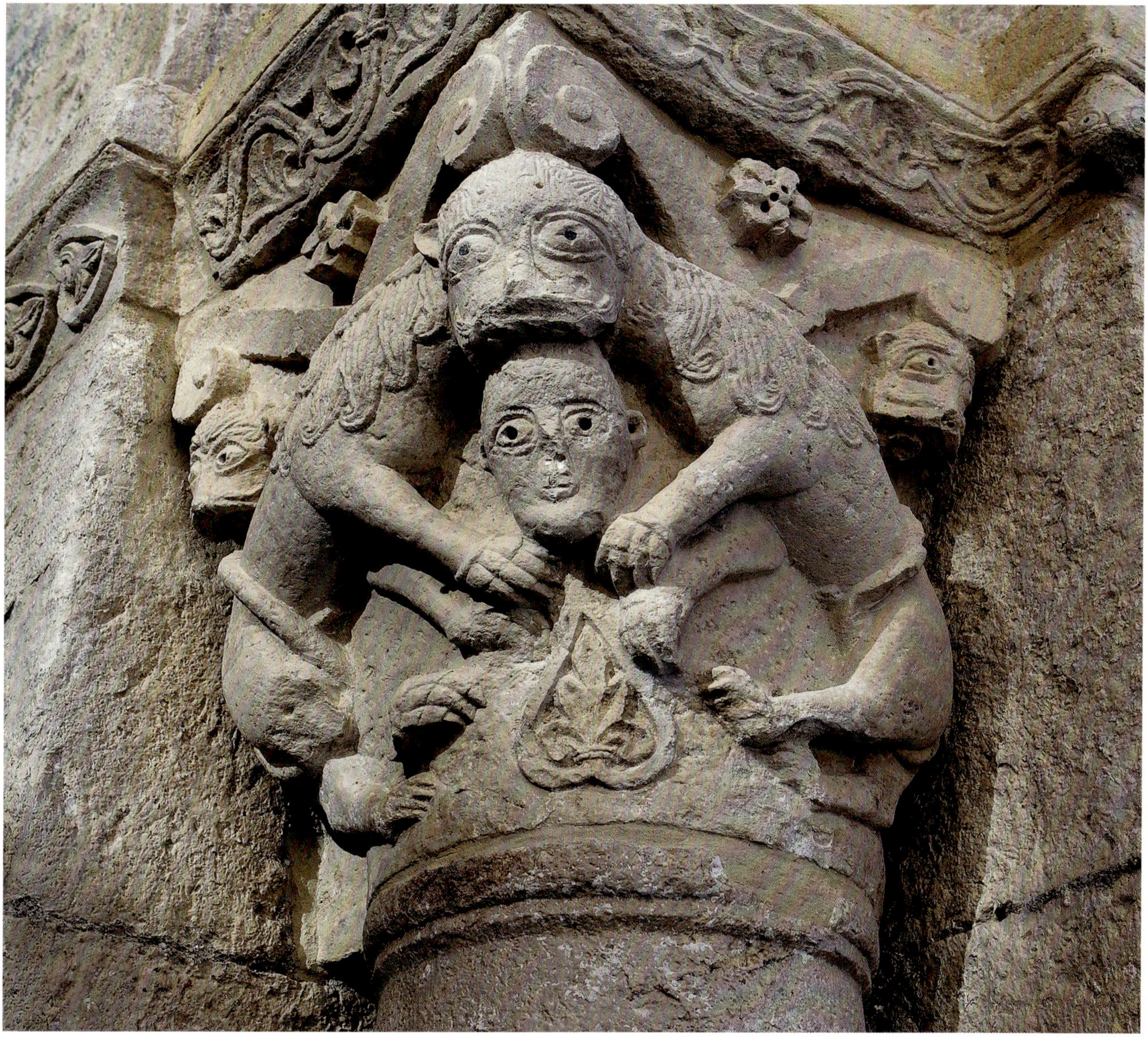

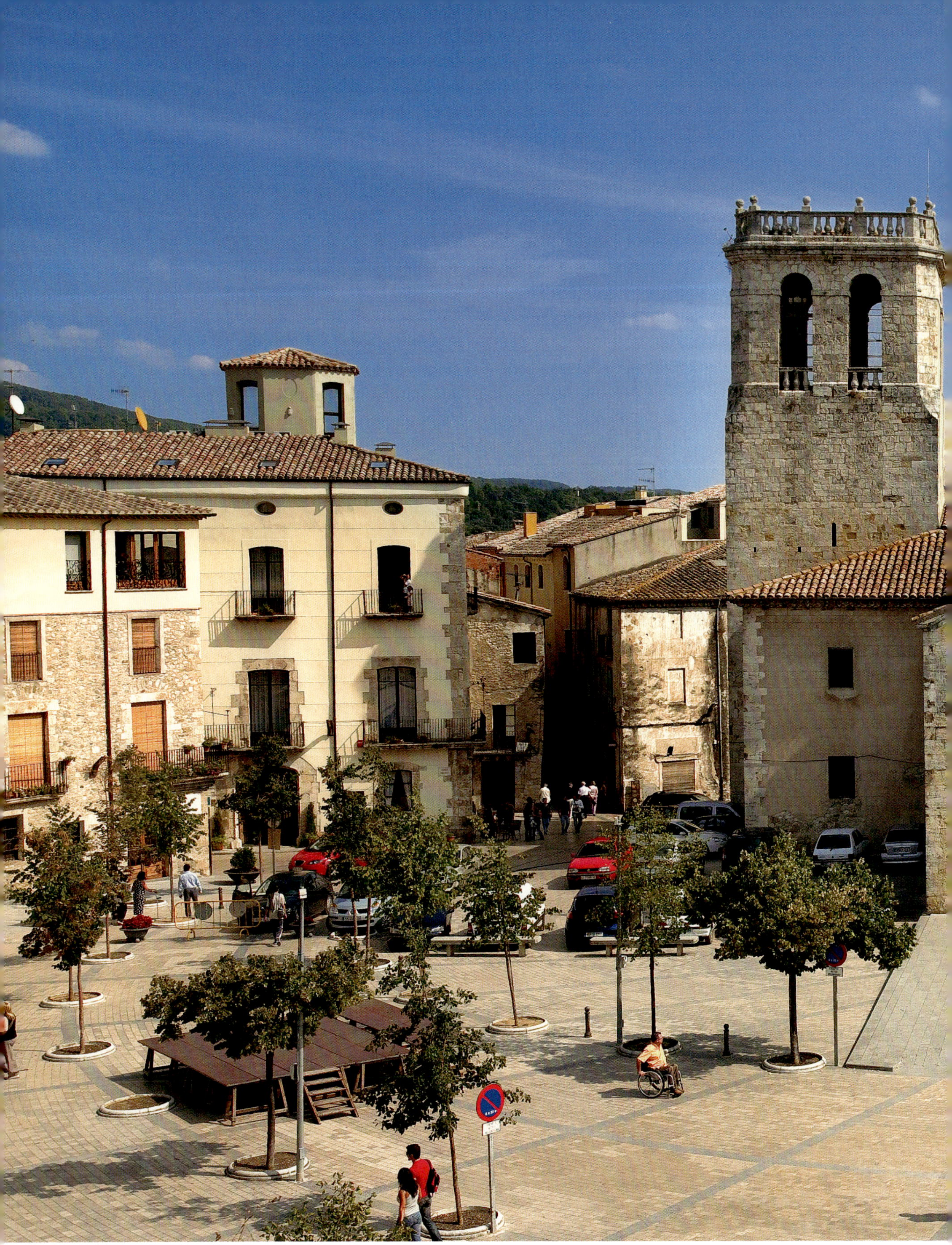

Prat de Sant Pere

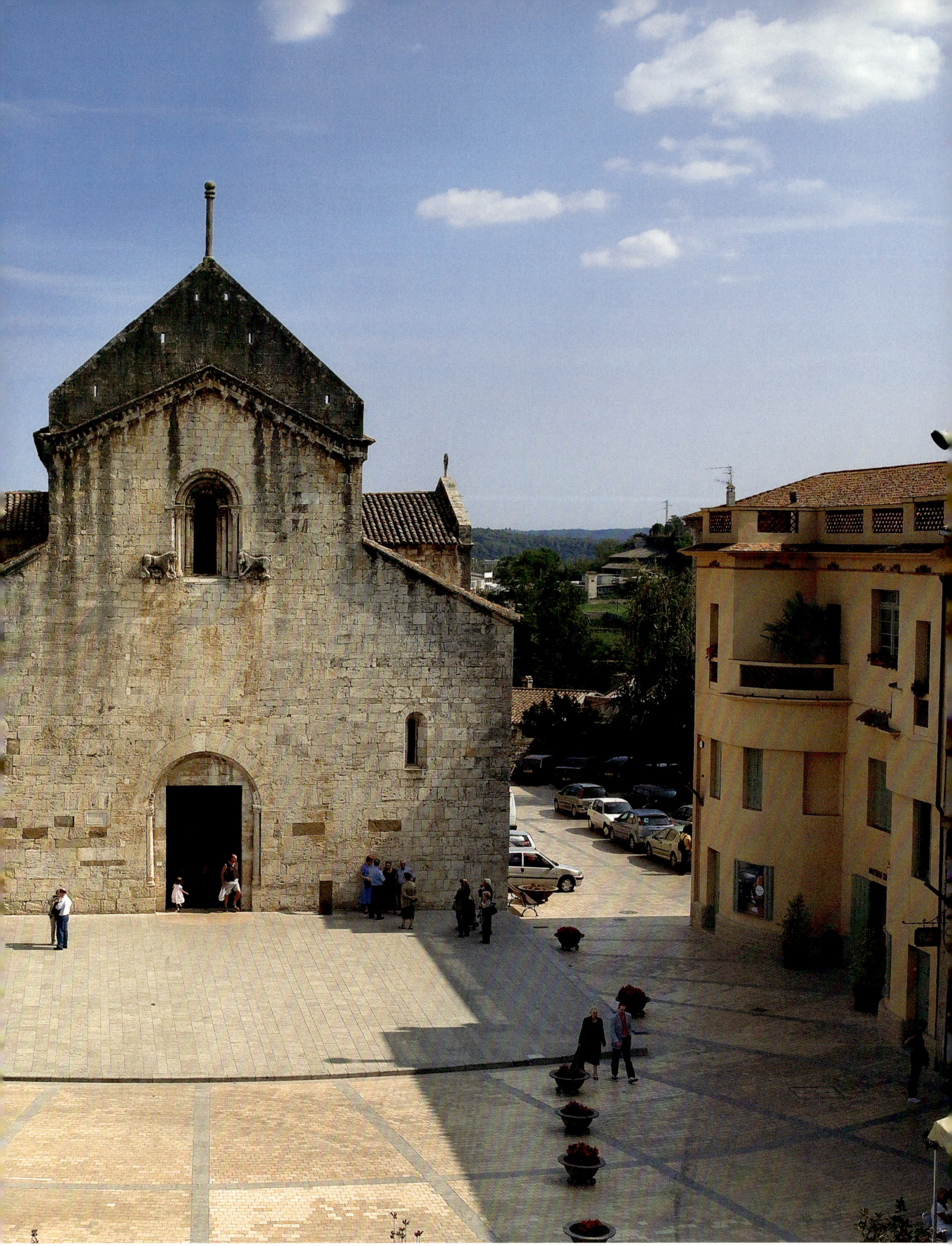

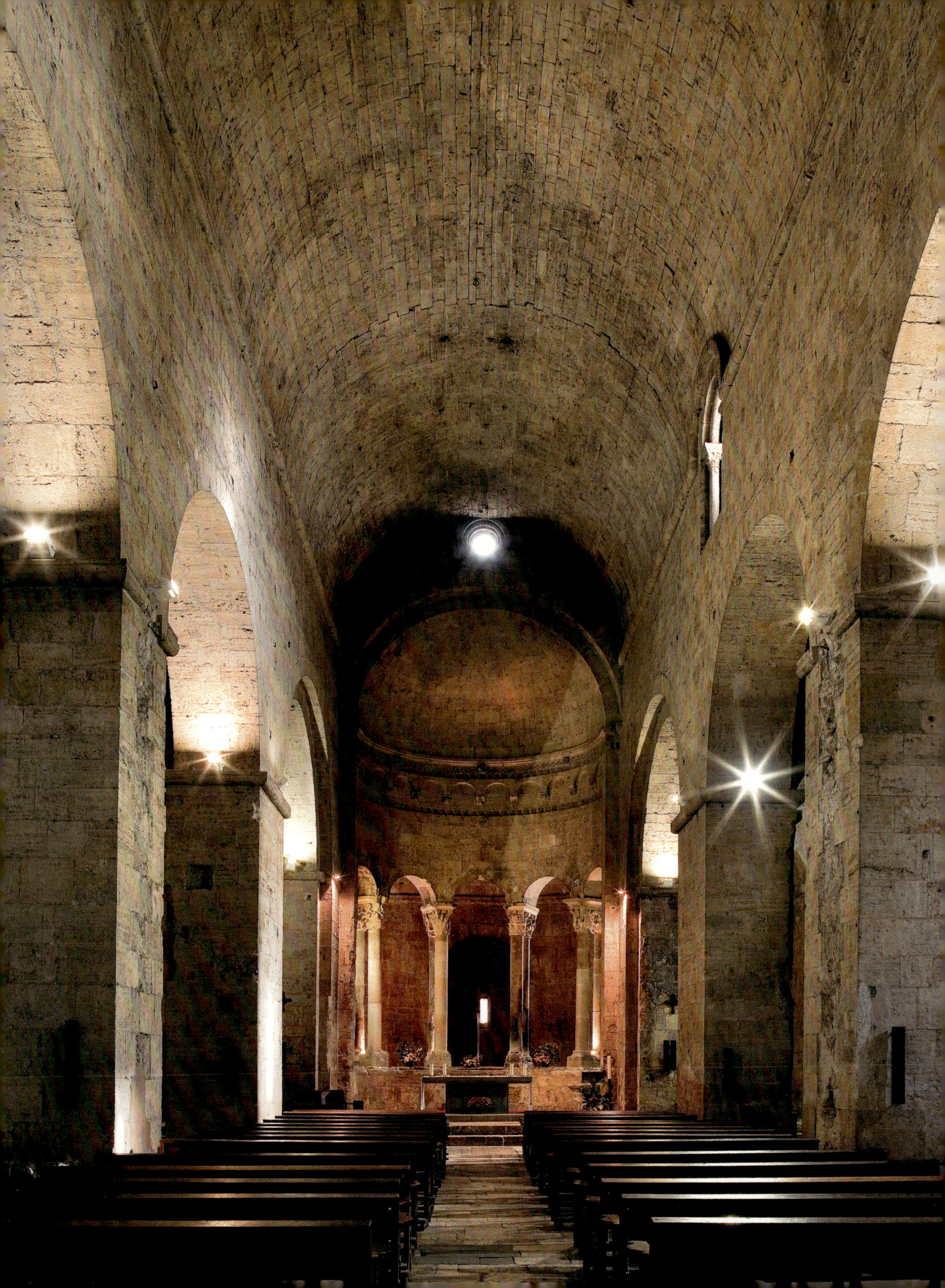

The Monastery and El Prat de Sant Pere

All that remains of the old monastery of Sant Pere de Besalú, after the sale of Church lands in 1835, is the church and some rooms attached to the north face, beneath the 17th-century Baroque bell tower.

The façade of Sant Pere has a quite unique large window in which one can appreciate the figures of two lions, symbol of the strength, power and protection that the Church provided against evil and paganism. The travertine stone used to build this monastery, just like the other medieval buildings of the town, comes from the quarries of Serinyà.

The square opposite, El Prat de Sant Pere, was the old cemetery of the monastery where all the faithful had the right to be buried. It has never been given the name of square. Popular superstition and magical beliefs have turned it into *prat*, meadow, despite the fact that there is no grass and it is in the middle of the town.

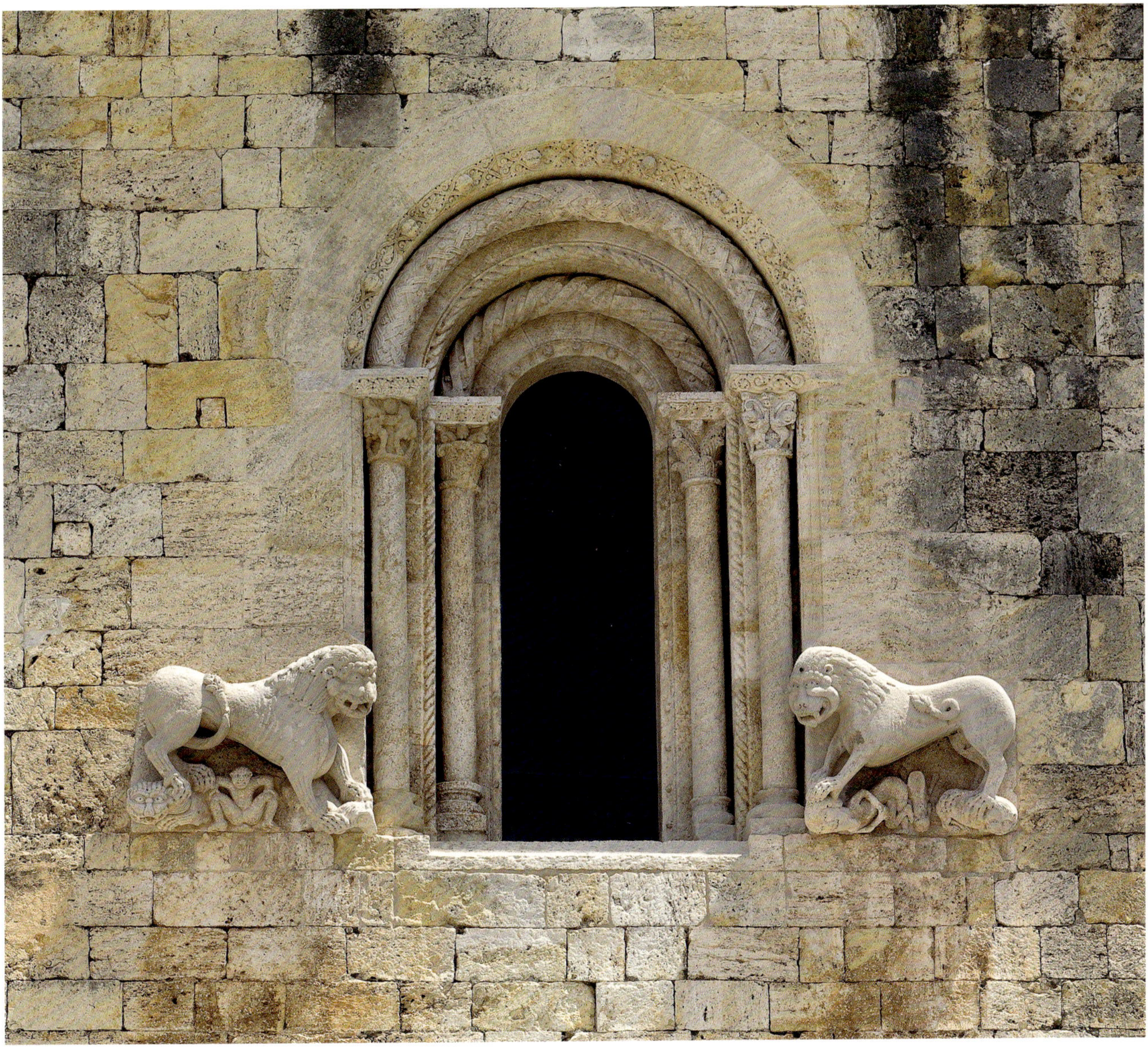

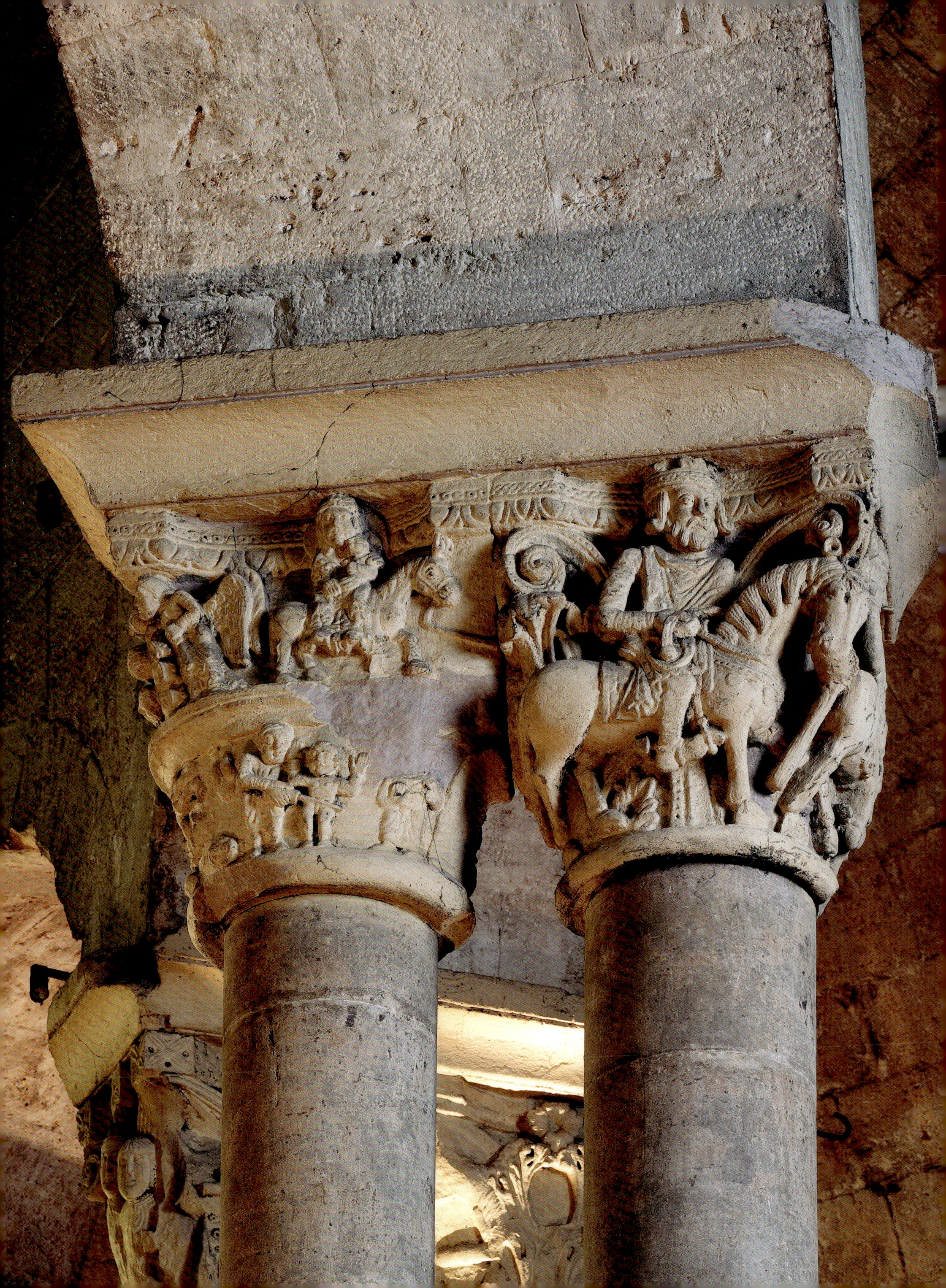

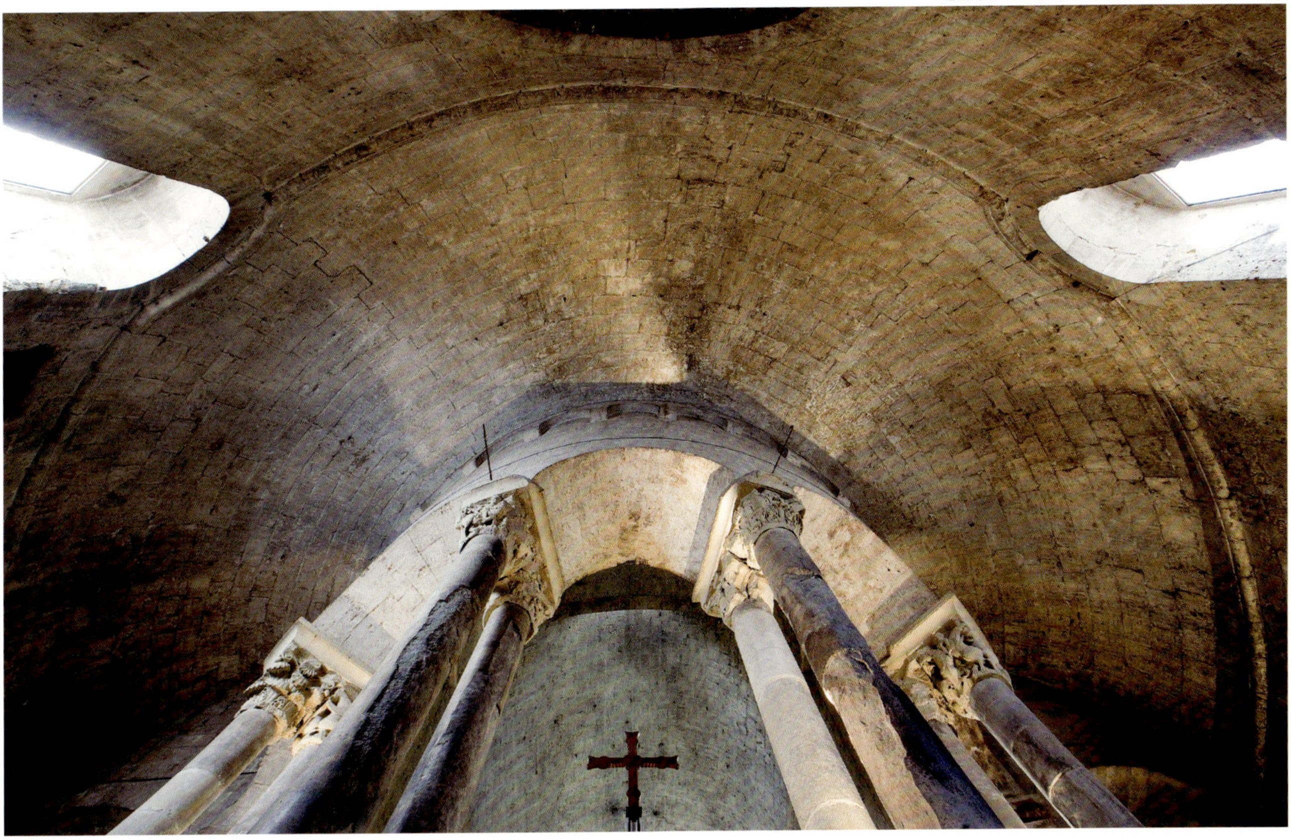

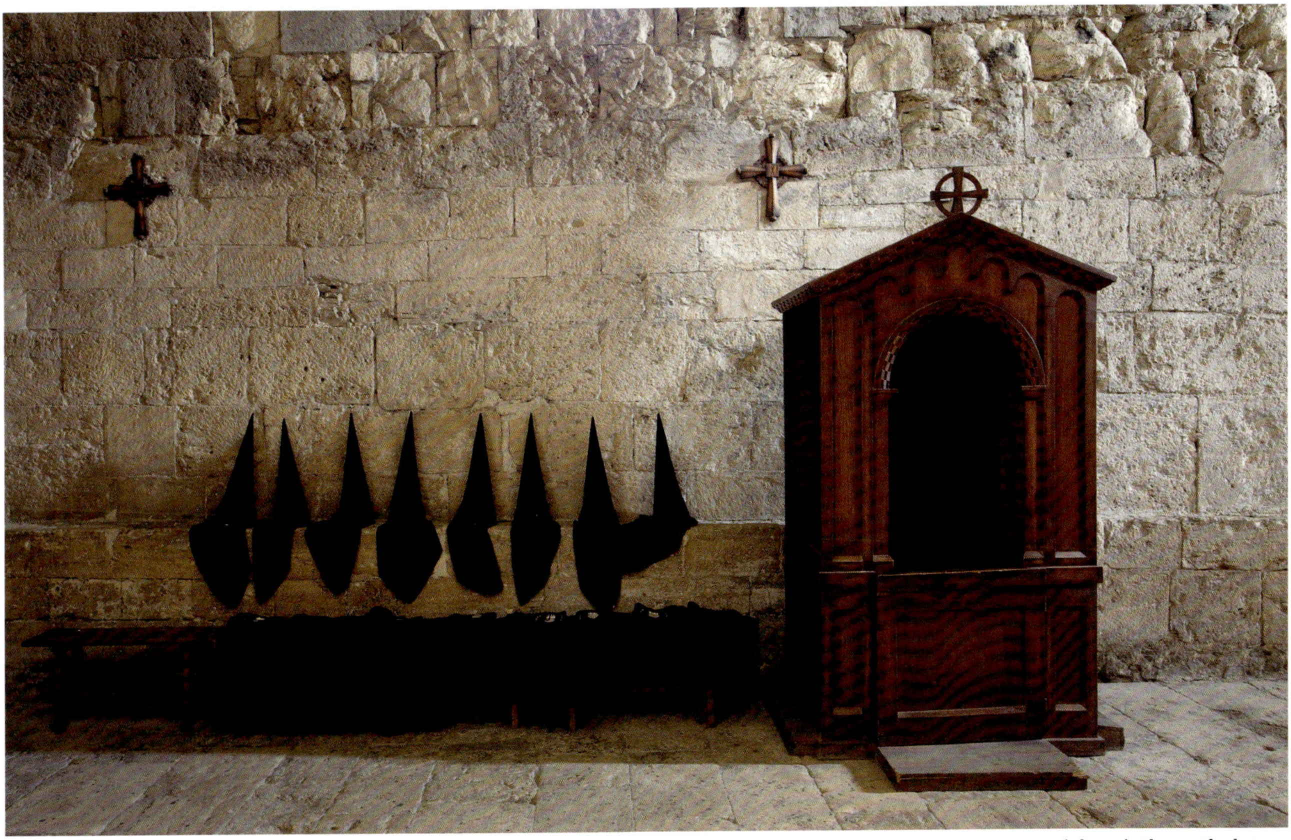

◂ Detail of the capitals

(above) The ambulatory

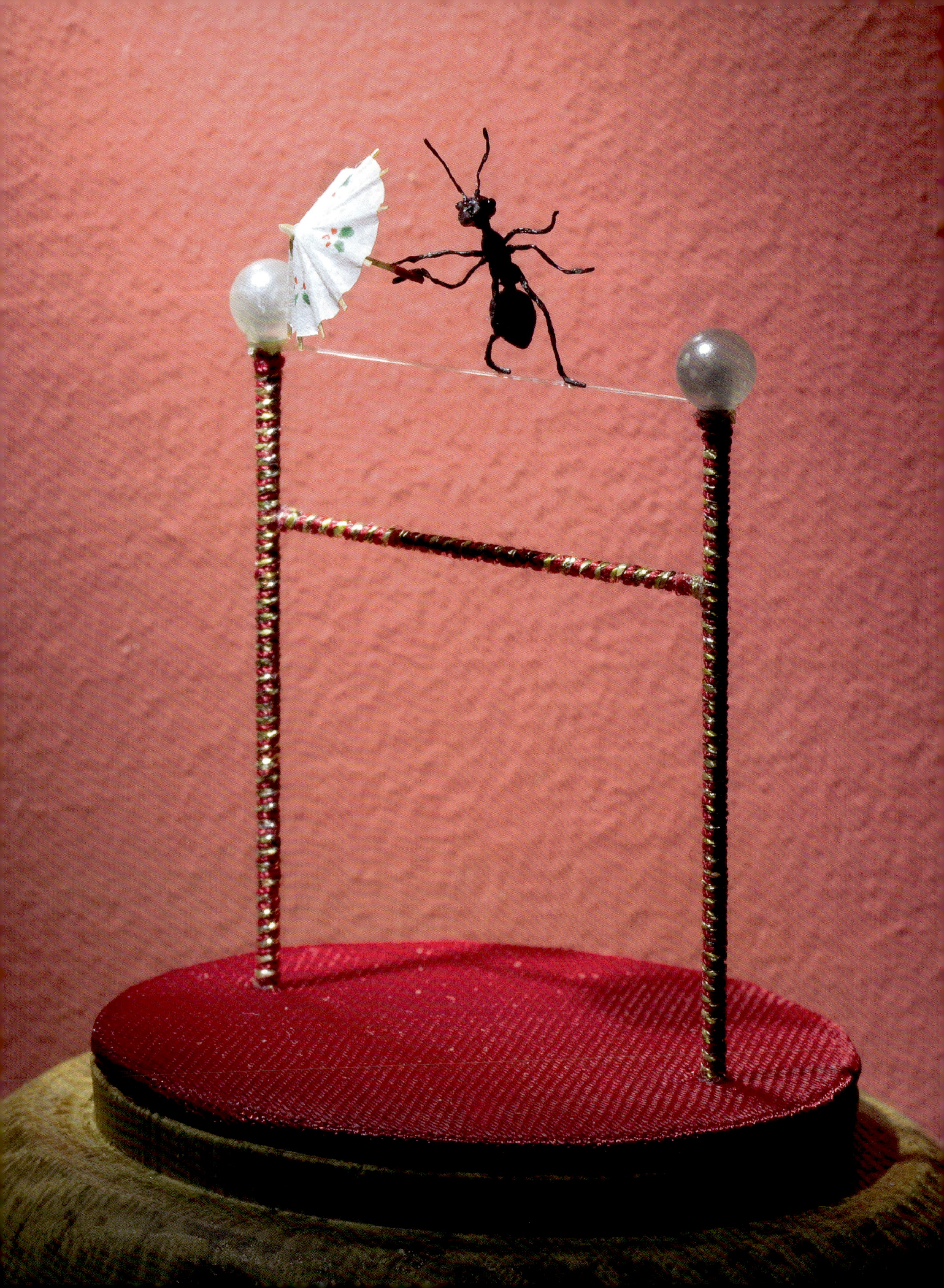

The Museum of the Miniature

It is in the Prat de Sant Pere. Visiting this museum is like entering into another reality, on another scale. It is discovering one of the most complete and varied collection of miniatures in Europe and the first in Catalonia, housed in a singular building. It is finding out about a series of magnificent works that will introduce us into several miniature worlds: a 19th-century pharmacy, a hairdresser's from the 1920s... It is observing more than 2,000 increasingly smaller items until reaching the unimaginable dimensions of micro-miniatures: you will be amazed before a caravan of camels on the hole of a needle, a series of jewels on an apple pip, and even the Eiffel Tower on a poppy seed.

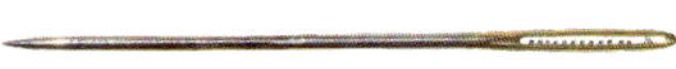

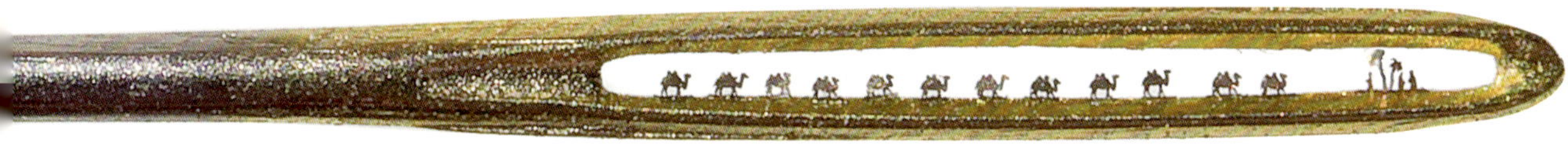

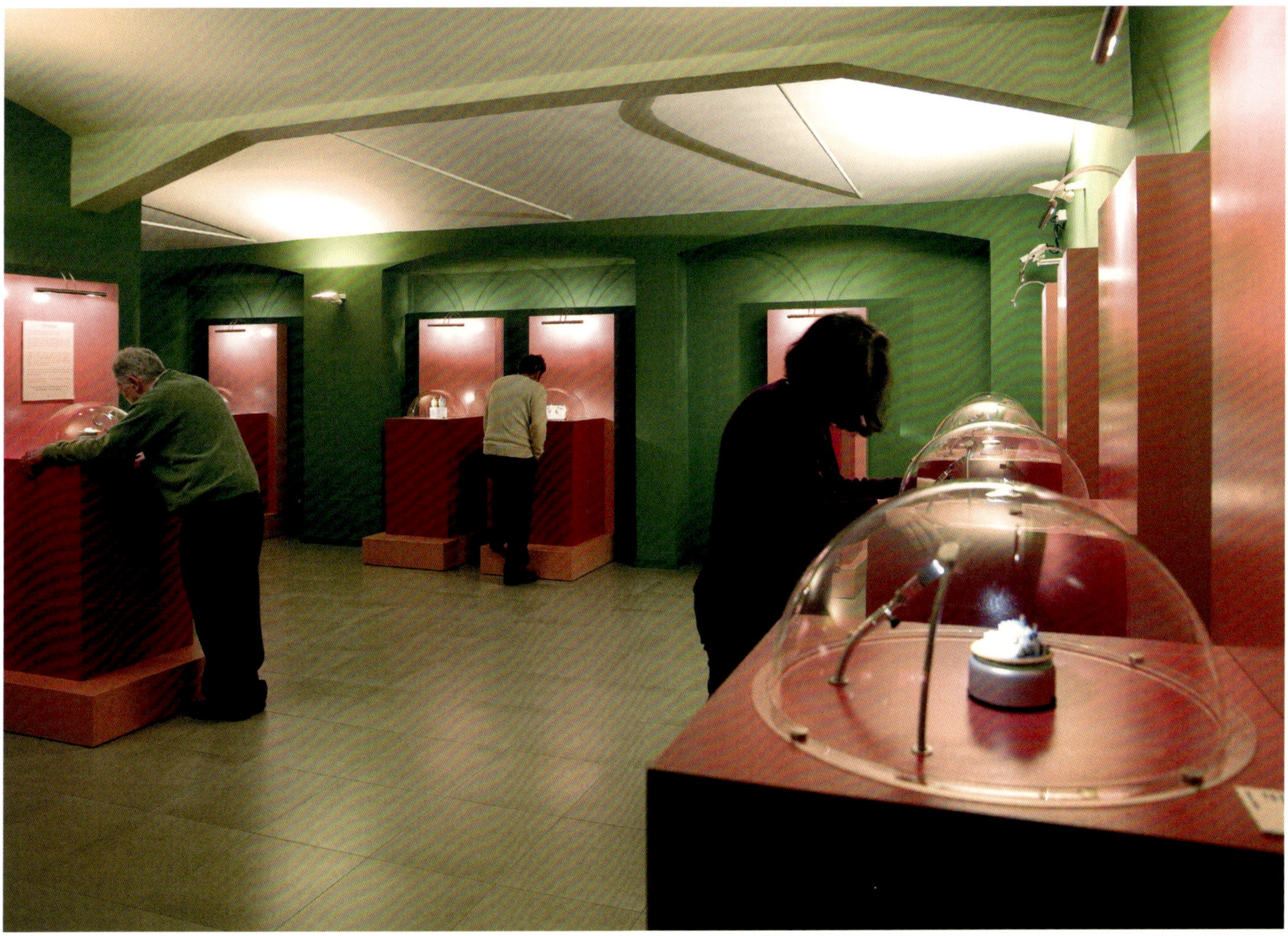

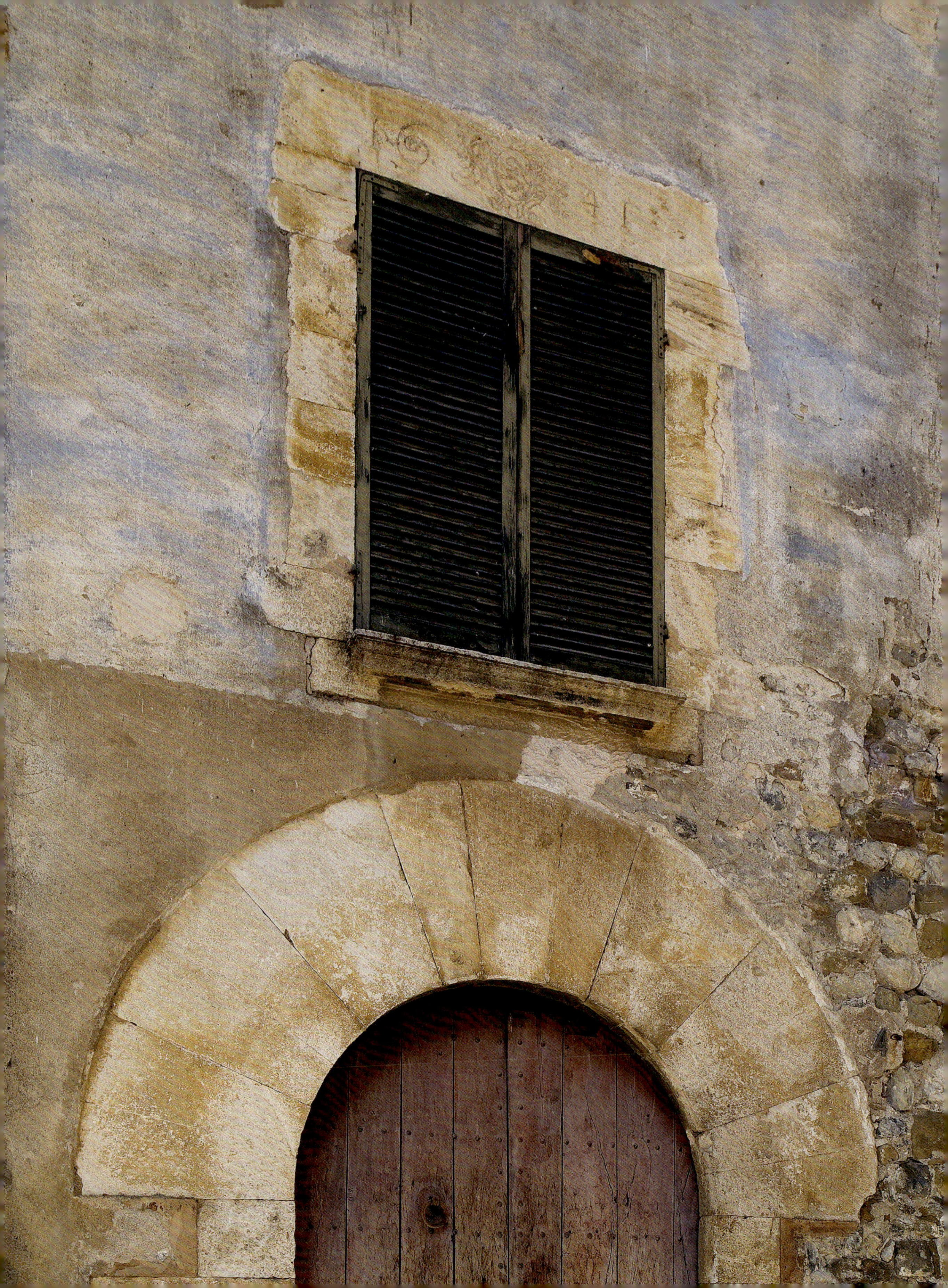

La casa Cornellà or Can Llaudes

Is considered one of the best-conserved Romanesque civil buildings in all Catalonia. It dates from the 12th century, and we should place the year of its construction post-1171, the year in which authorisation was given to build El Prat de Sant Pere. Of the entire structure of the house, there is no doubt that the most important element is the courtyard. The interest in Casa Cornellà within the whole of medieval civil architecture is exceptional since it is the only clear example, conserved and prior to the 14th century, of the type that was dominant in civil urban architecture of the Gothic period. It is currently private property.

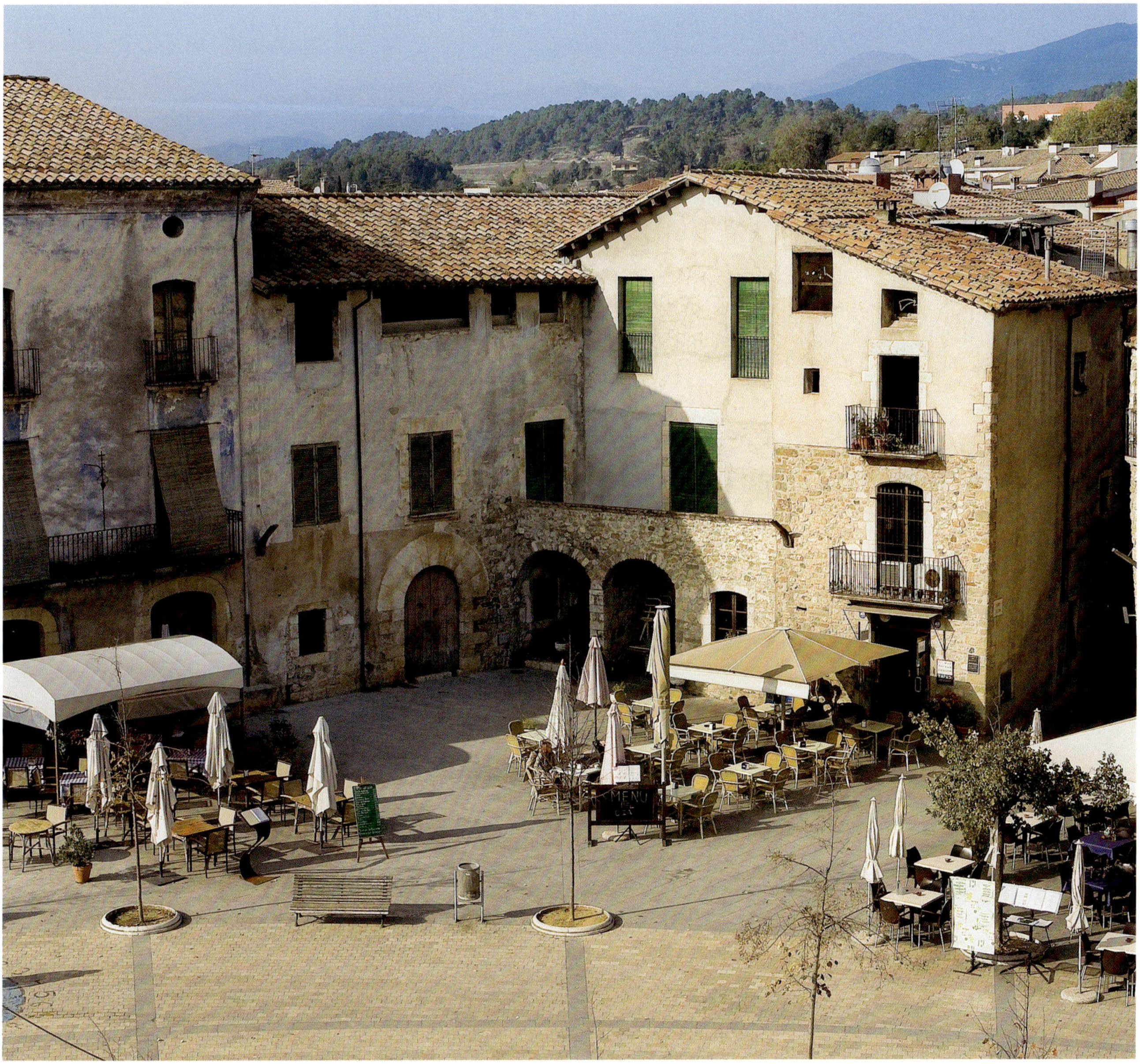

Central courtyard of Casa Cornellà ▸

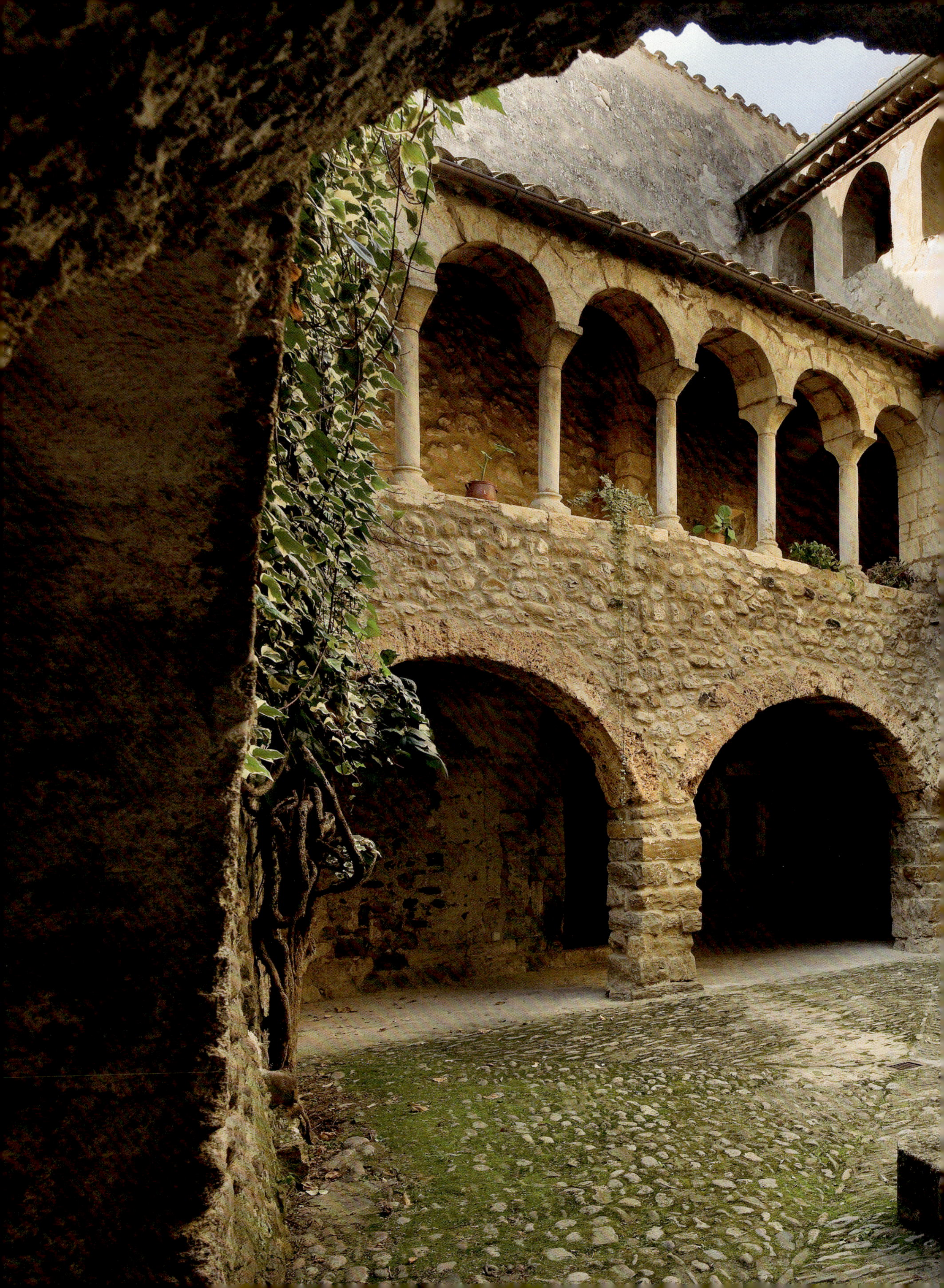

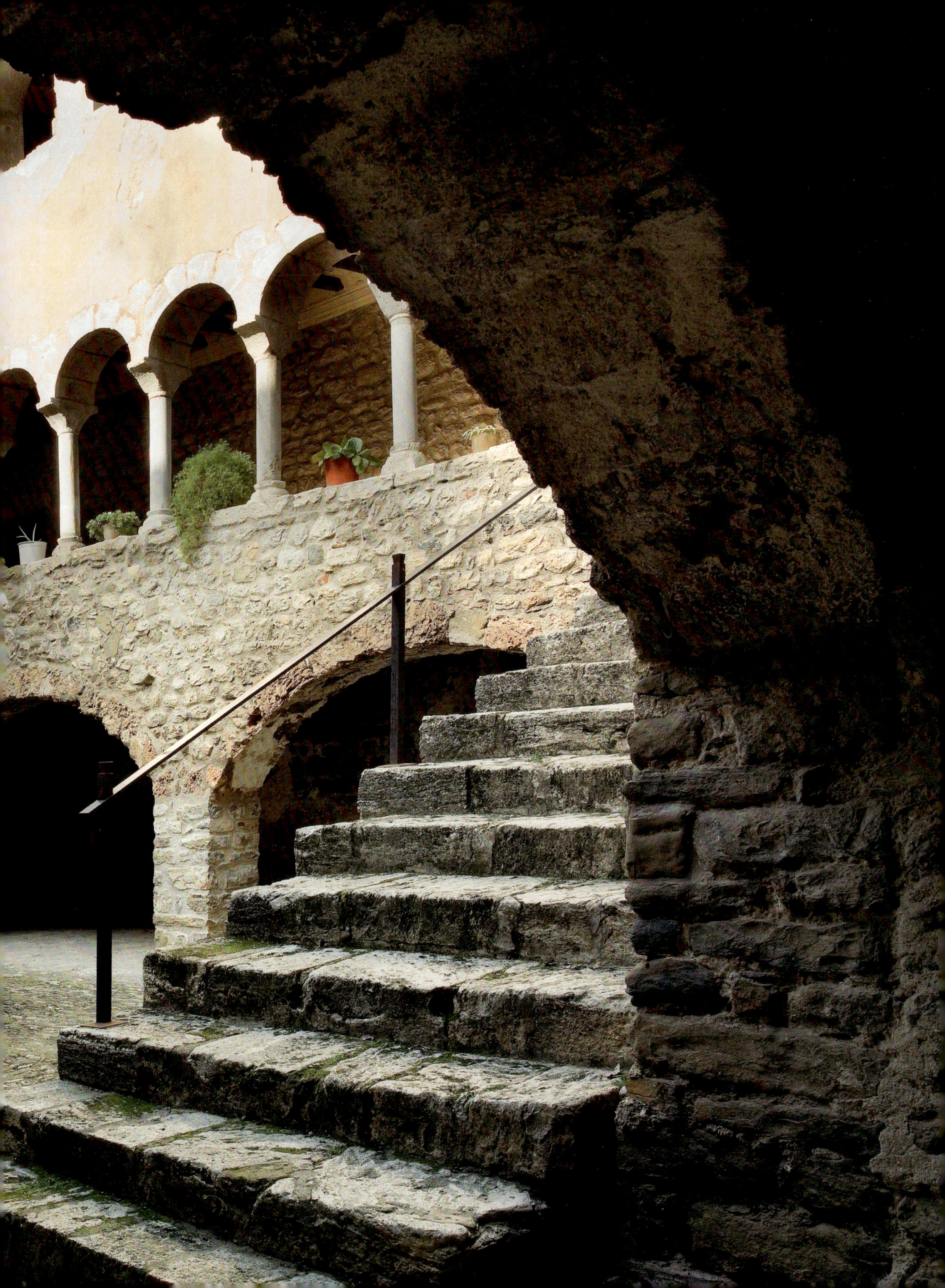

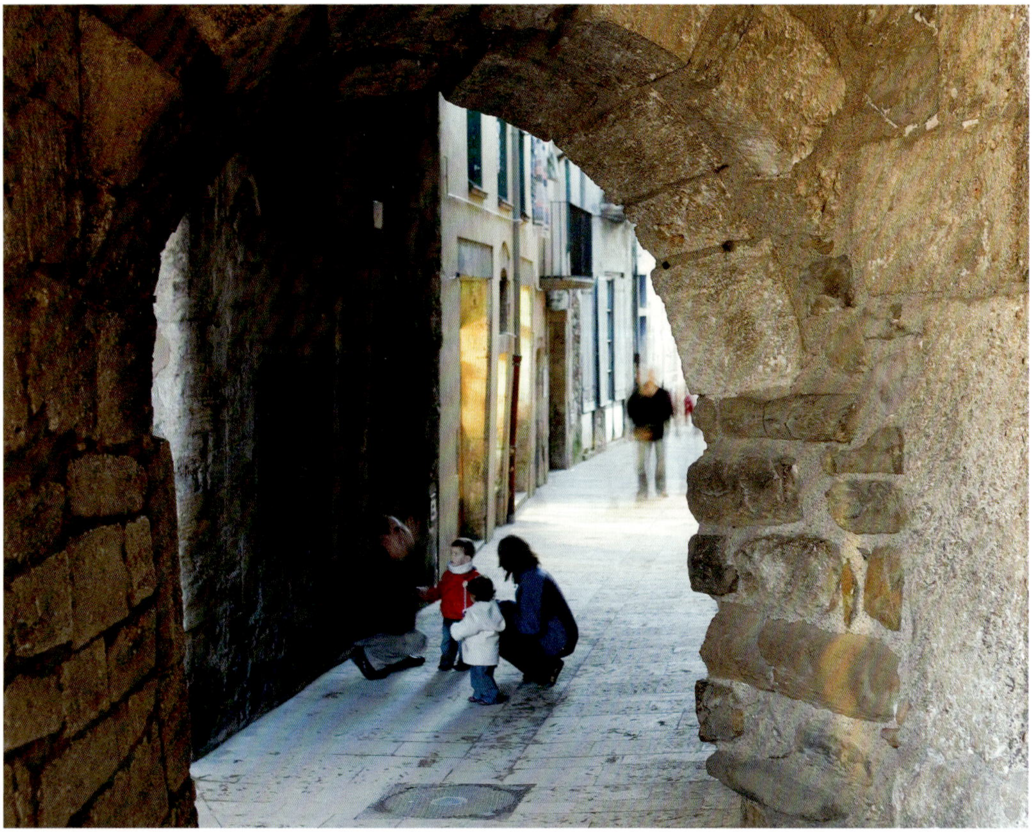

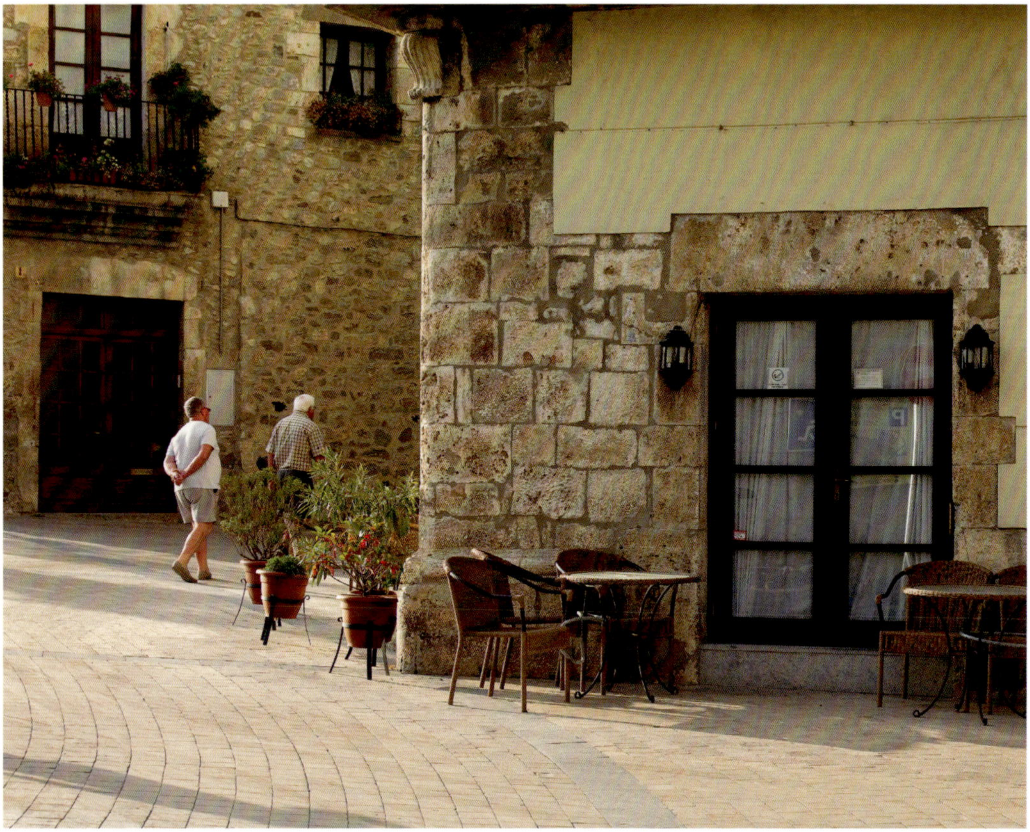

The three arches ▸

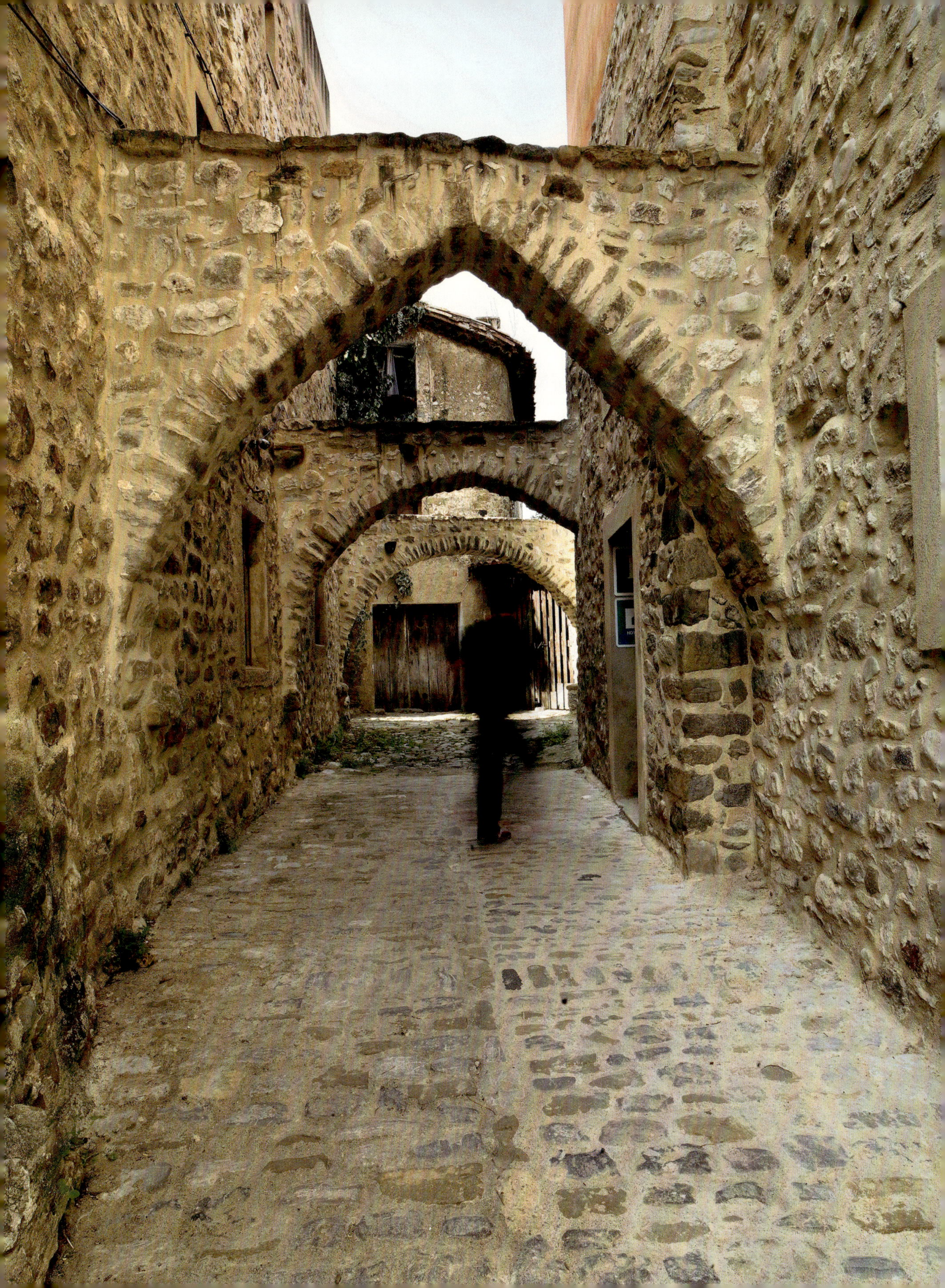

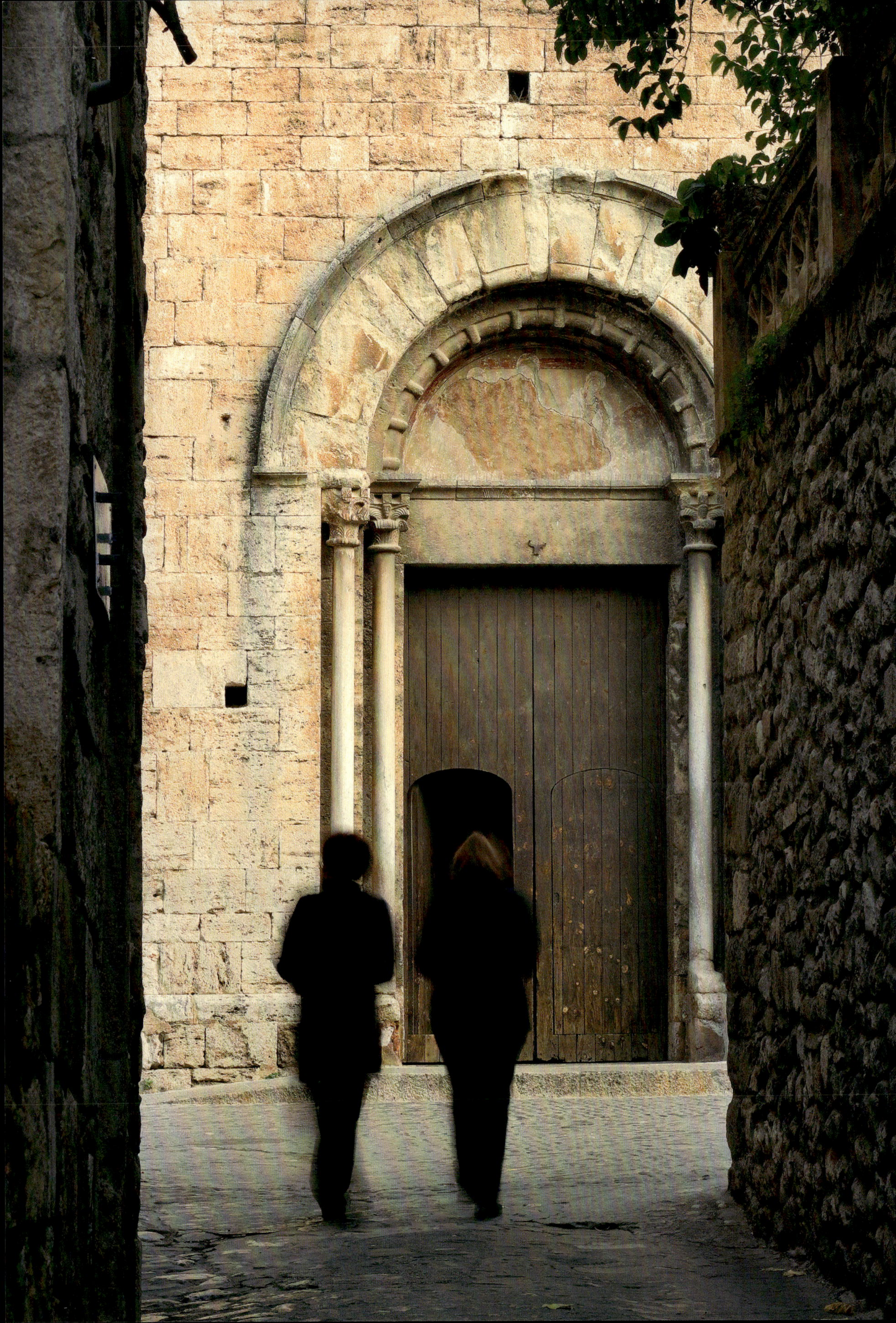

The church of Sant Vicenç

Documented in 977, in the period of Count-Bishop Miró, is currently the town's parish church. Inside, in the main presbytery, right by the gospel, we find the Gothic tomb of Pere de Rovira who brought the relics of Saint Vincent to Besalú in 1413. The tombstone is attributed to Pere Oller, one of the great sculptors of the time, and comprises three images: the central body of the recumbent and two smaller bodies of mourners in the upper and lower part.

Inside a Gothic side chapel is kept the Relic of the True Cross, loaned by Francesc Cambó in 1923, as replacement for the first one, brought by Bernat Tallaferro from Rome in 1017 and stolen in 1899.

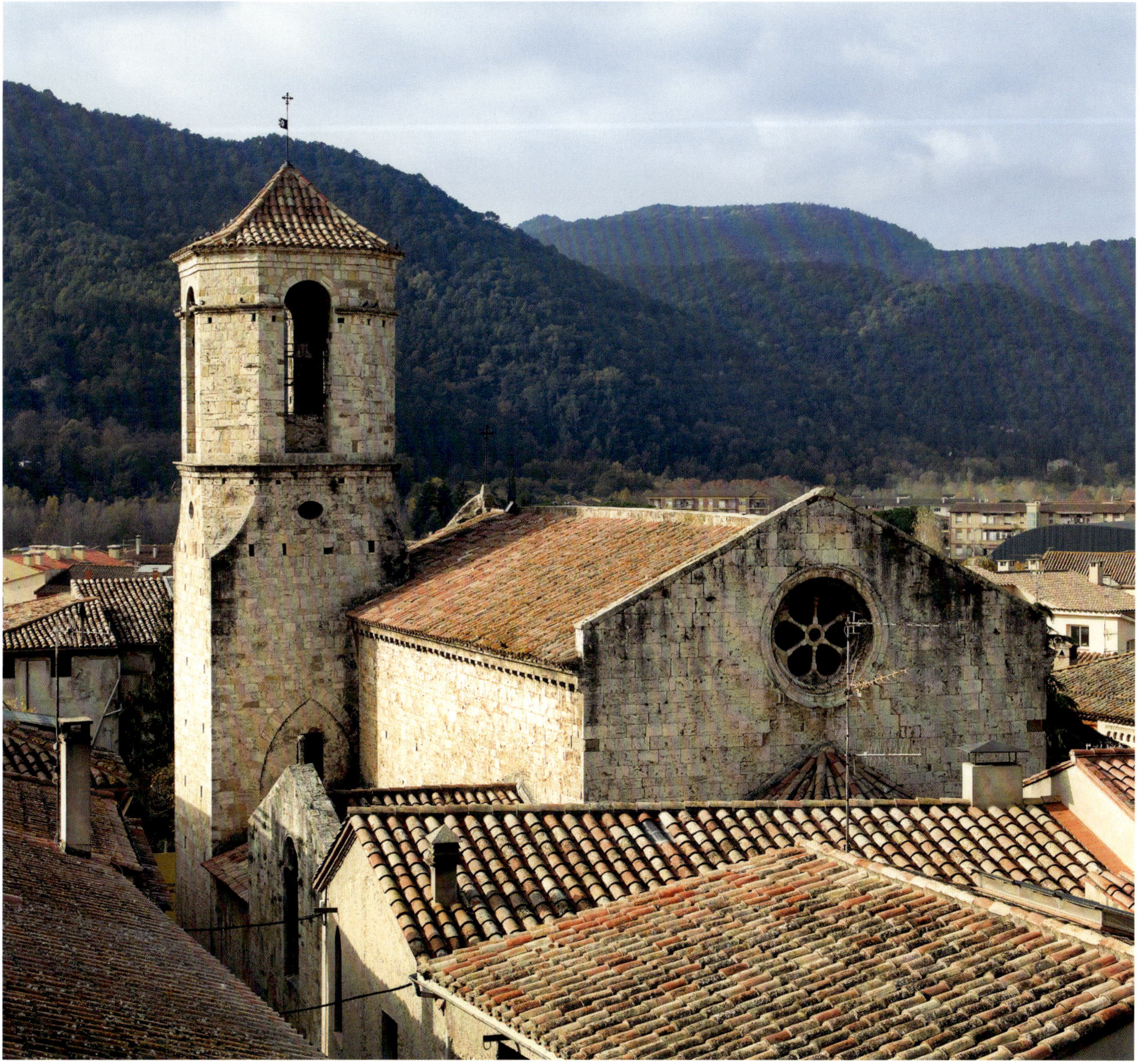

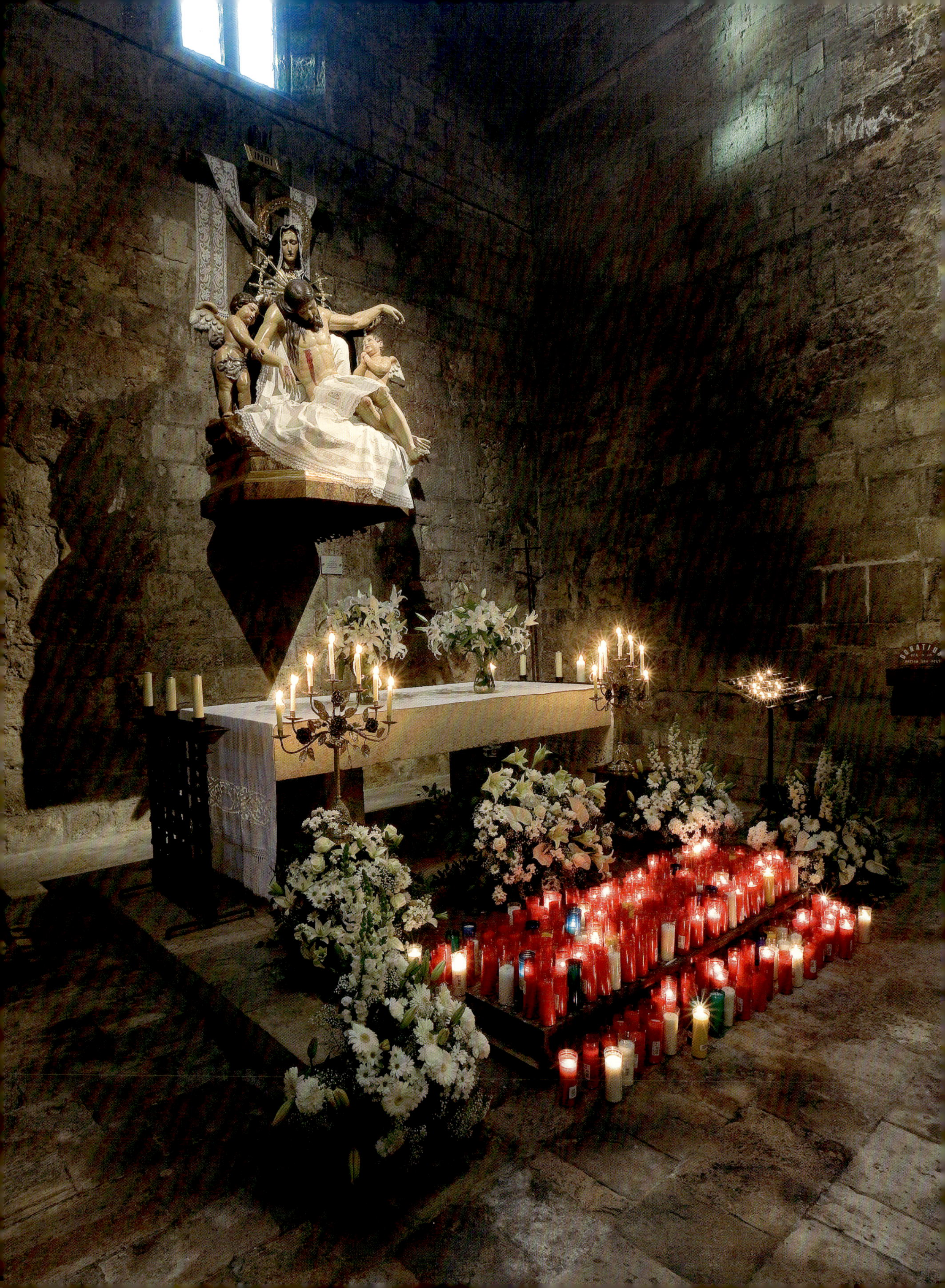

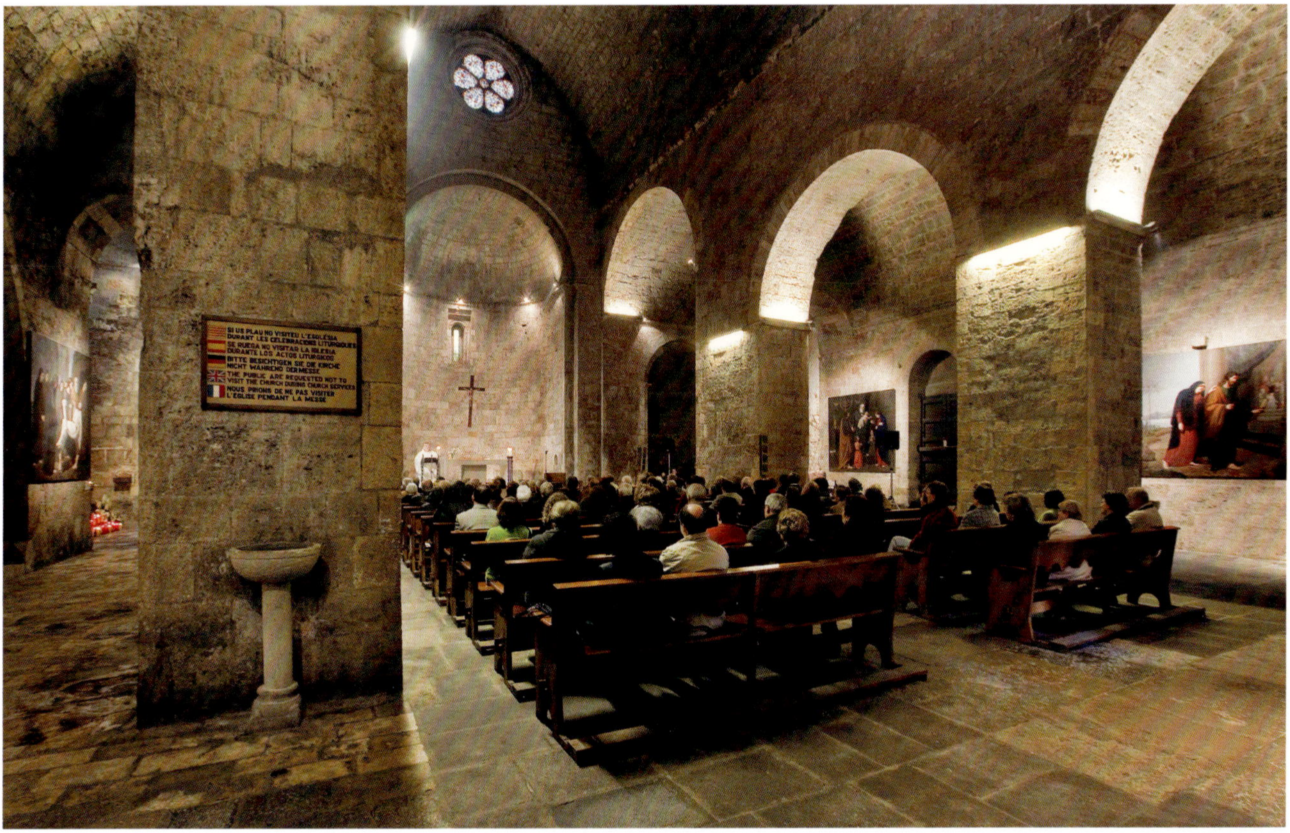

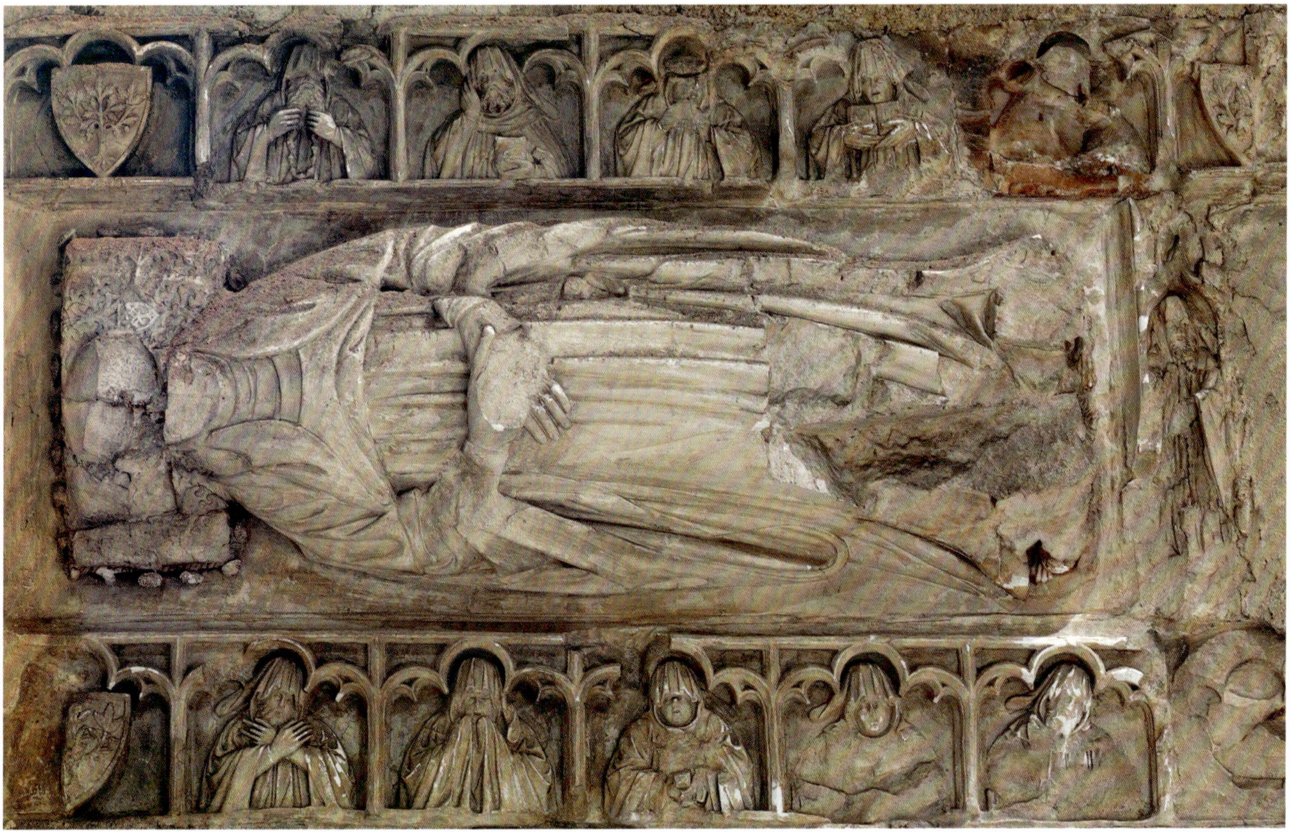

◂ Virgin of the Dolors

(above) Central nave of Sant Vicenç. (below) Gothic tomb of Pere Rovira

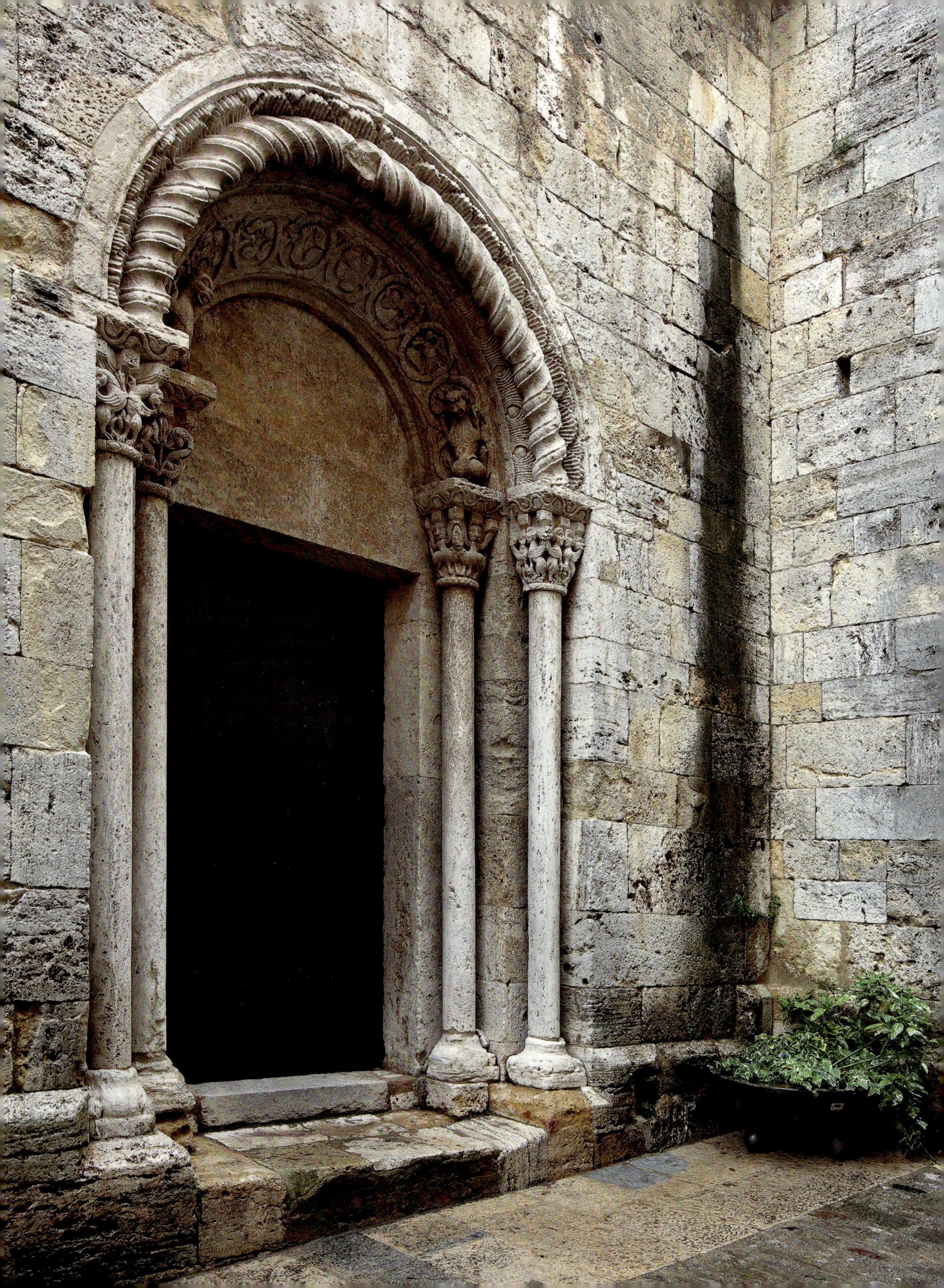

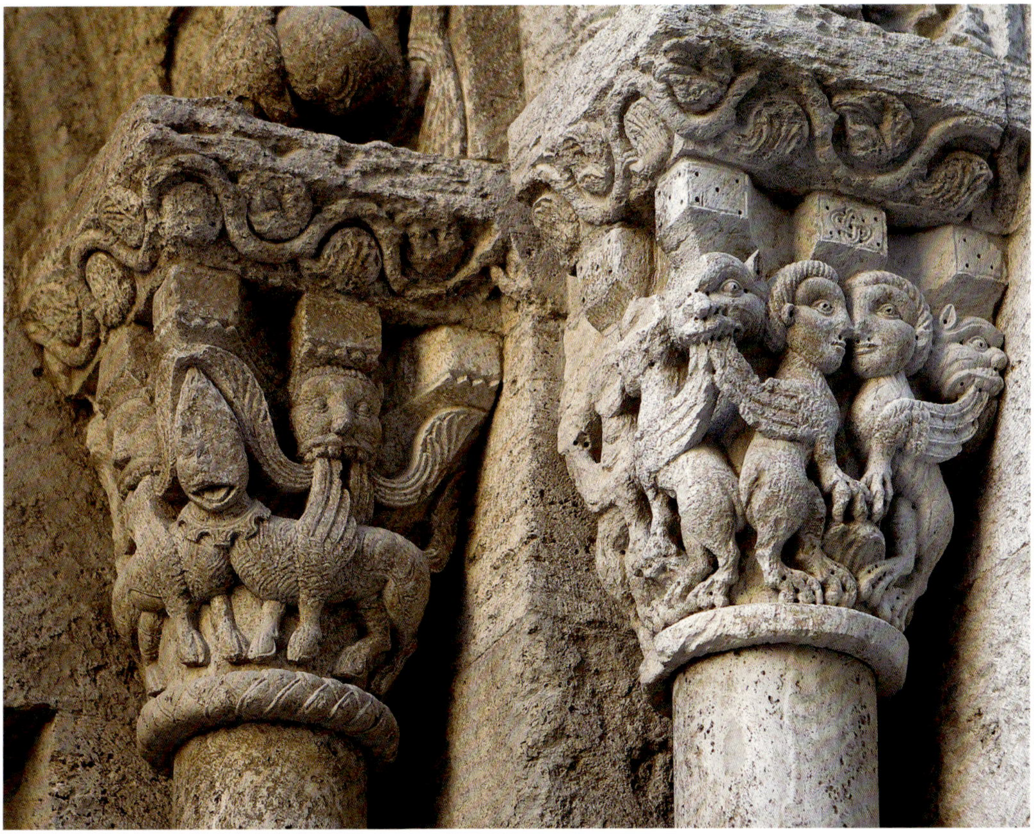

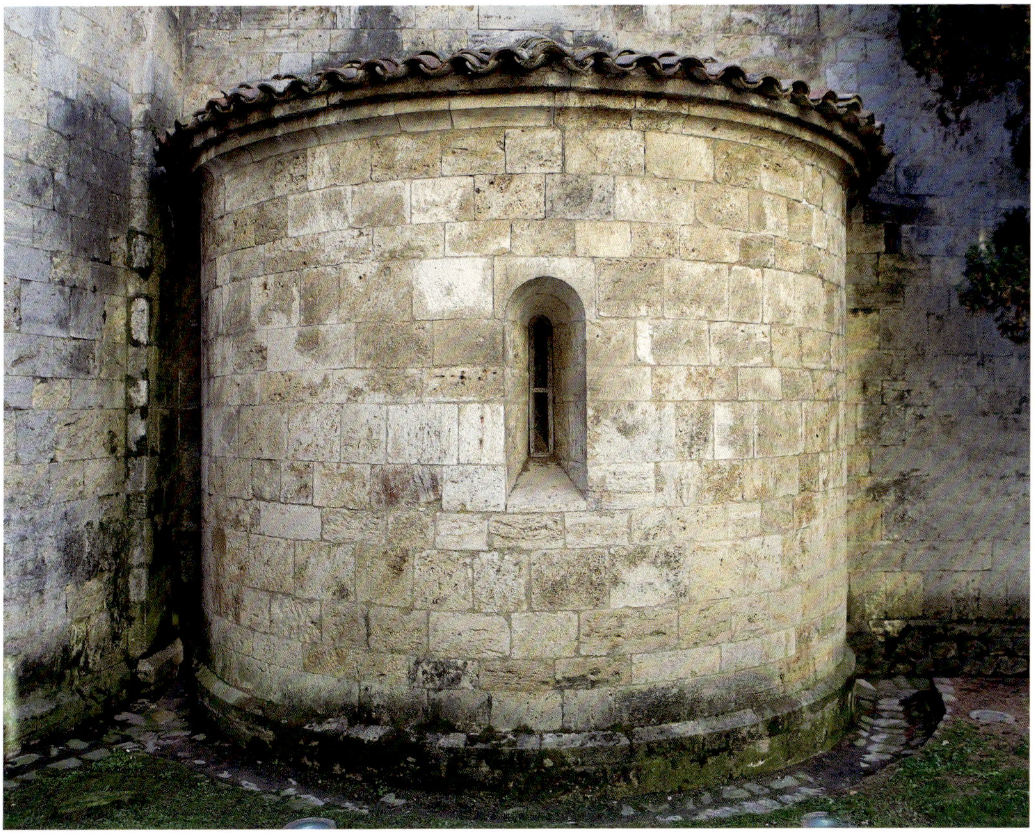

◂ **Sant Rafel Doorway**

(above) Detail of the capitals. (below) Apse of Sant Vicenç

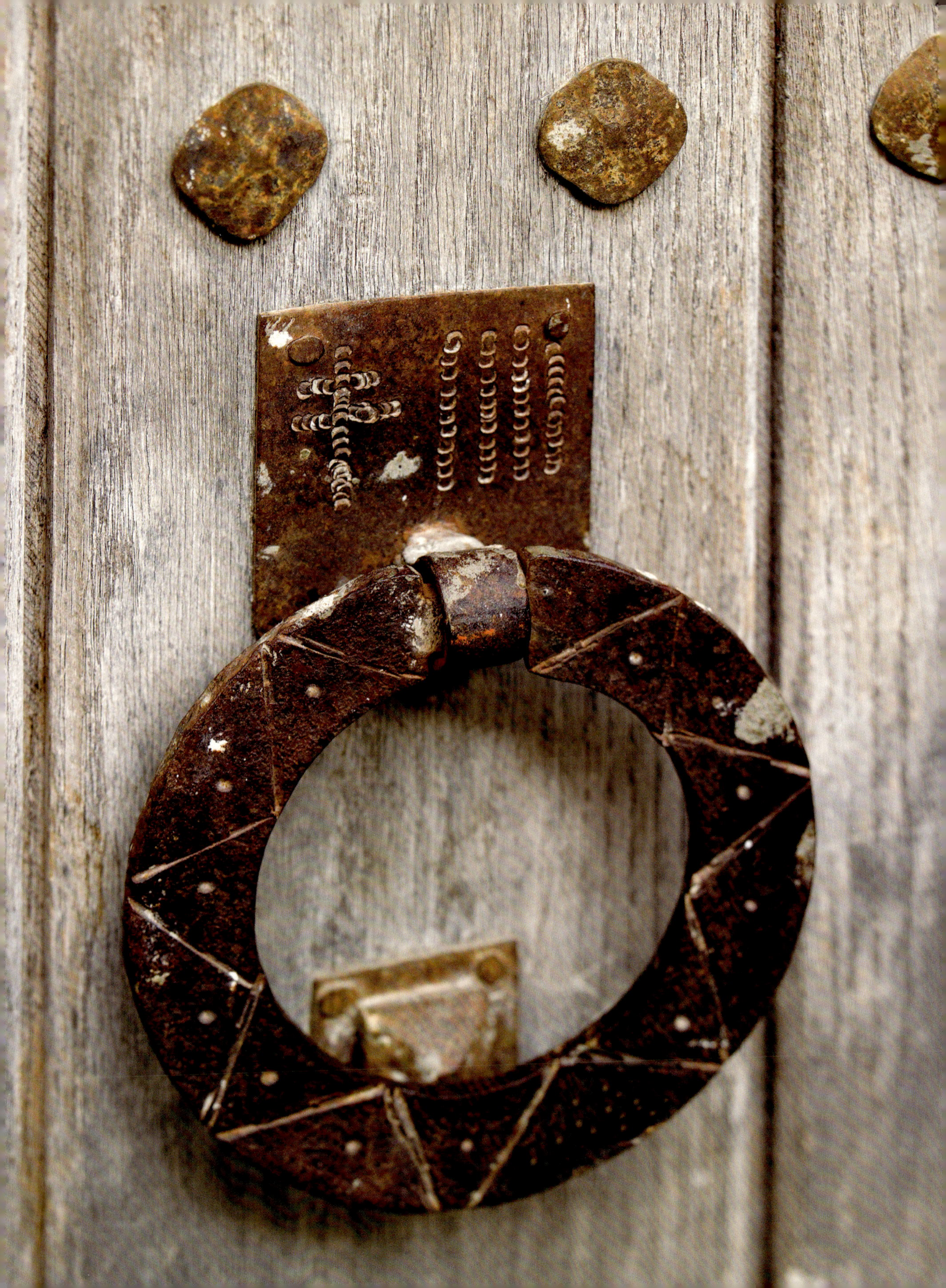

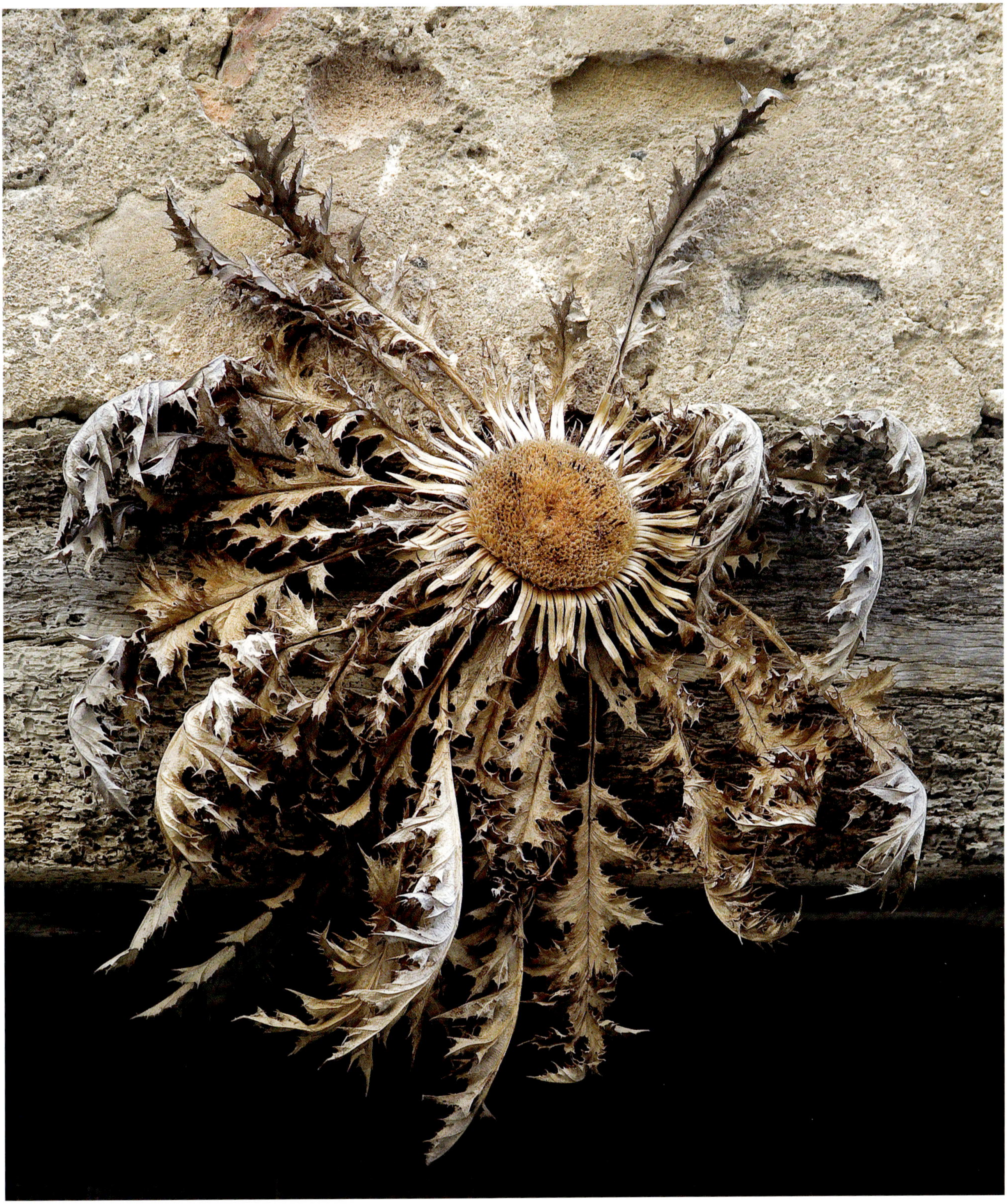

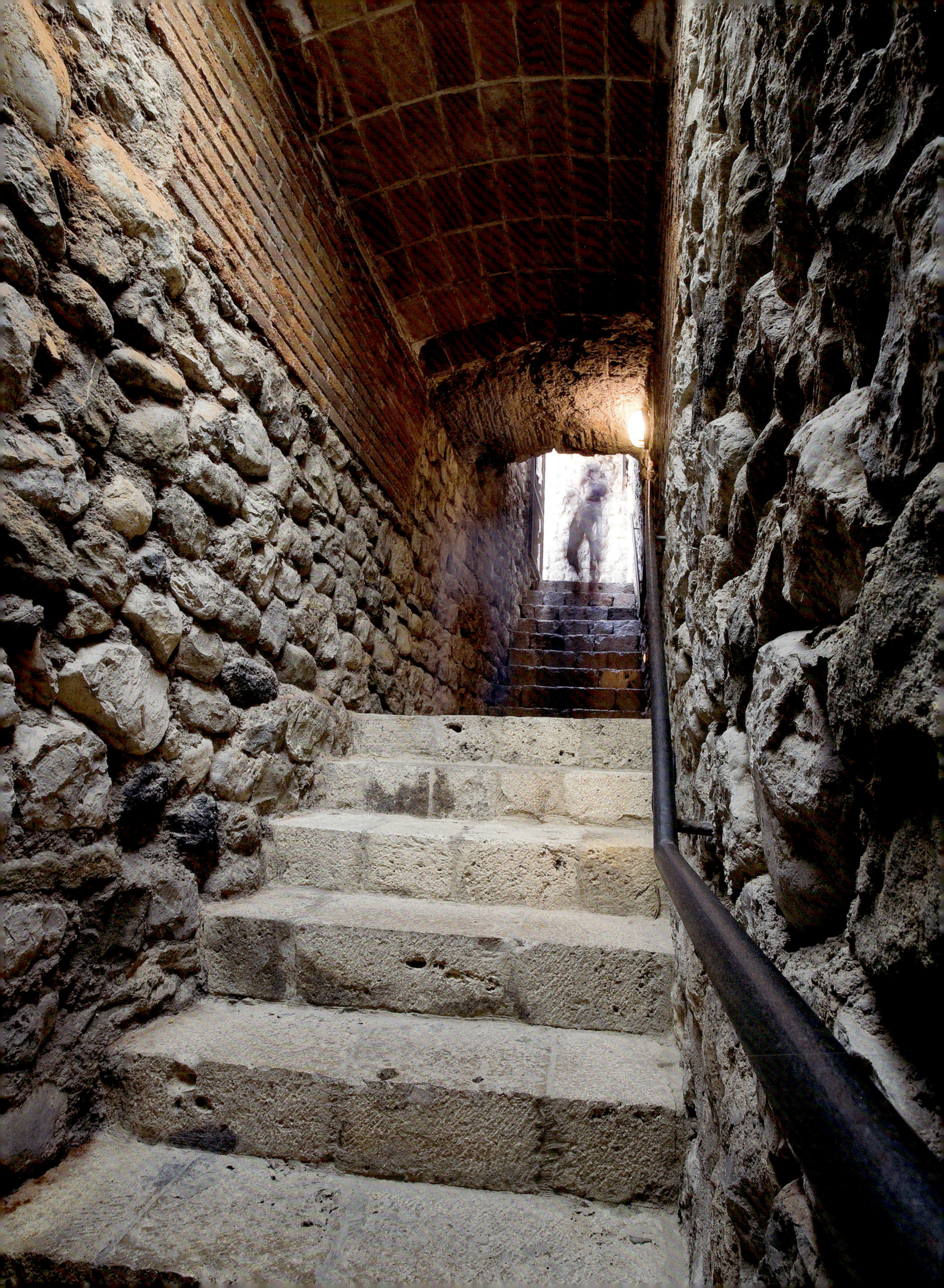

The miqveh and the Jewish quarter

The miqveh or ritual bath of purification was discovered by coincidence in 1964. The building coincides with the place where the synagogue was documented. On finishing the excavation works the assessment of two rabbis was required who corroborated the discovery. The pools of the baths had to be filled with water from a spring, river, sea or lake without any type of channelling, in a totally natural way, the reason why it was often situated a few metres deep.

In the Jewish district, we can see that the doors on some houses still have the receptacle for the mezuzah, on the right-hand jamb of the door, where a rolled up parchment with two prayers from Deuteronomy was placed. The mezuzah is one of the most characteristic and deeply-rooted characteristics of Judaism, through which their houses were differentiated from those of their neighbours. Practicing Jews usually kiss the mezuzah with their hand on entering and leaving home.

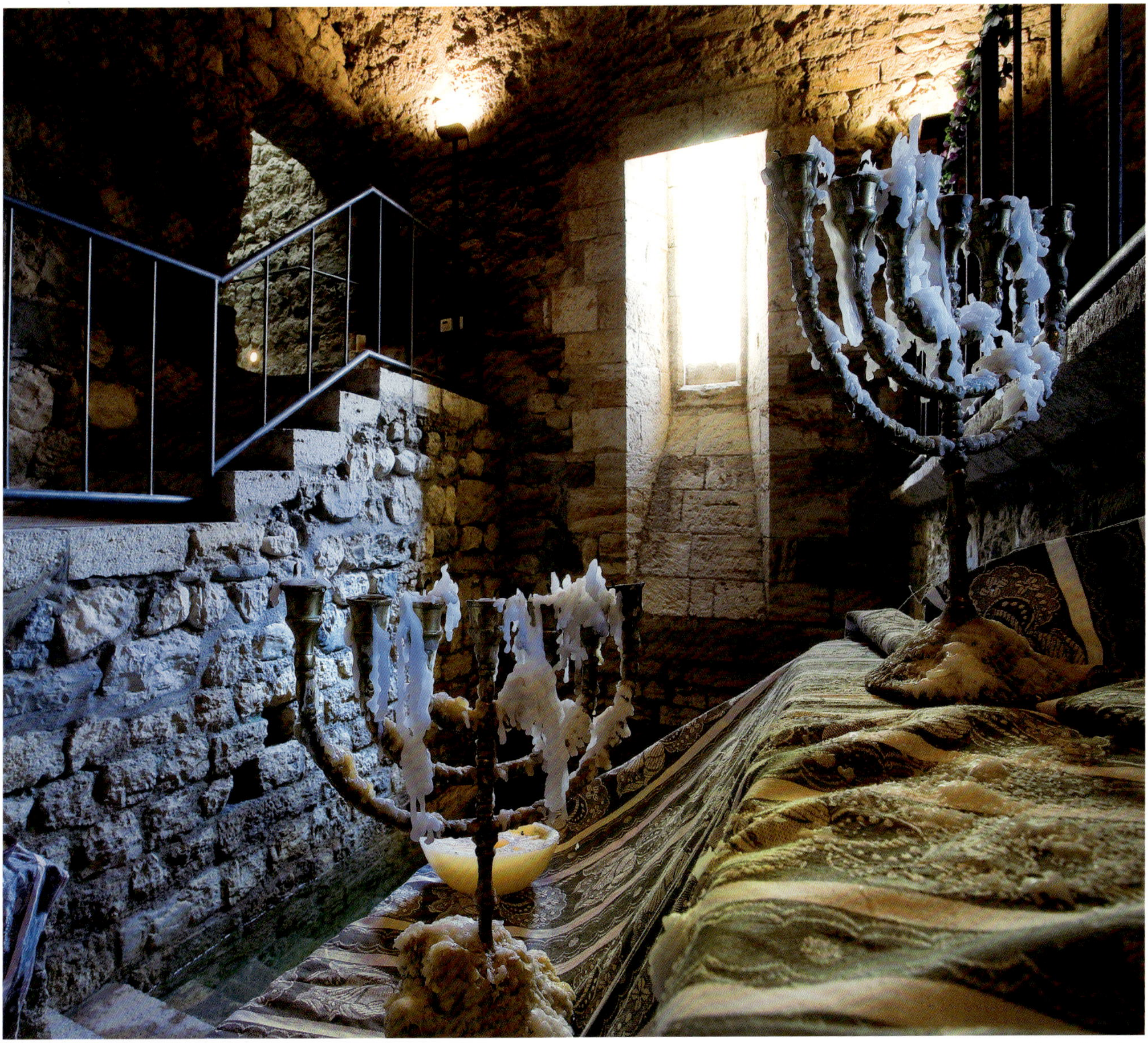

▲ **The miqveh** ▶

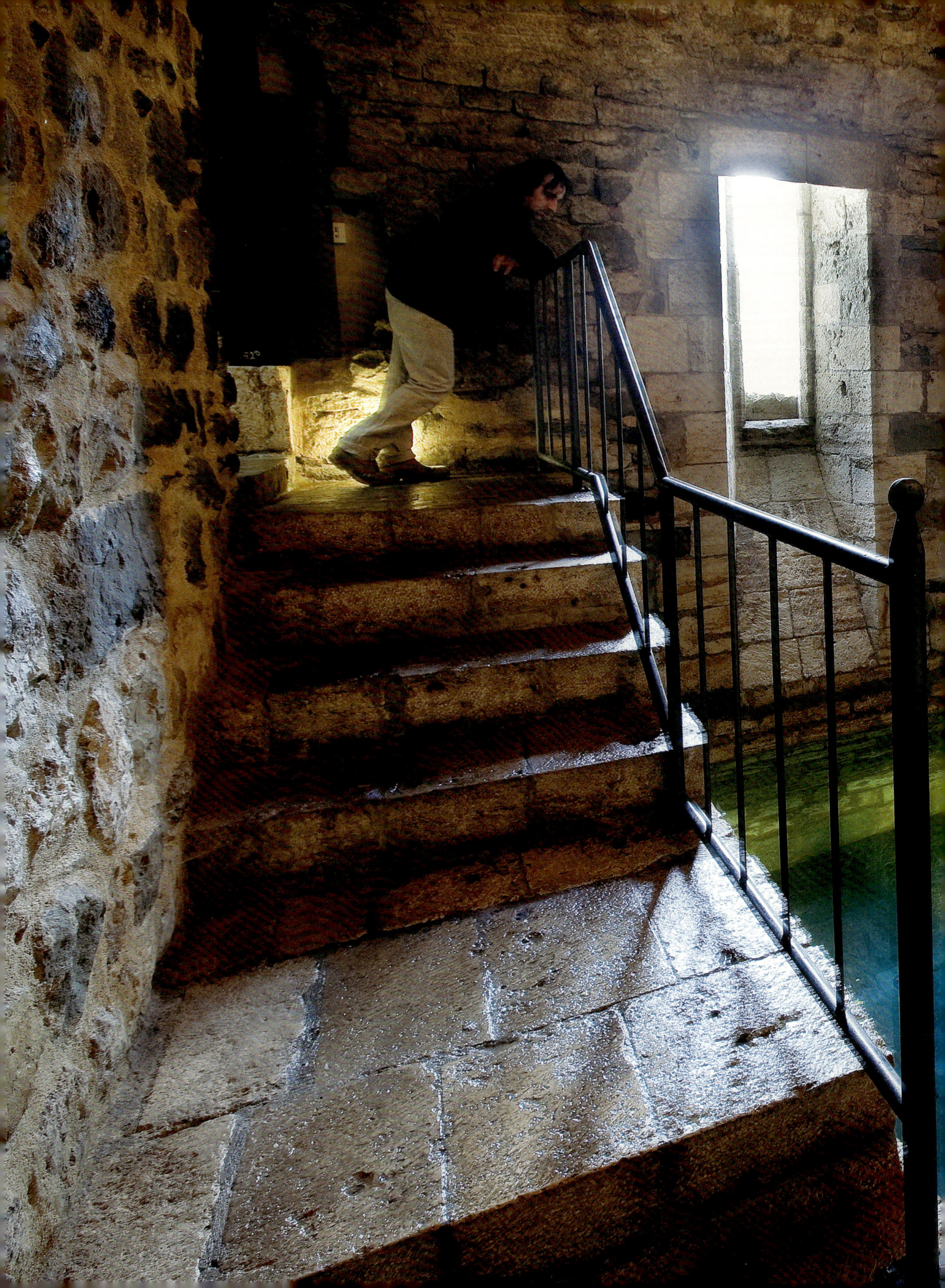

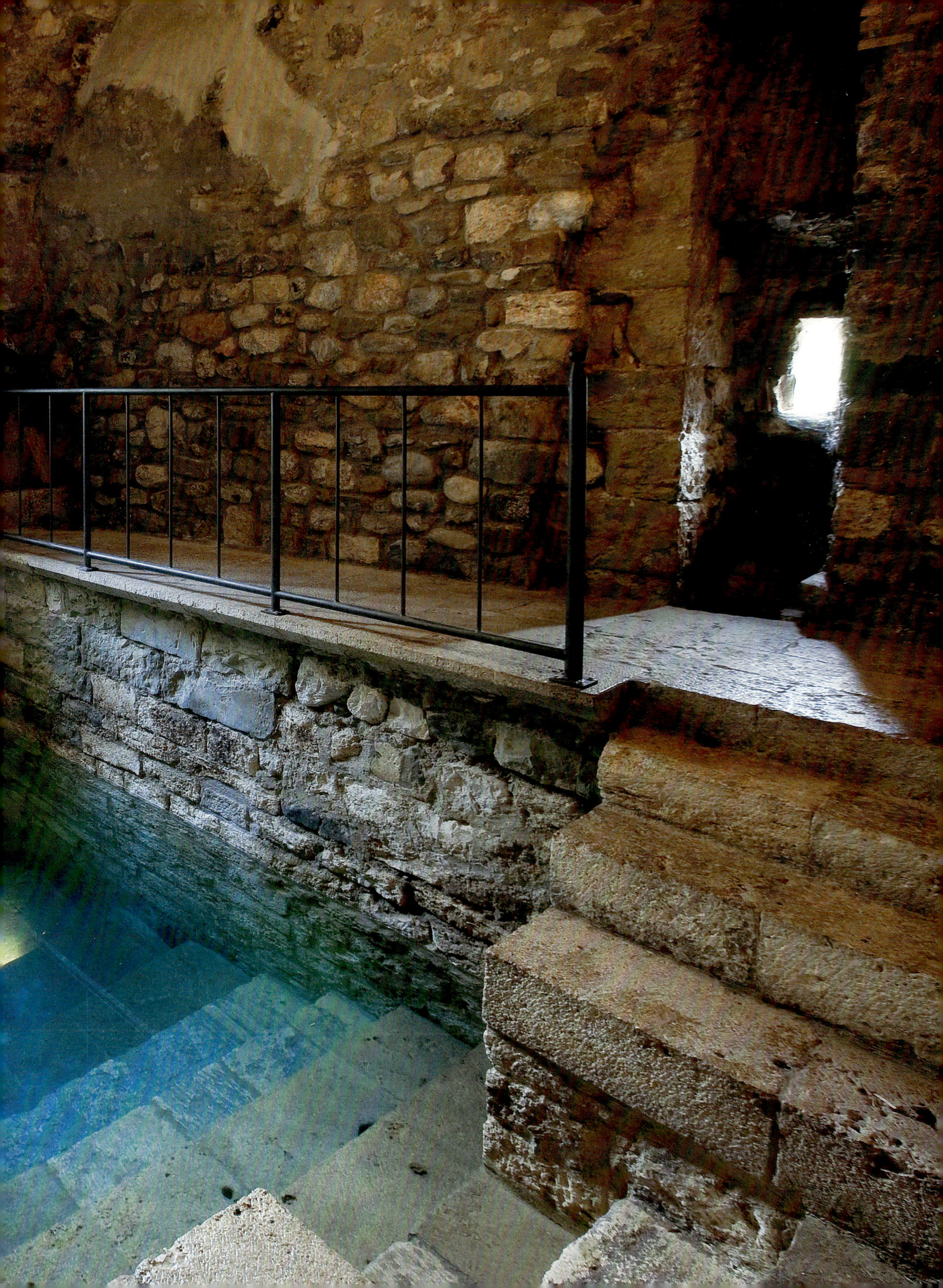

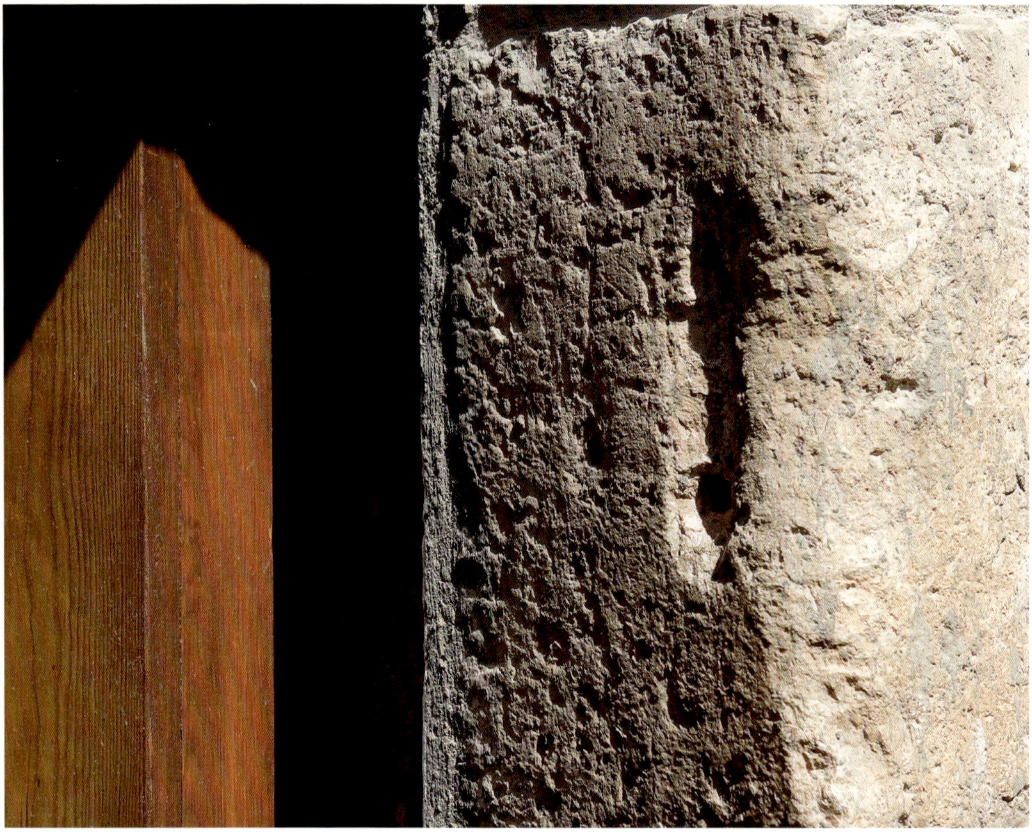

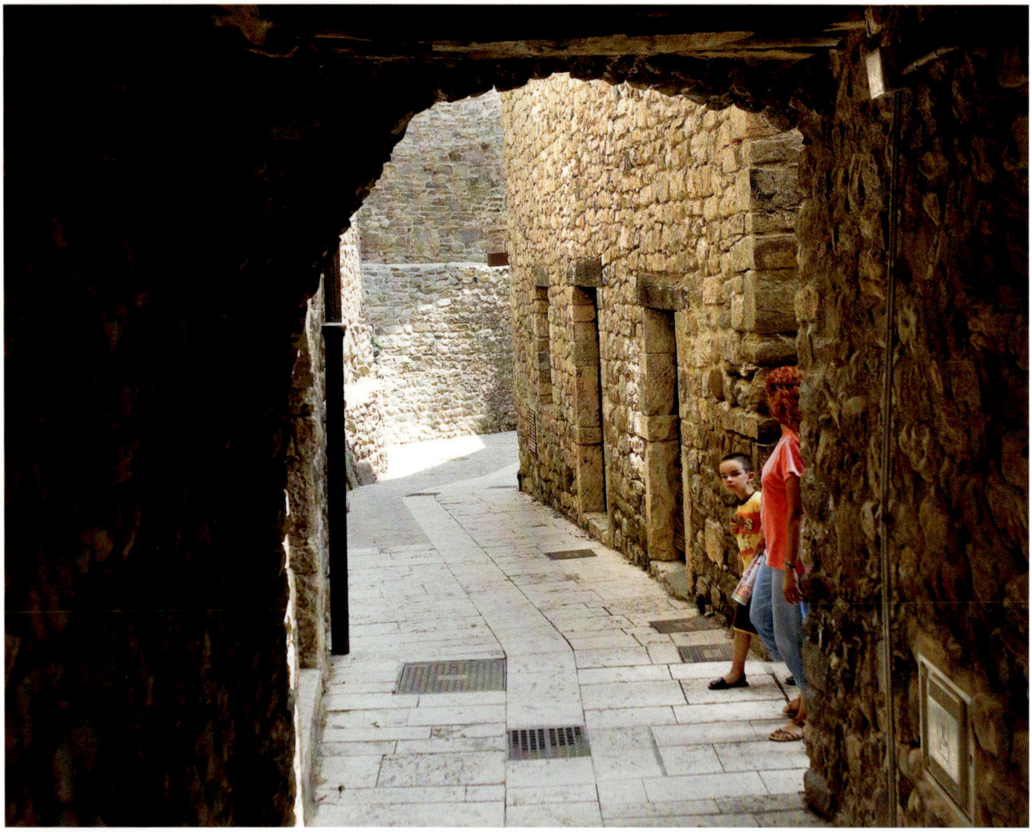

(above) Mezuzah

The Jewish quarter

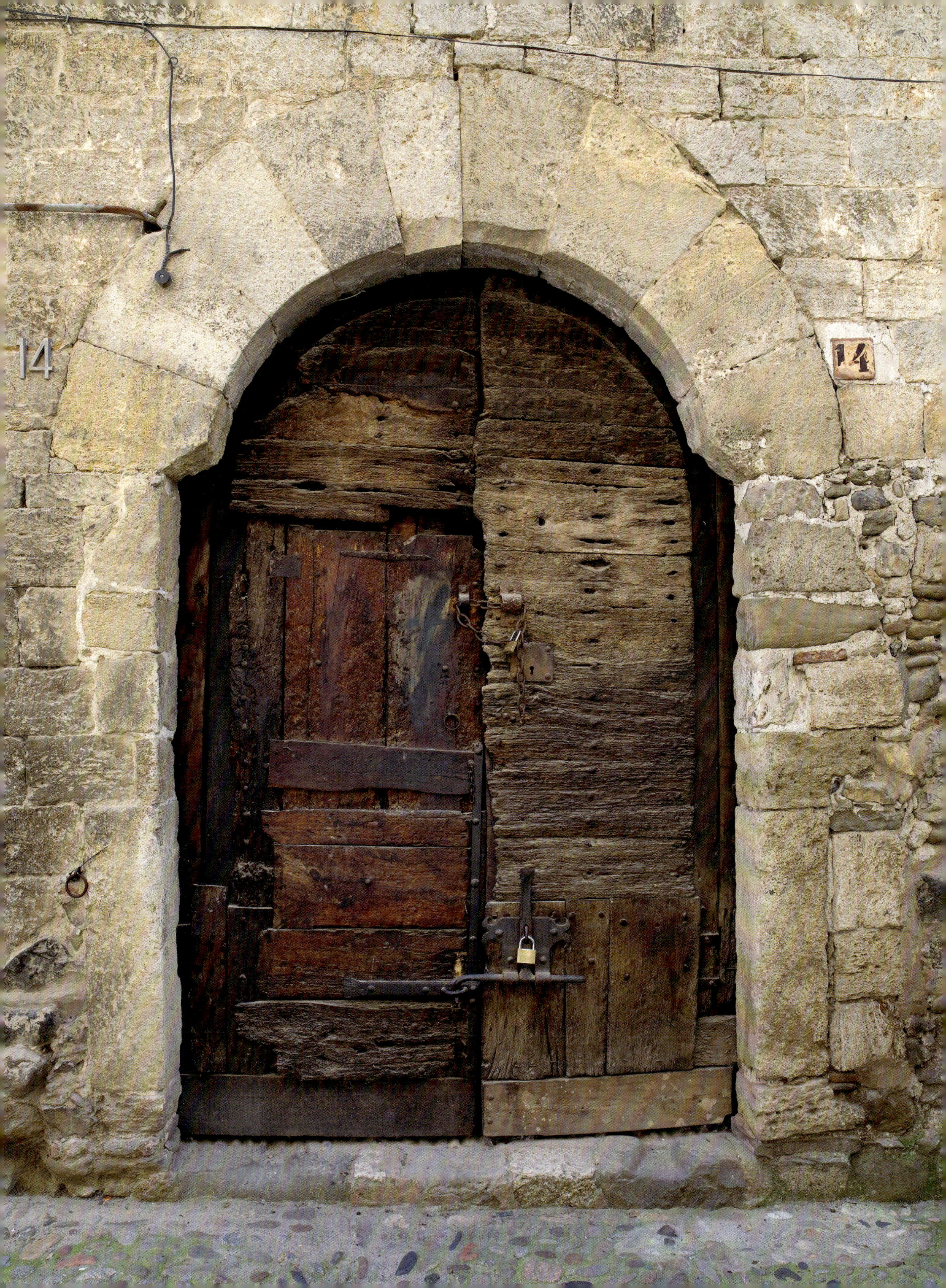
14
14

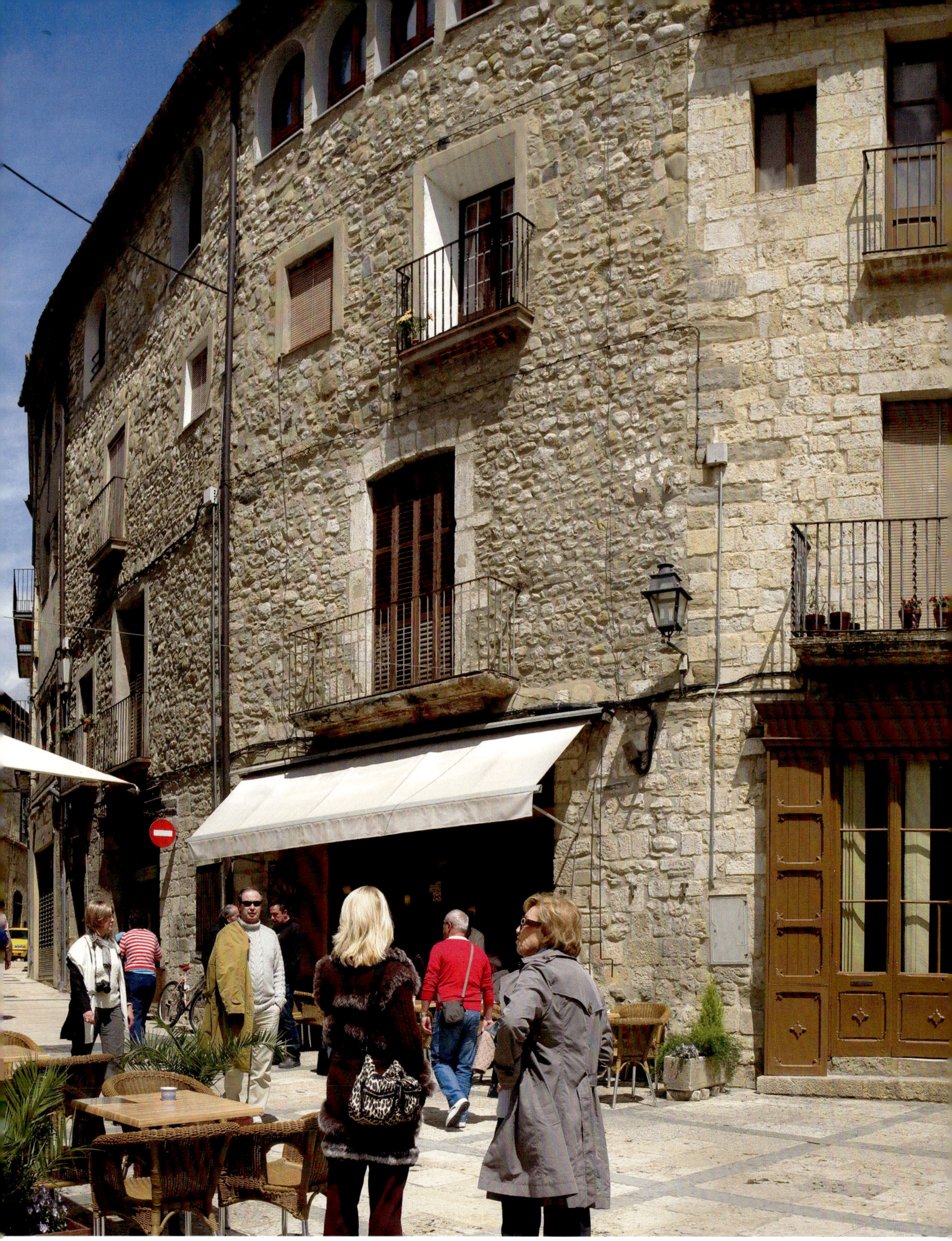

Plaça de la Llibertat

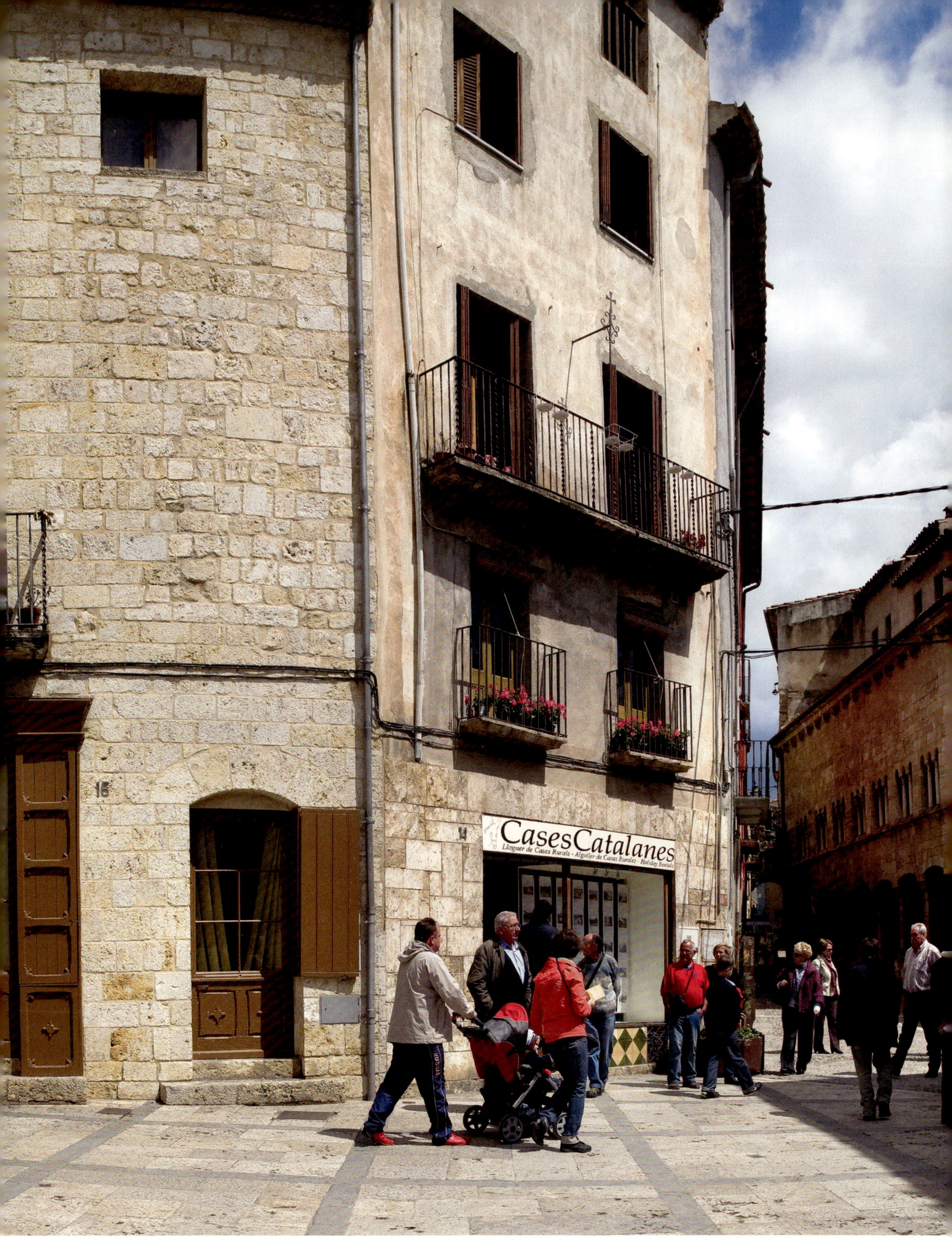
15
14
CasesCatalanes
Lloguer de Cases Rurals - Alguiler de Casas Rurales - Holiday Rentals

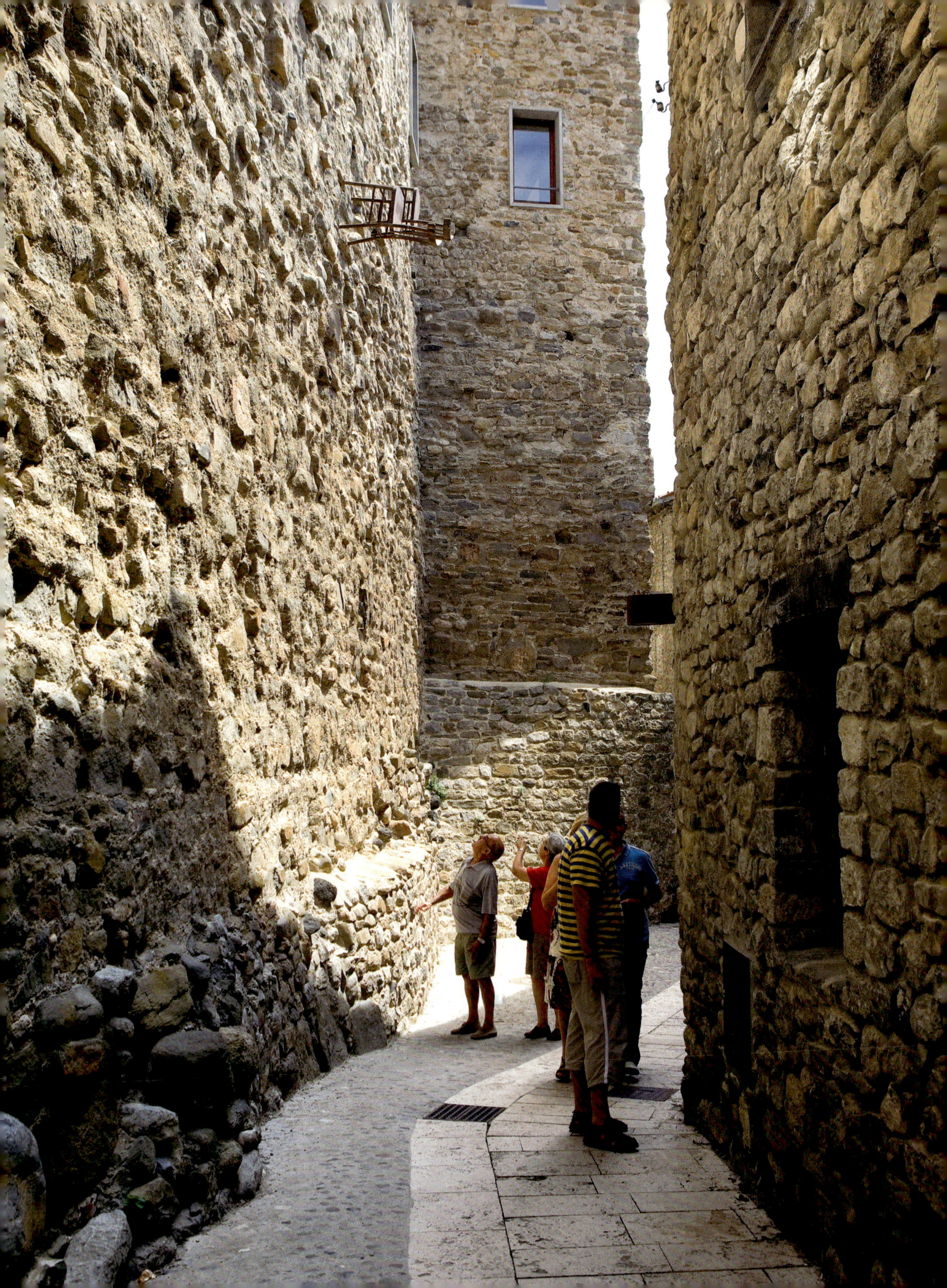

Streets and alleyways

They form an urban layout, which added to the civil and religious architecture, along with the important Jewish legacy, make the town of Besalú an historic-artistic centre recognised as such as from 1964. Besalú is a unique complex of historical buildings, and not only for its emblematic buildings, but also for its urban structure; cobbled streets, arches, stairways and corners that have survived the passing of time, the urban changes, and the tastes and needs of each historical period.

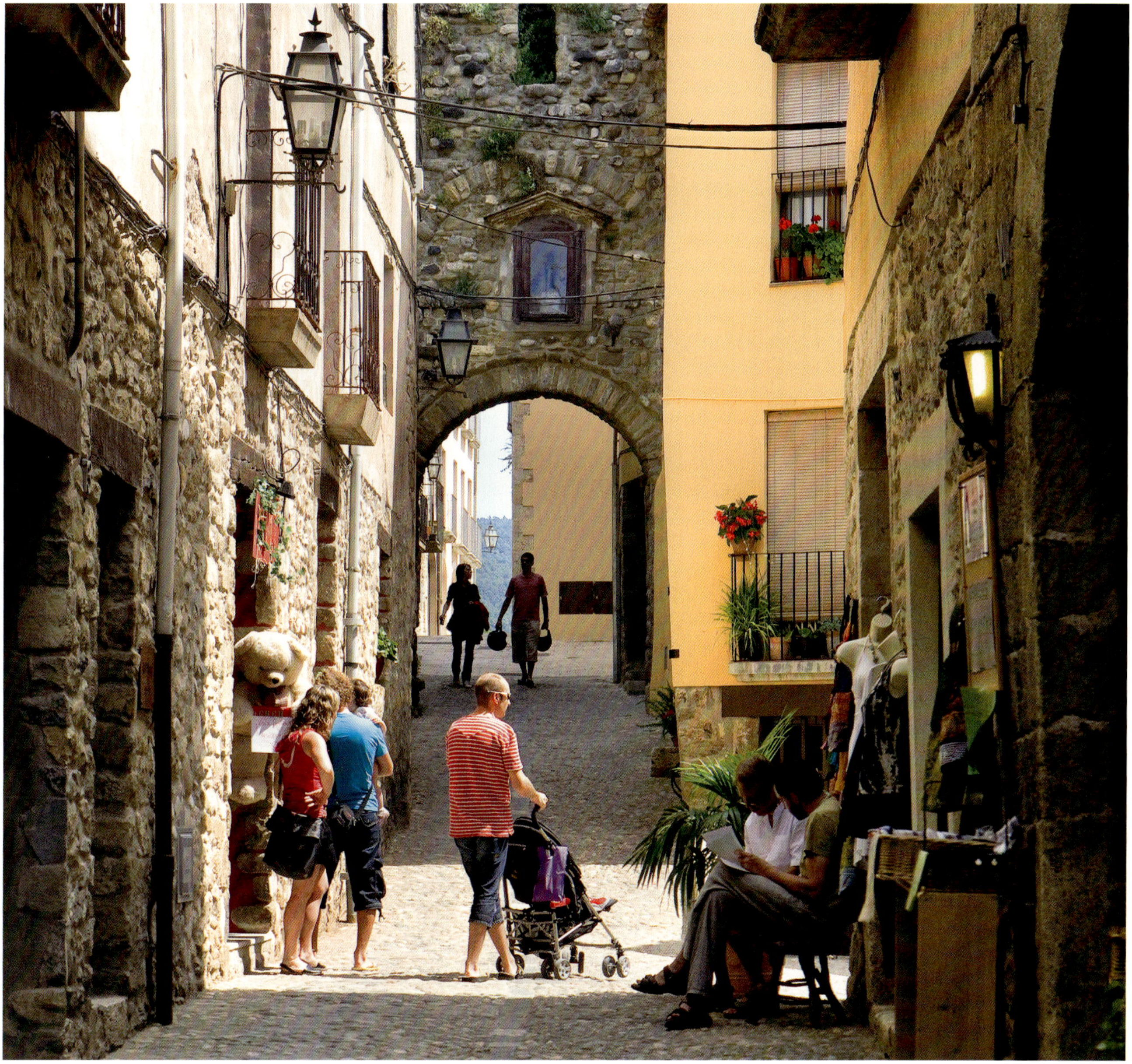

◂ Carrer Rocafort

Portal de la Força

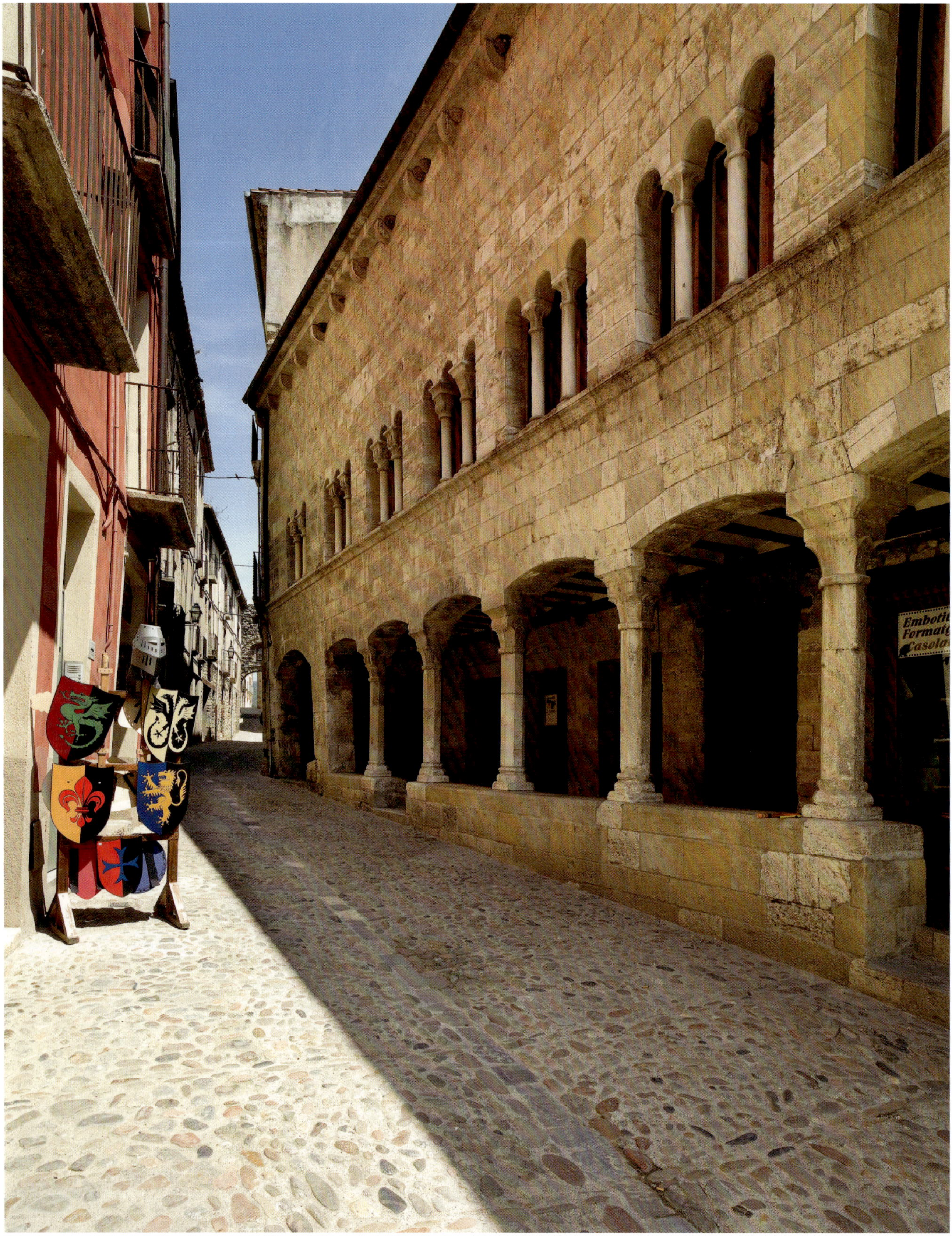

Carrer del Comte Tallaferro

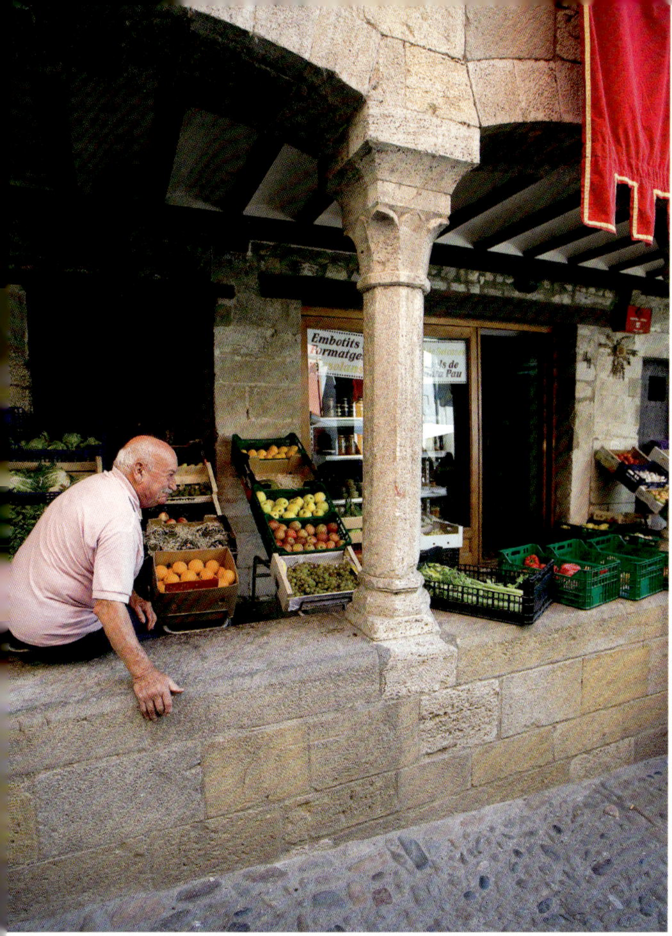
Embotits
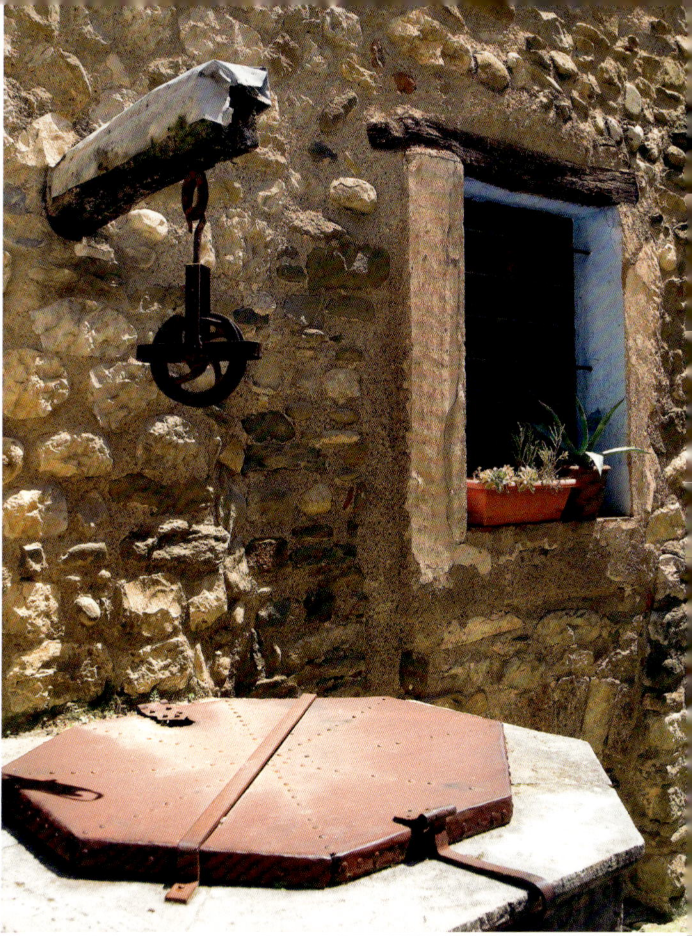
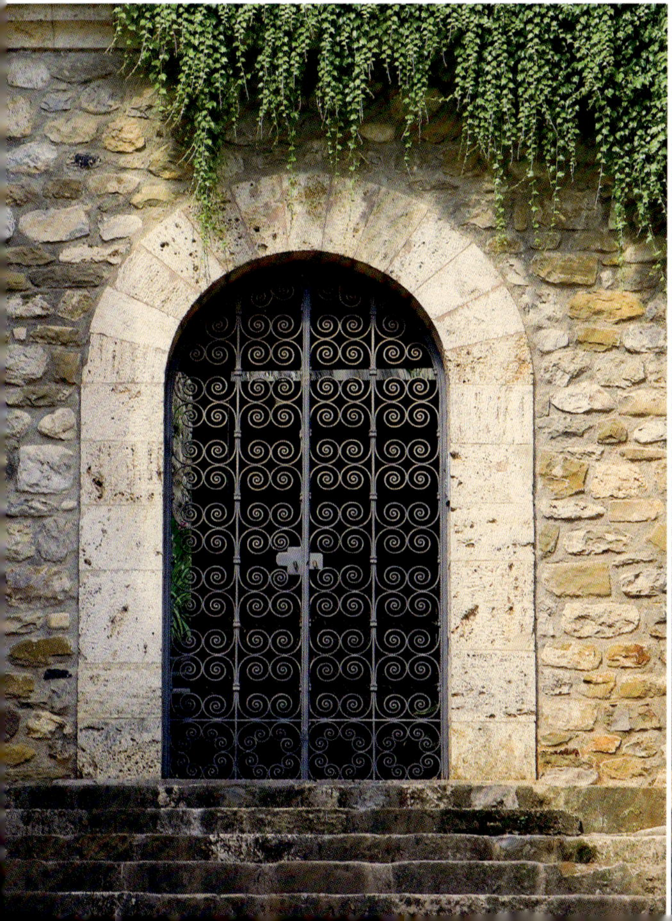
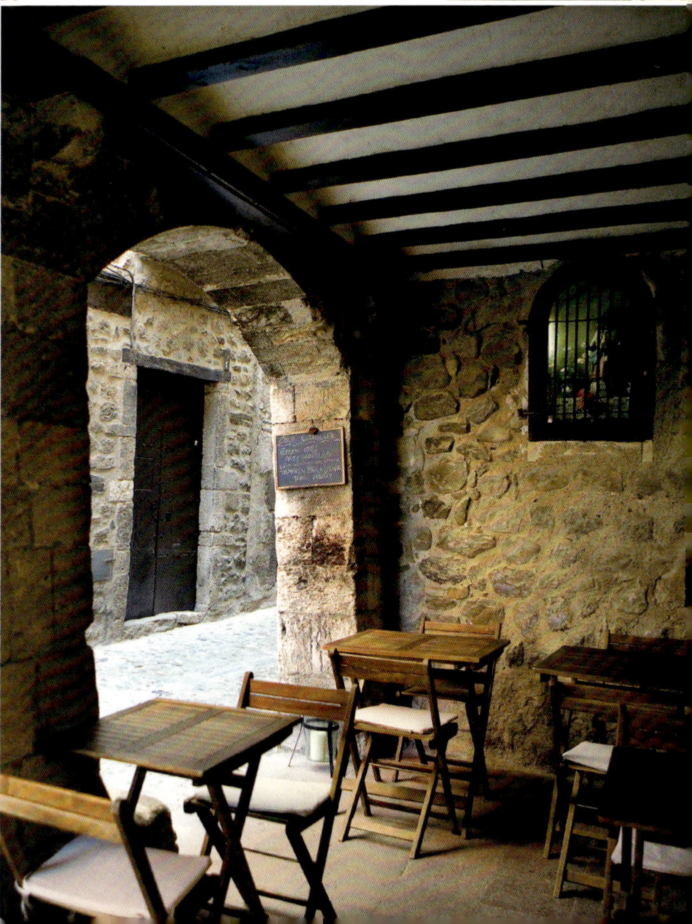

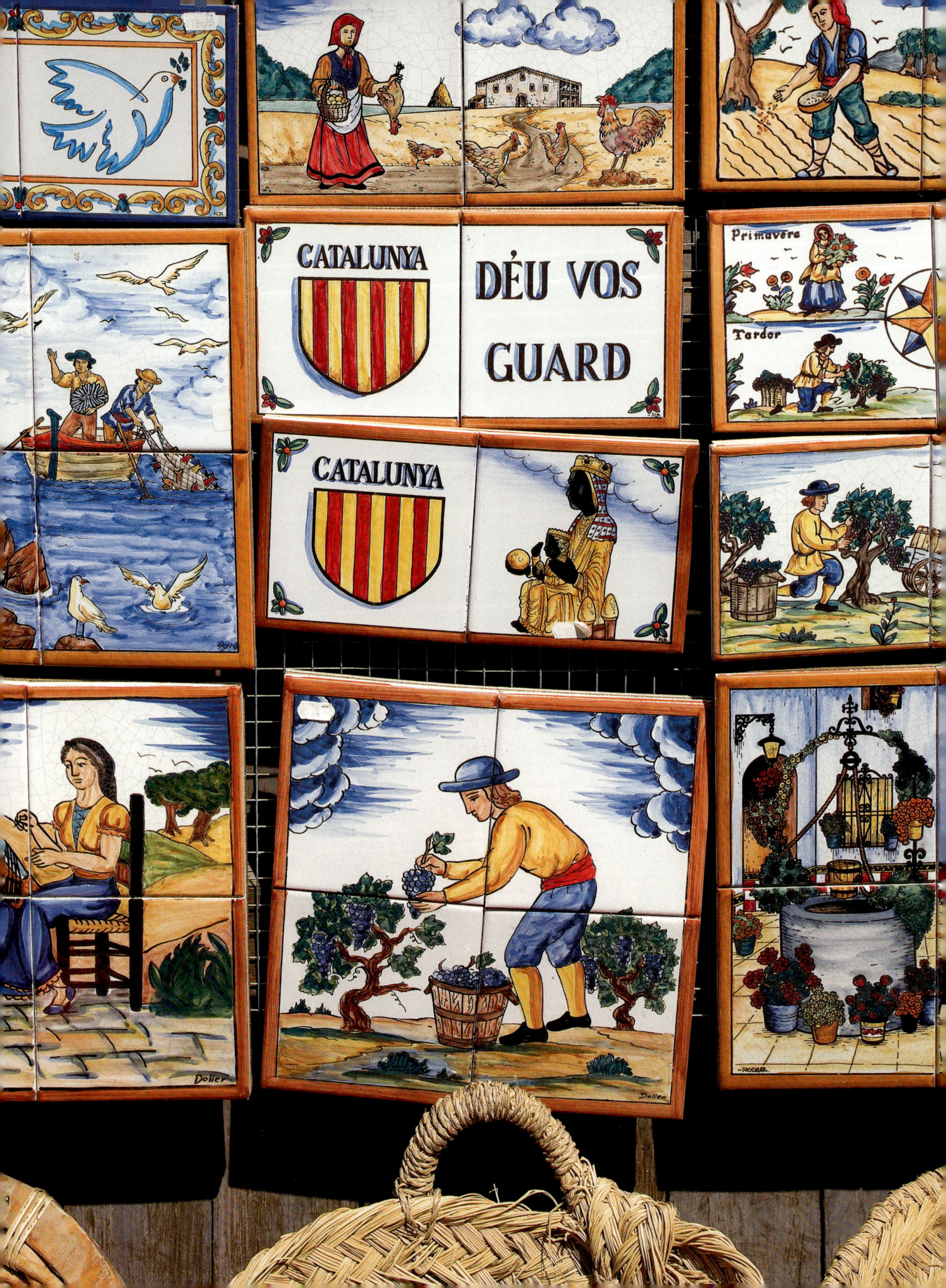
CATALUNYA
DÉU VOS
GUARD
Primavera
Tardor
CATALUNYA

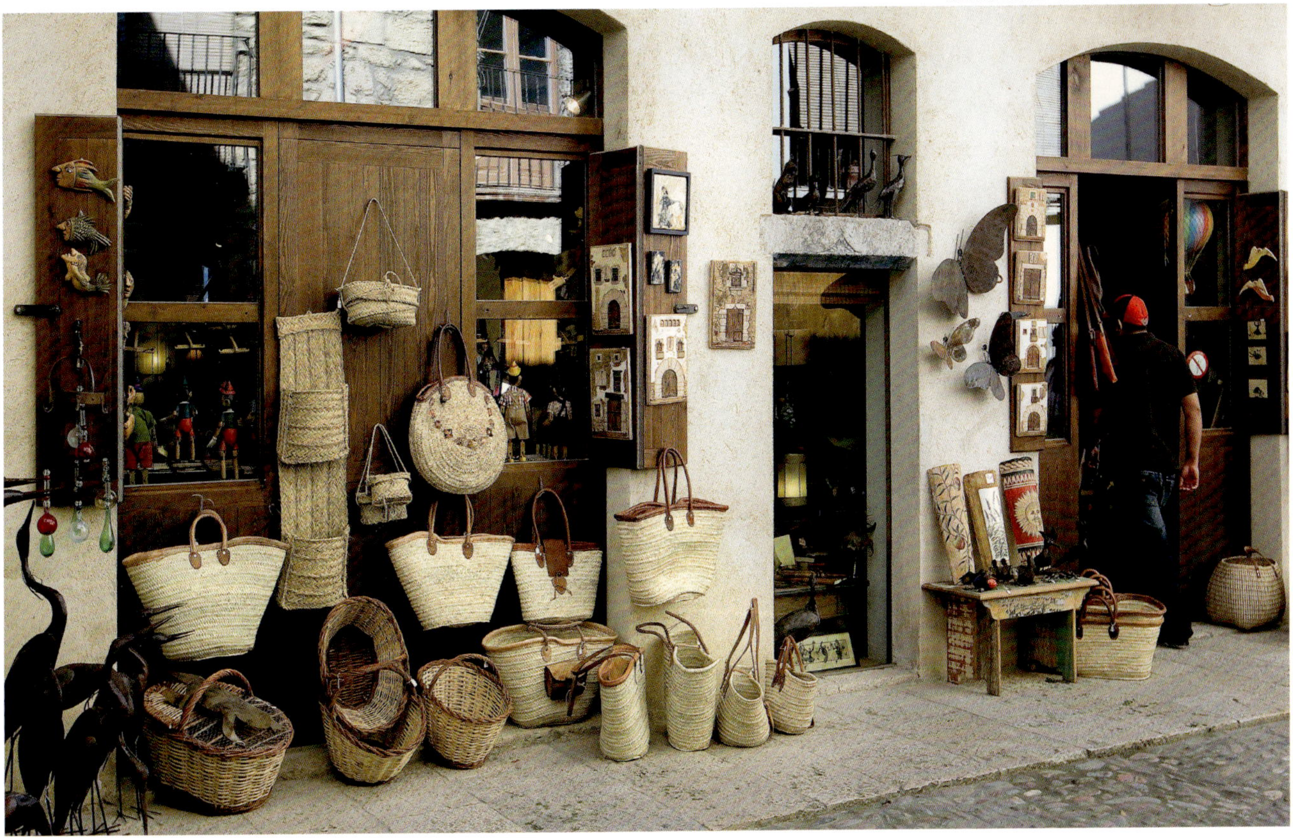

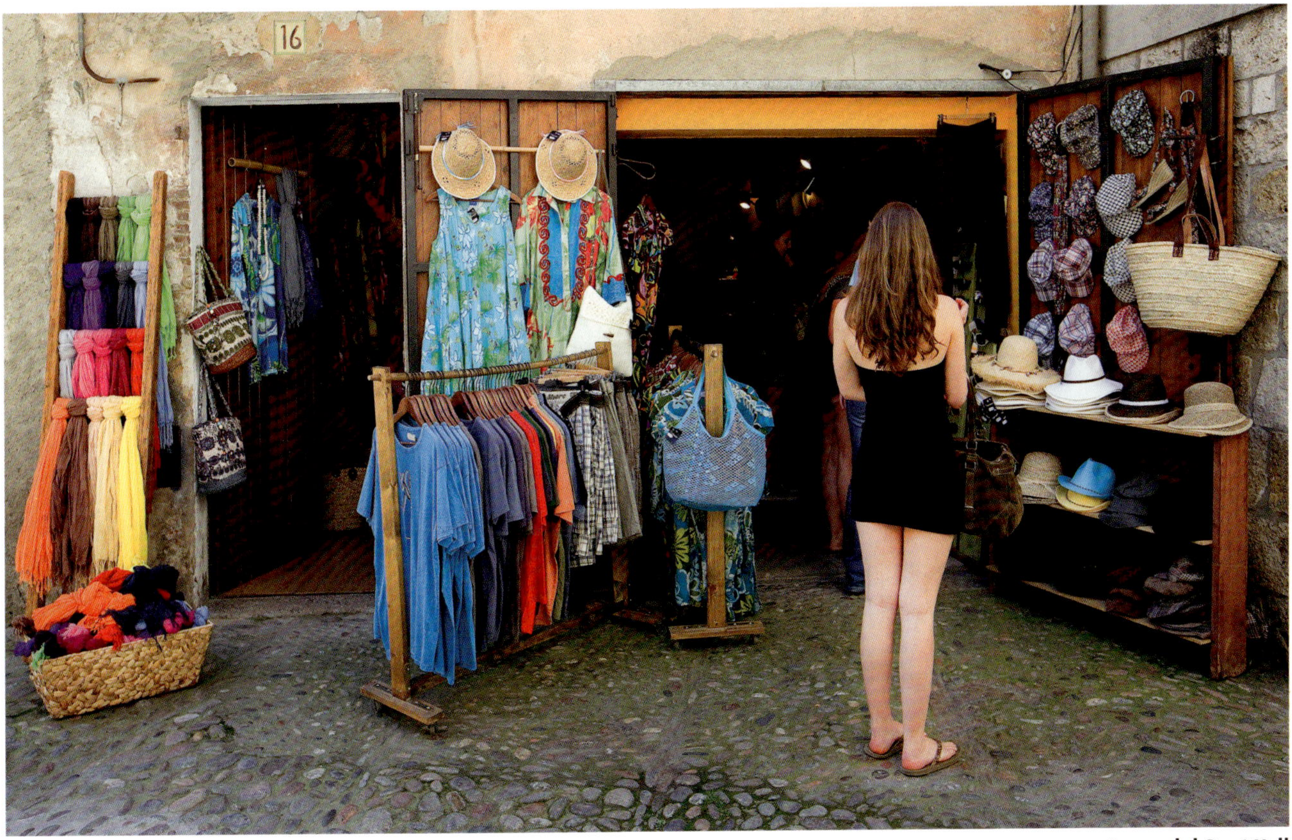

Carrer del Pont Vell

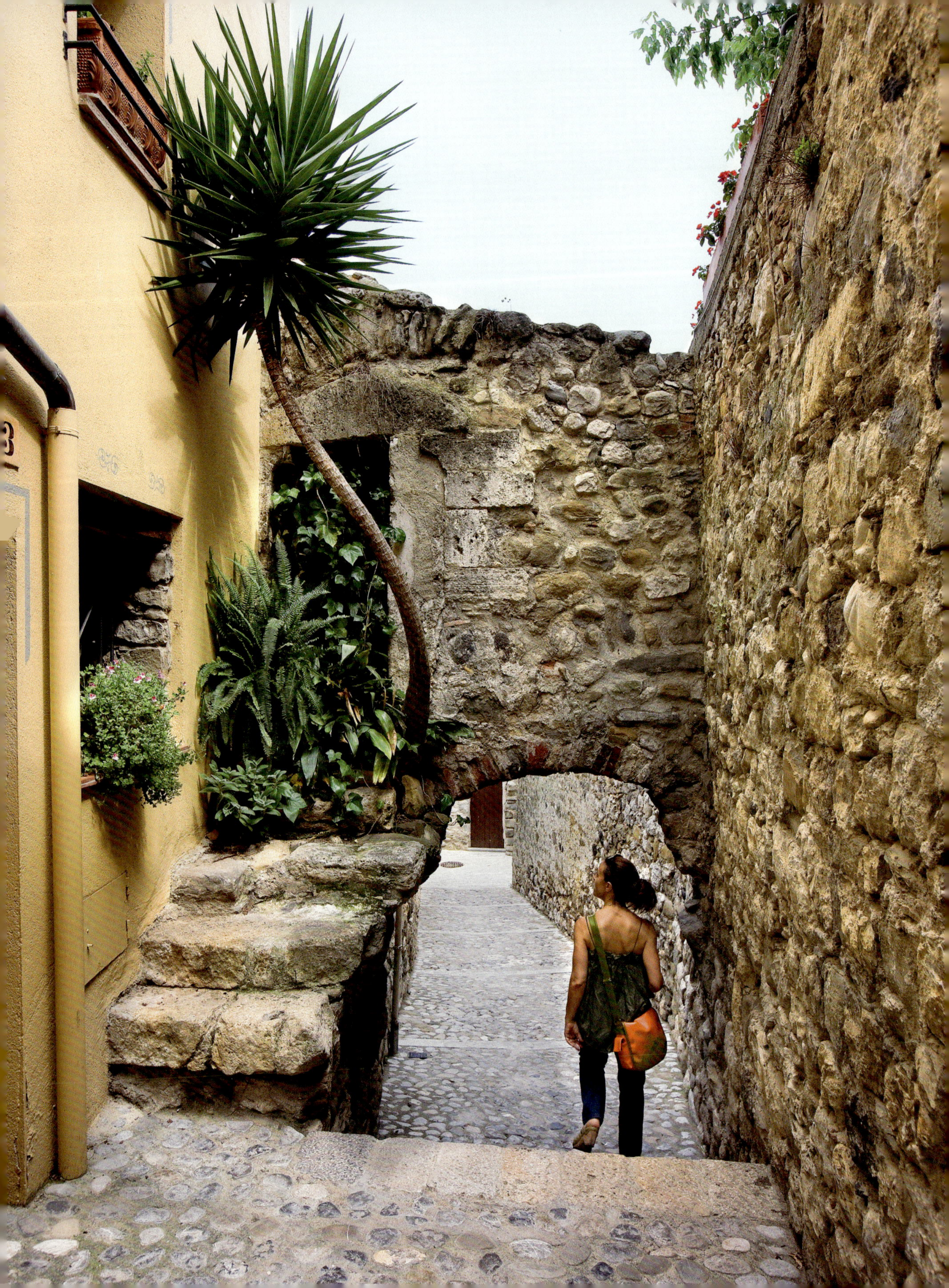

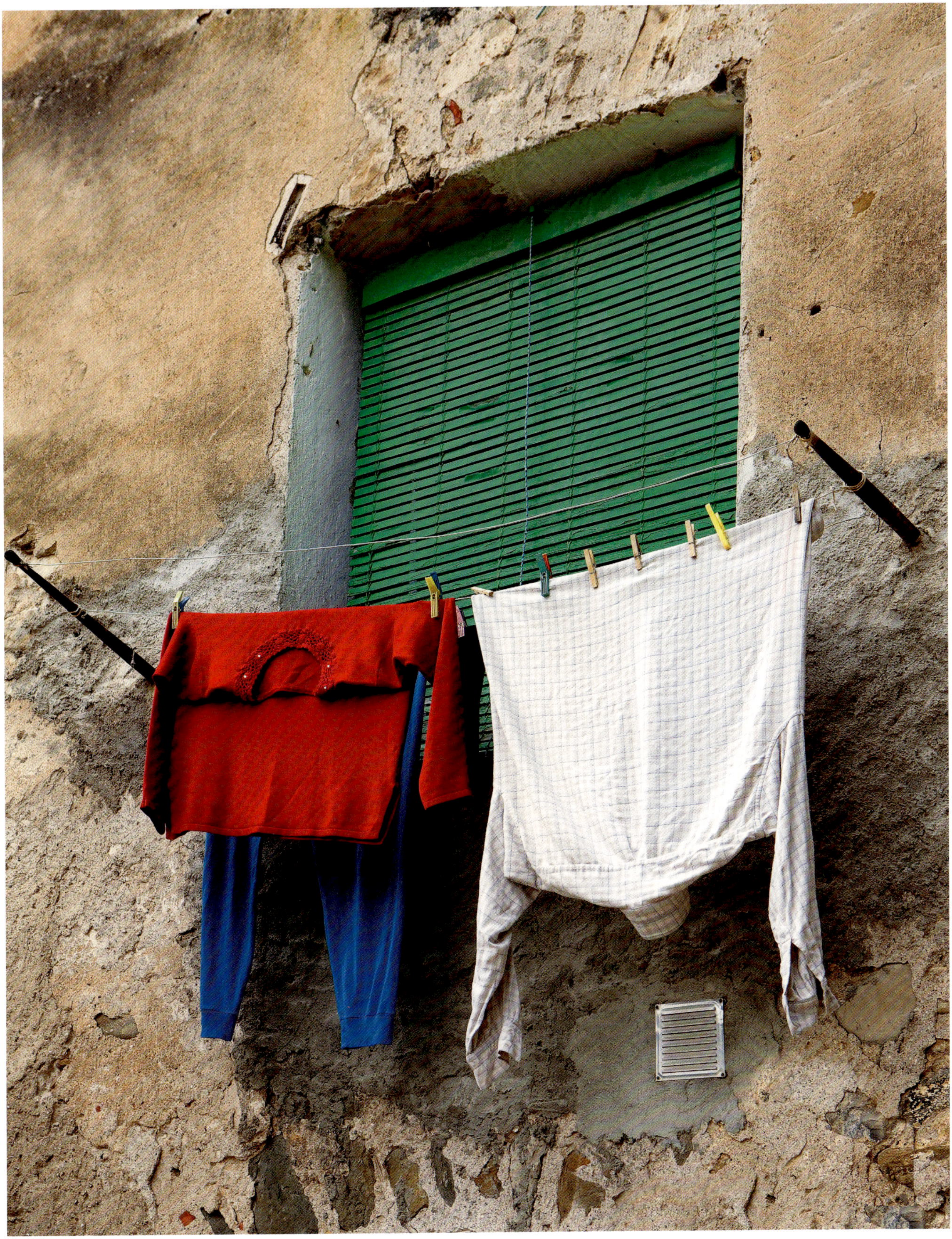

◂ **Portalet City Wall**

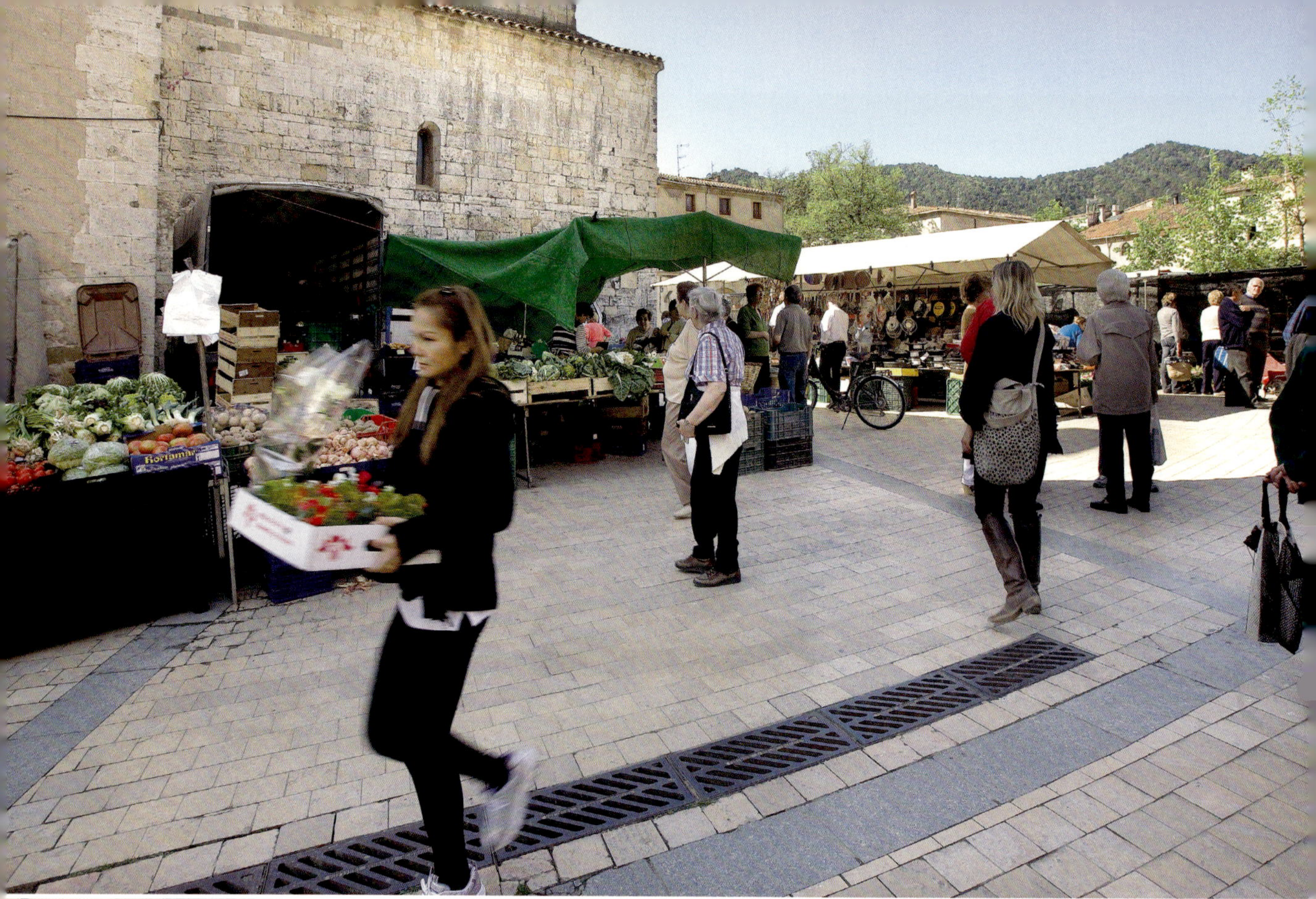

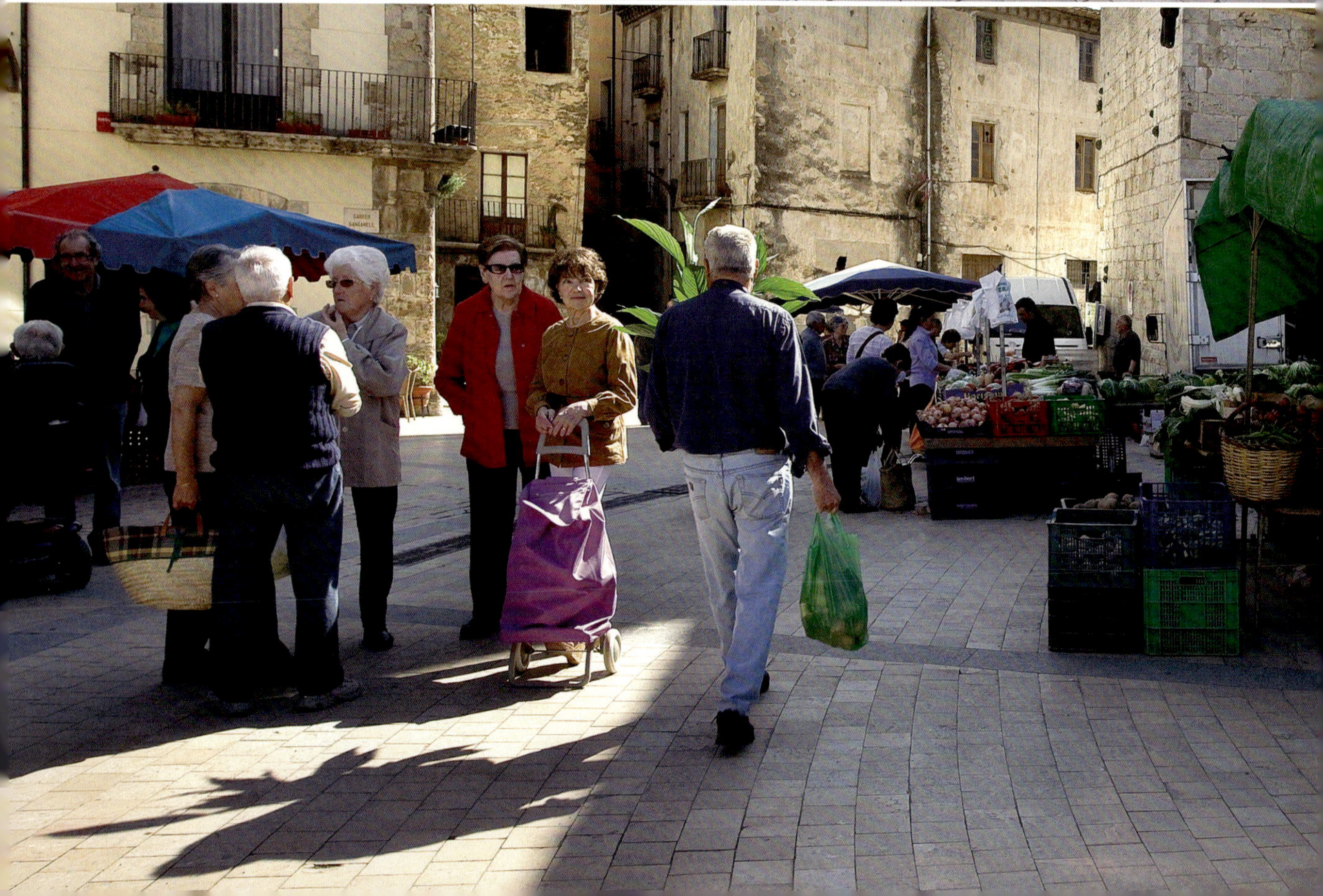

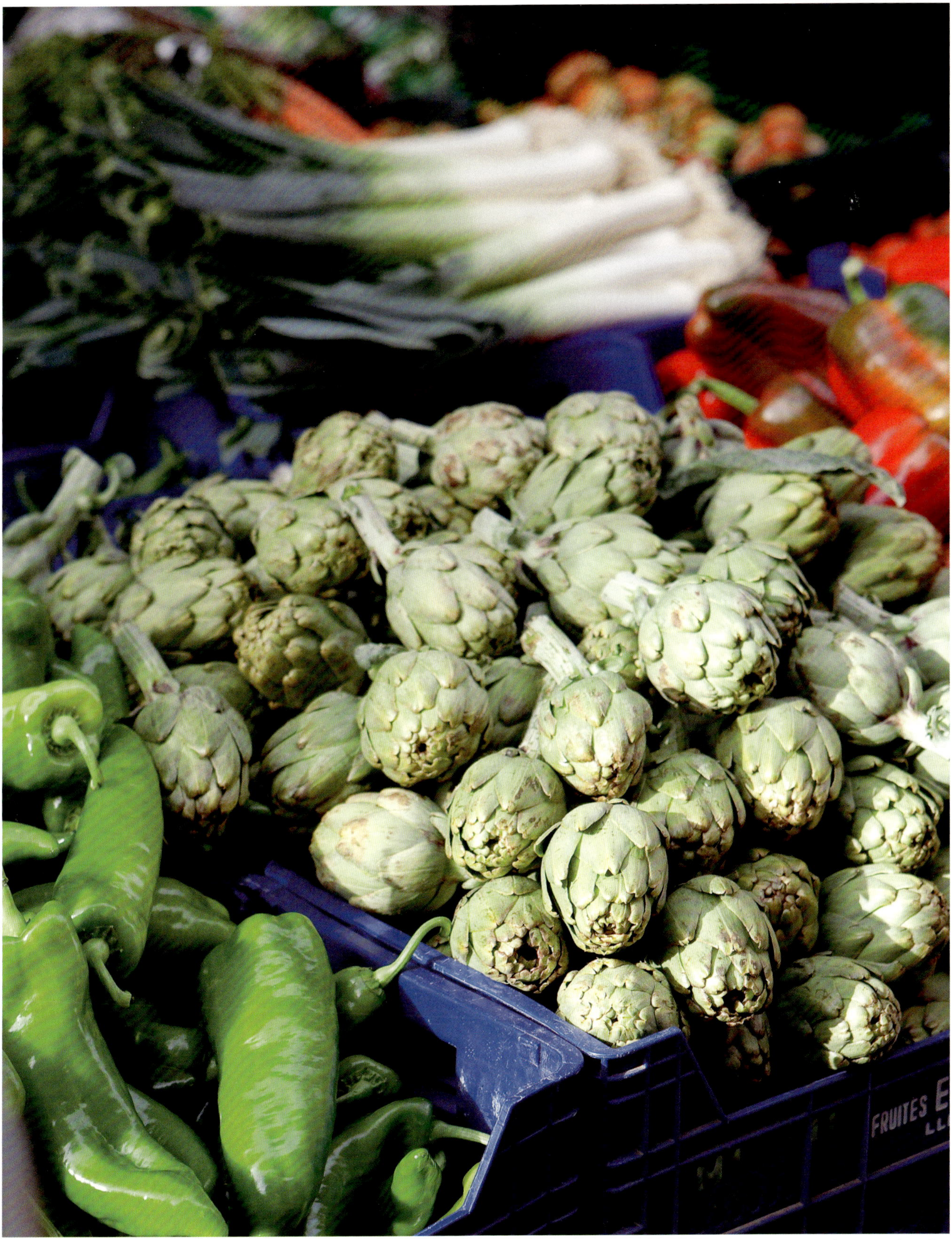

Tuesdays, market day

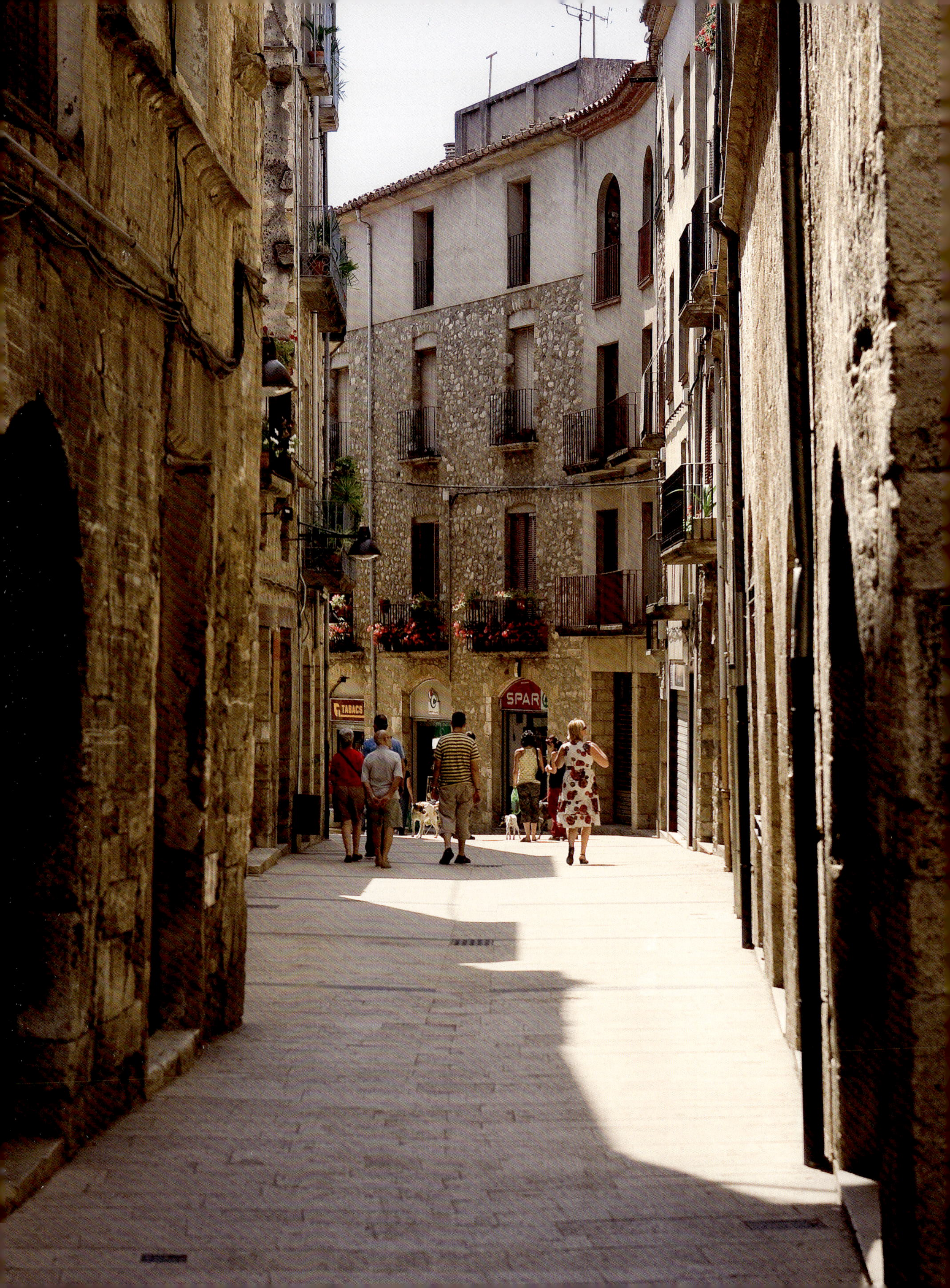
TABACS
SPAR

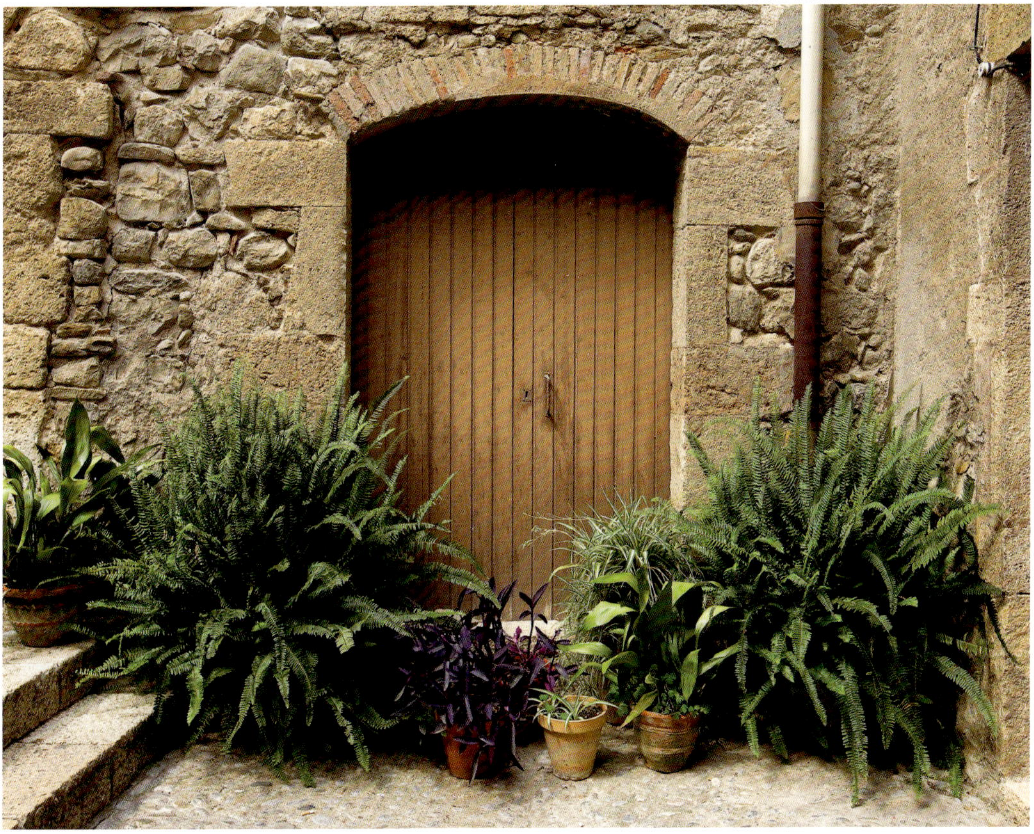

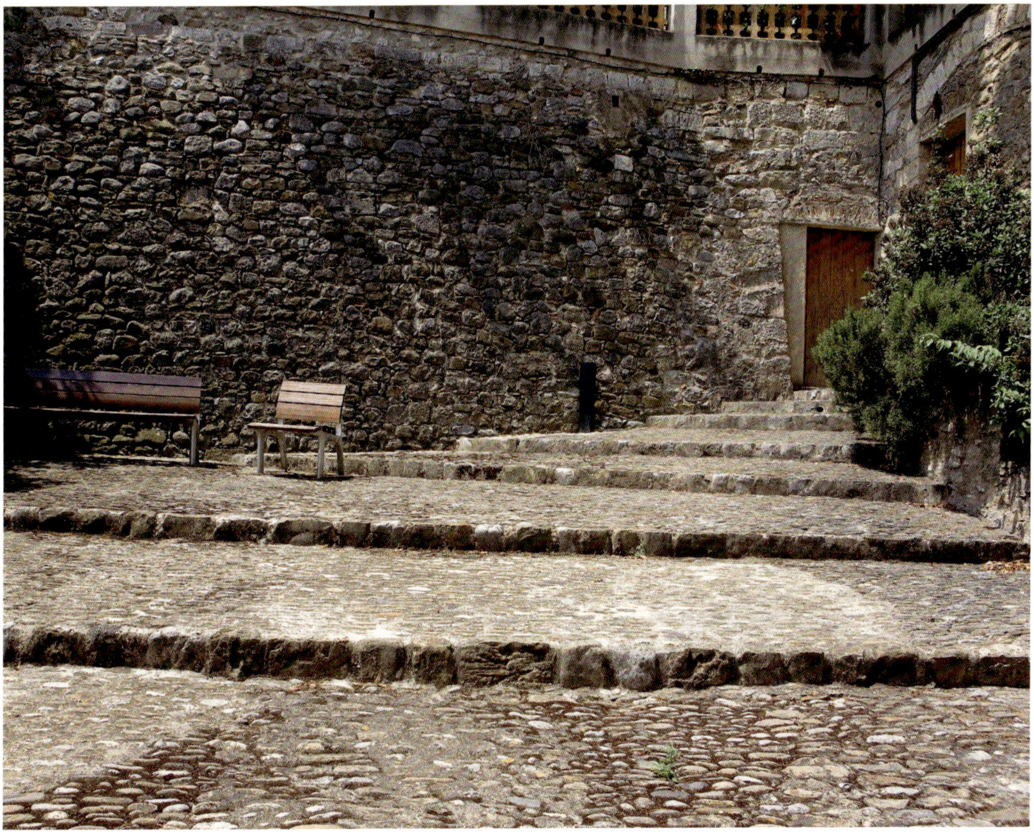

◂ Carrer Major

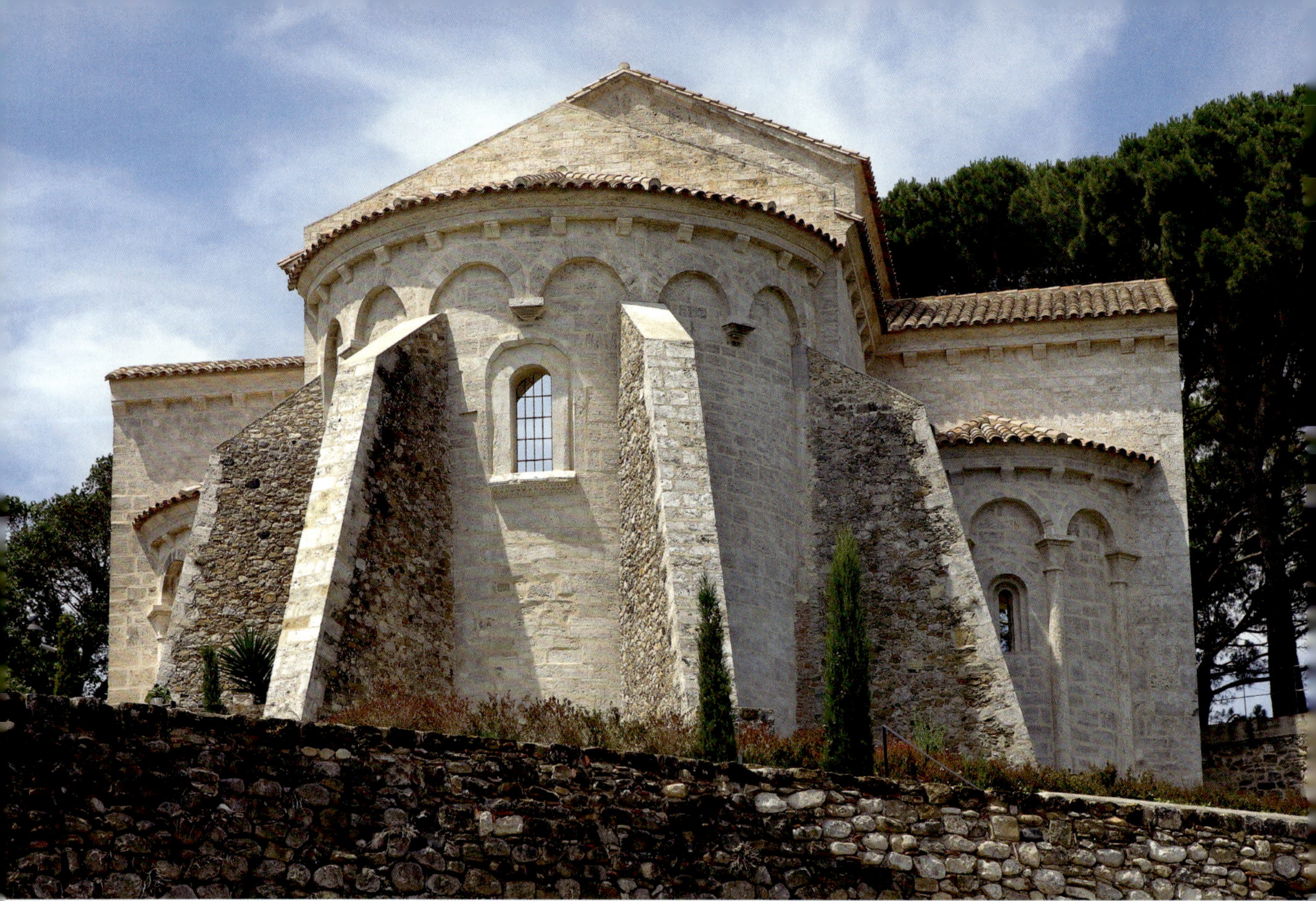
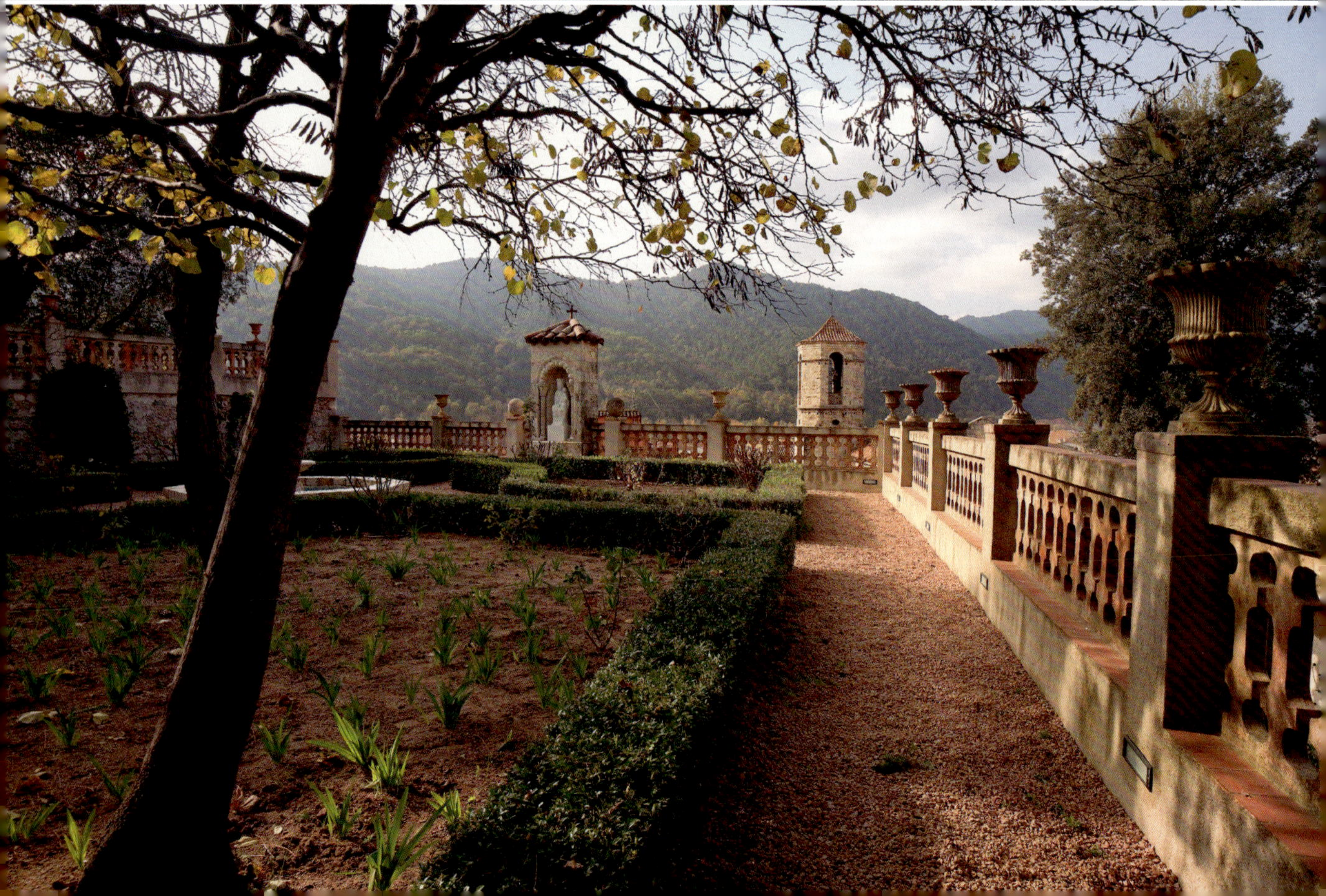

The collegiate of Santa Maria

Is situated within the precinct of the old count's castle, of which very little remains. Originally, it was built as the church of the castle, but on the disappearance of the county of Besalú as an independent entity, the church became an Augustinian canonry. The original building was raised in the 10th century, but in the 12th century experienced a profound reconstruction that led to a church with a basilica ground plan with three naves. The little that remains today belongs to that period: a head with transept and three apses which feature the characteristic Lombardy arches and Romanesque capitals. This canonry was extinguished in the 16th century, and the church was transformed into a collegiate, and in the 19th century, with the sale of Church lands, what remained passed into private hands, and this meant that it was abandoned and a large part of its architectural elements sold.

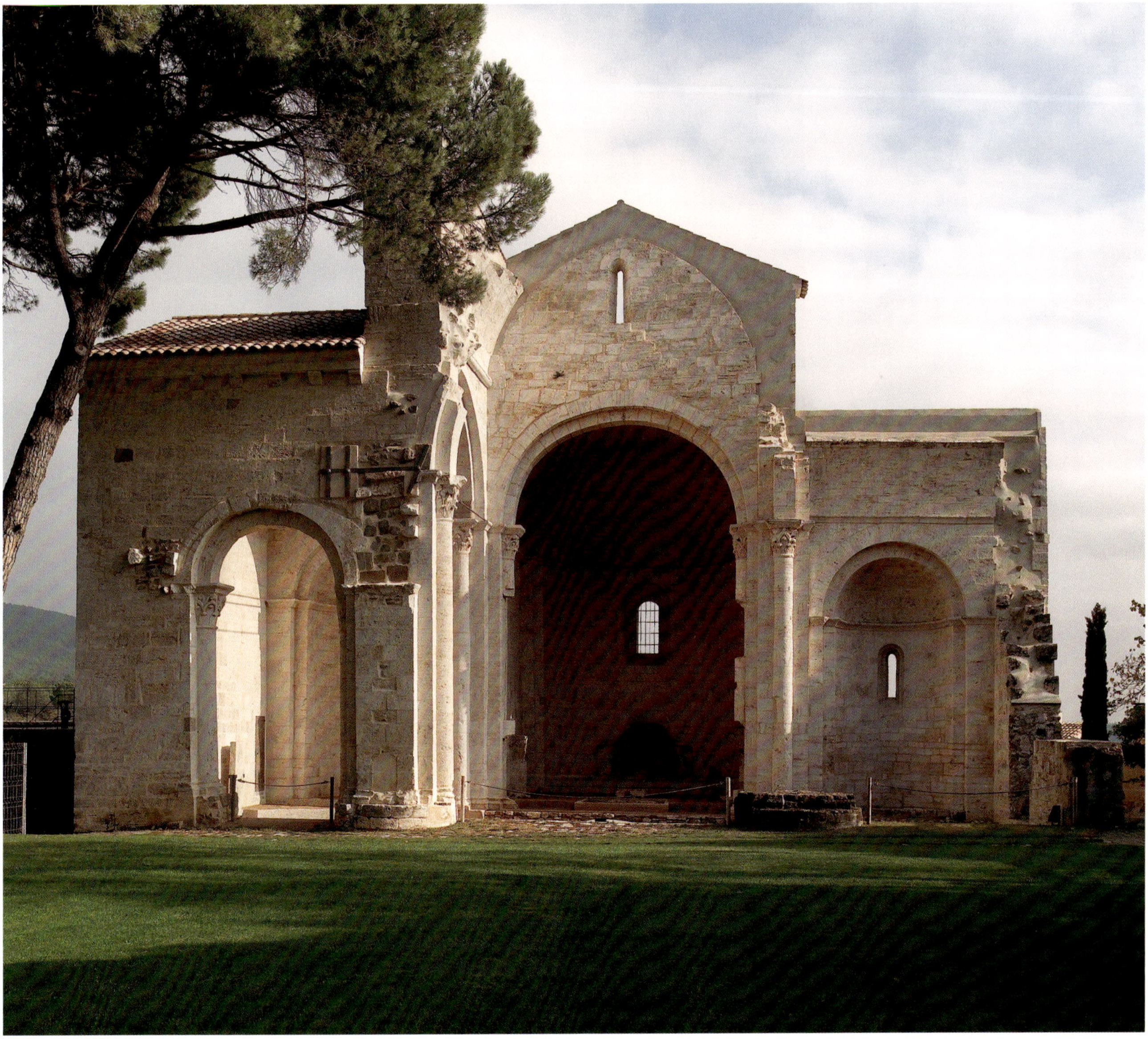

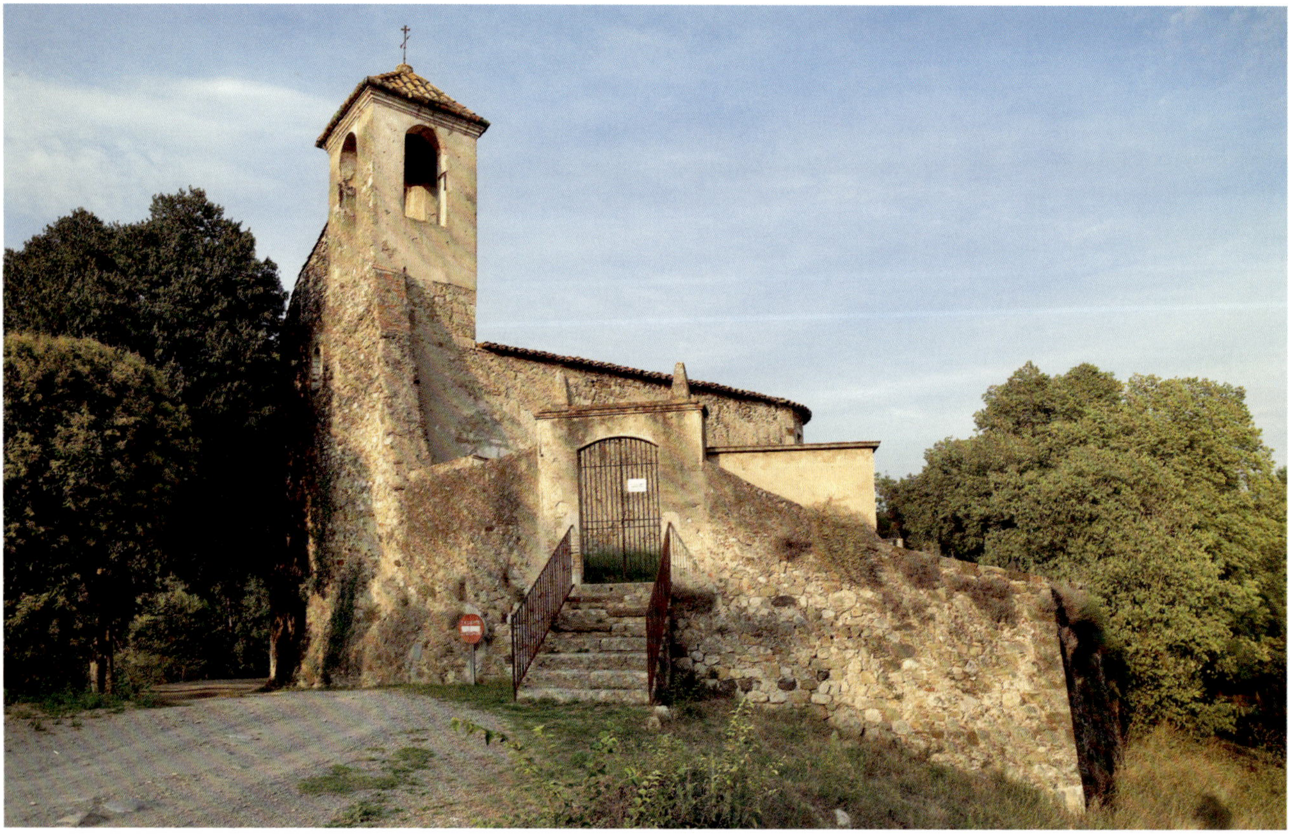

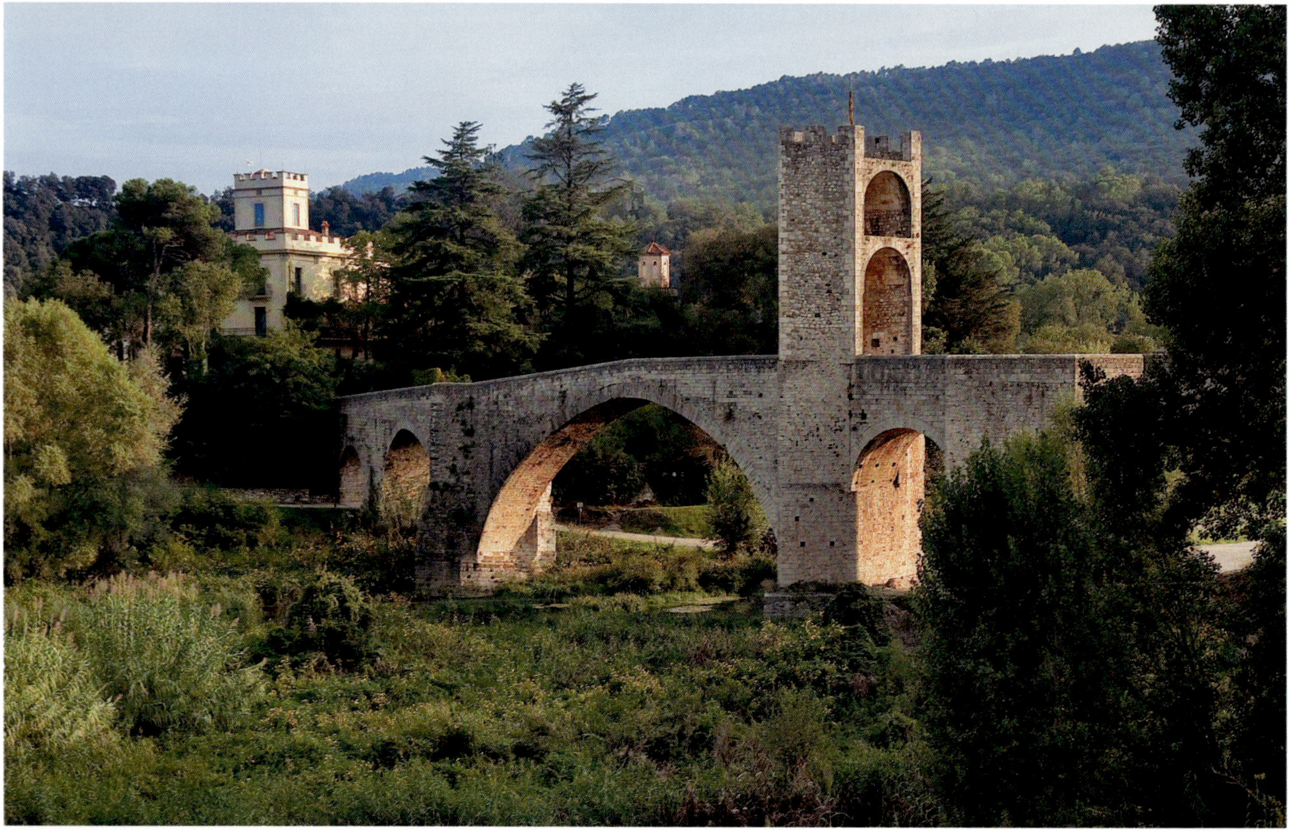

(above) Sant Martí de Capellada. (below) The fortified bridge

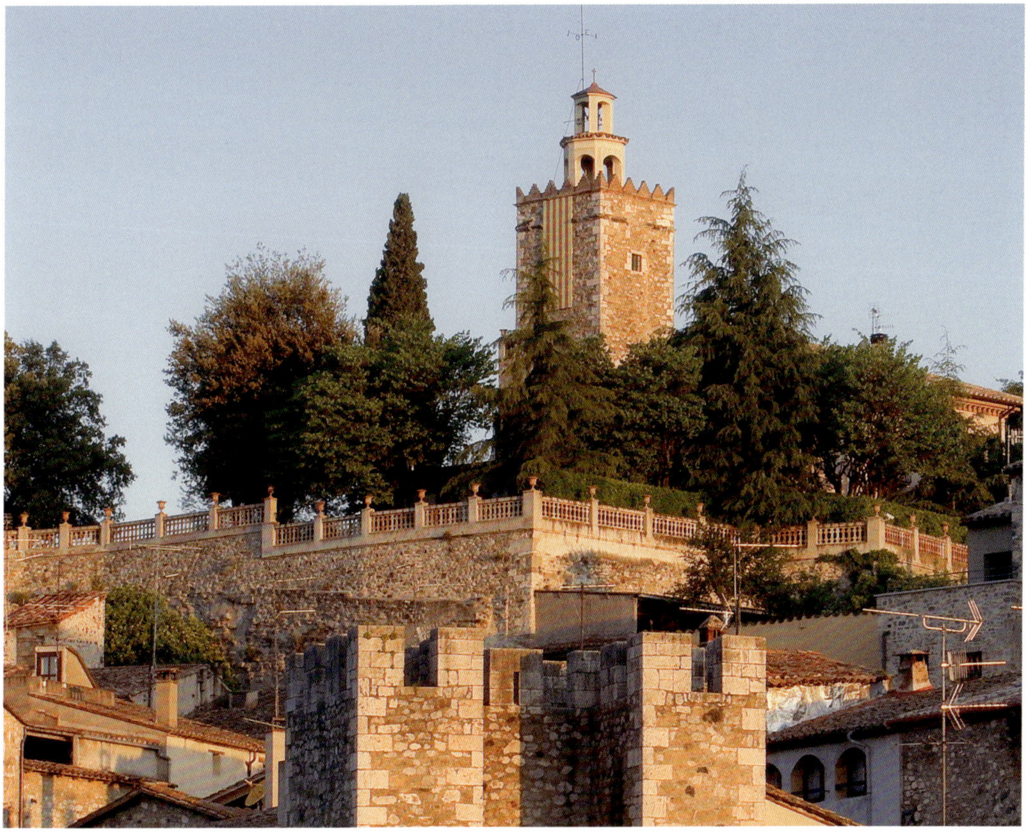

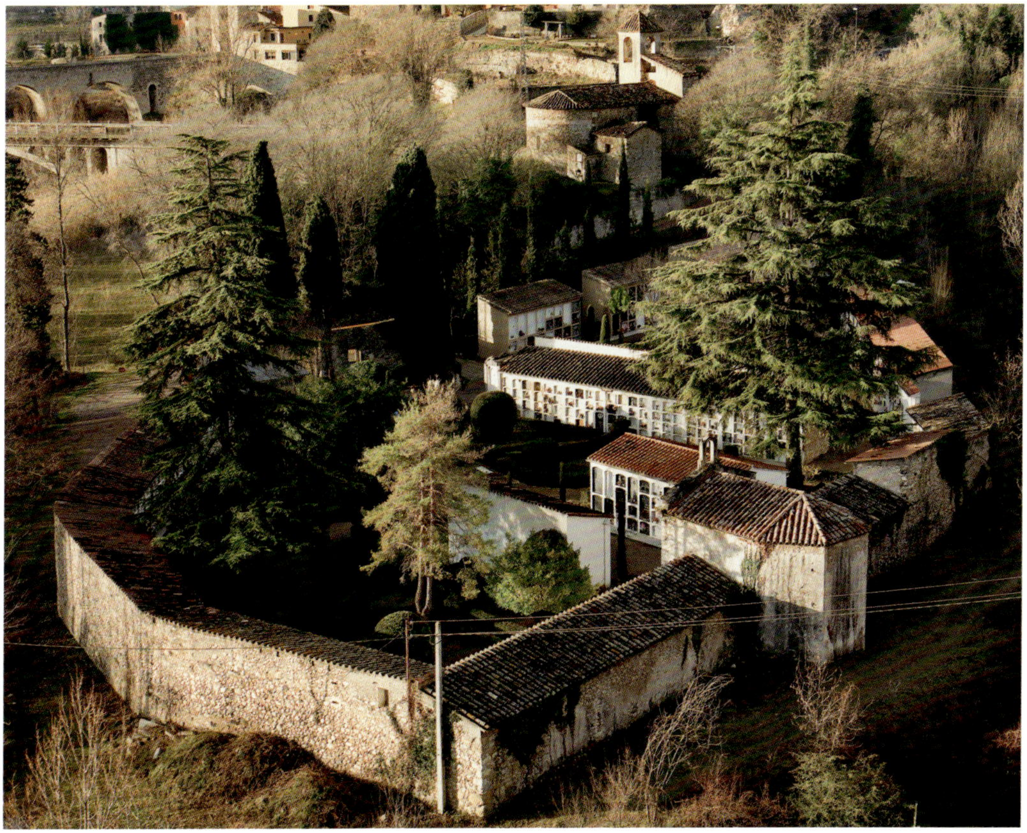

(above) Tower of the count's castle. (below) The cemetery

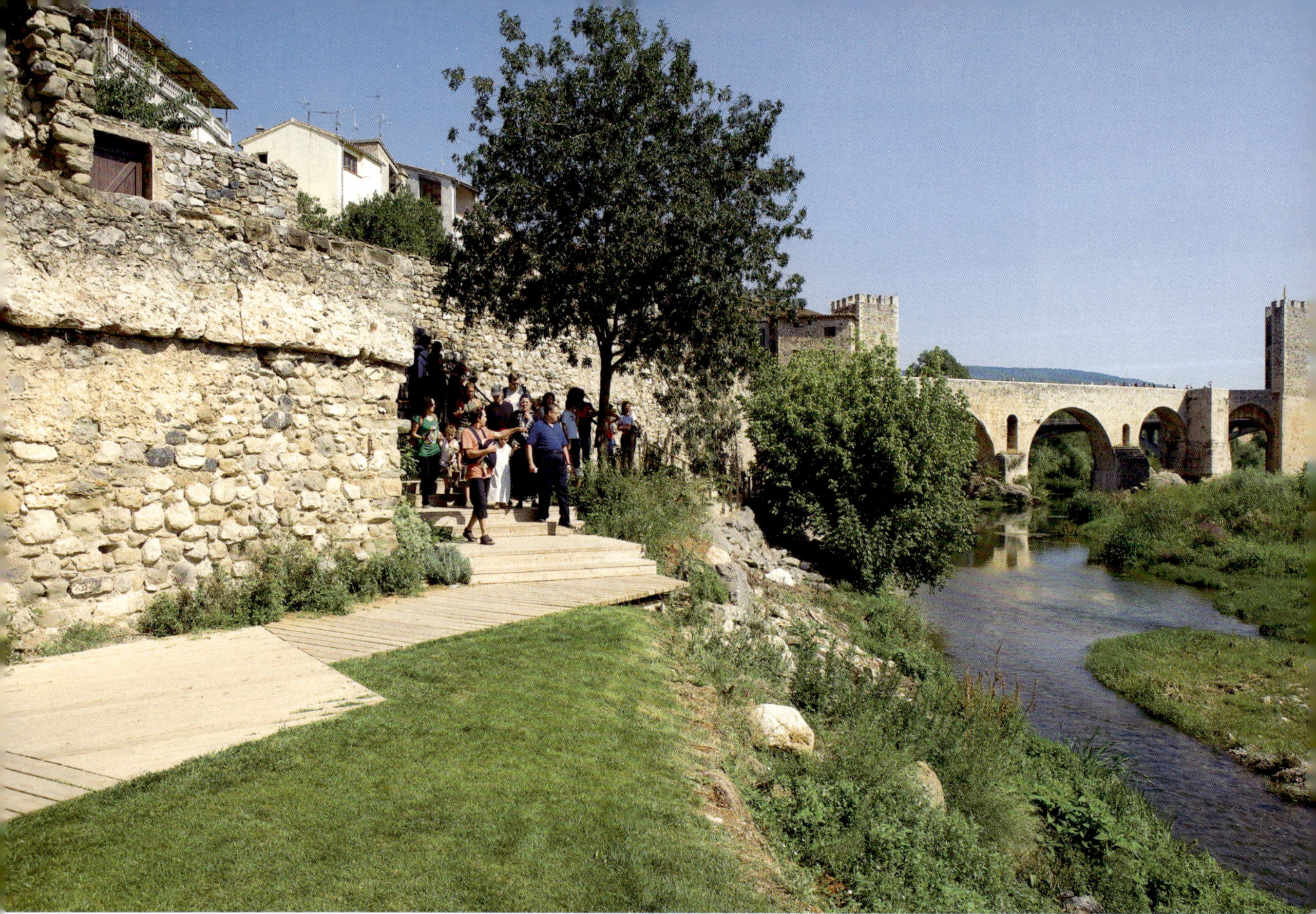

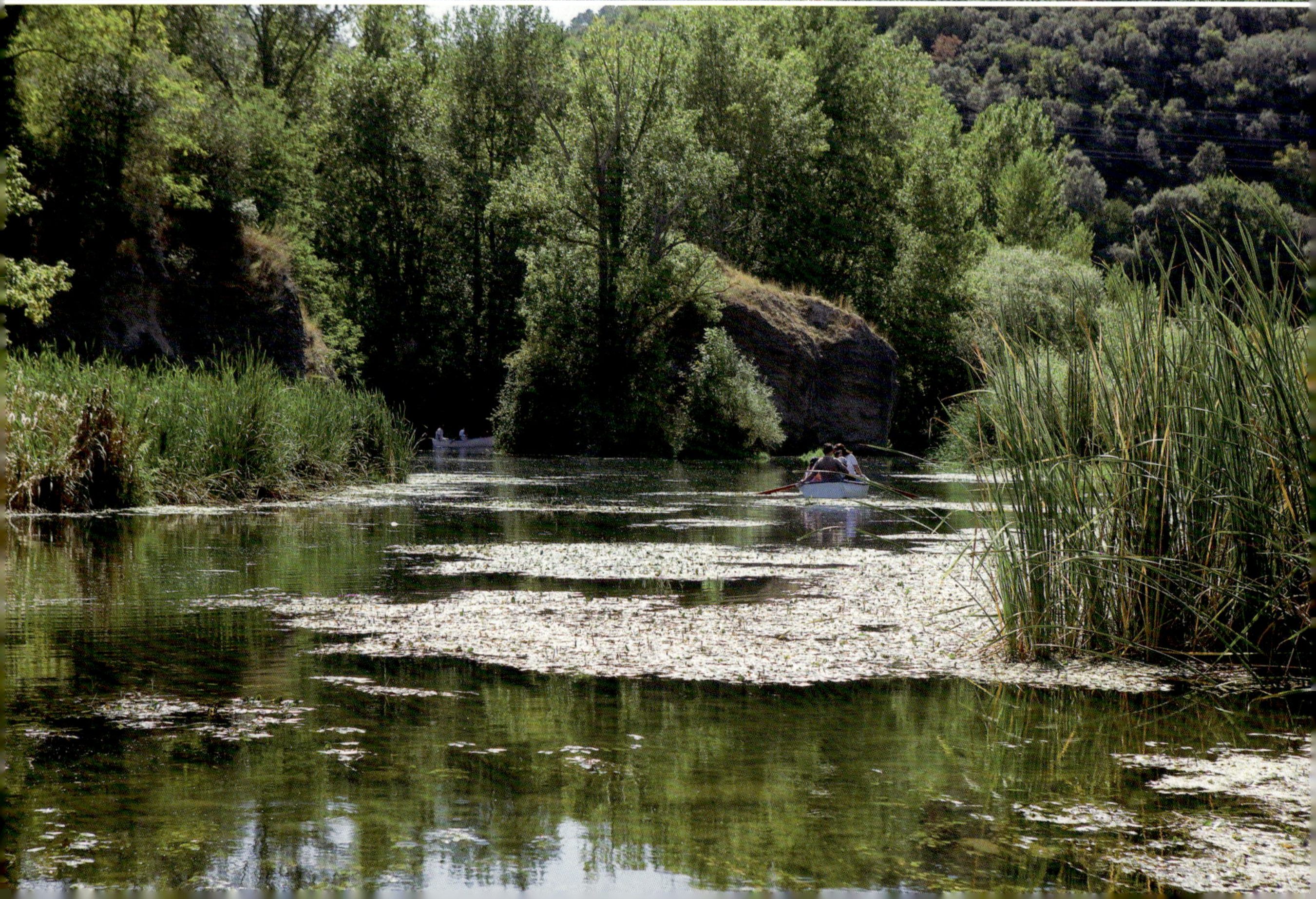

The green ring

It is a riverside route in which one can do different activities and which enables you to link up all the aspects of the town of Besalú. It can be done on foot and dropping down to the orchards that the Benedictine monks tended in former times, and which are now tended by local people. The Porta dels Horts, with Saint James the Apostle presiding over the threshold, allow us access to this space that also includes the Jardí de la Ratafia, where aromatic plants are grown which are used to make this traditional liquor. Beside the orchards, the Molí d'en Subirós, recently restored and turned into a museum, enables us to get a very approximate idea of how these types of installations worked.

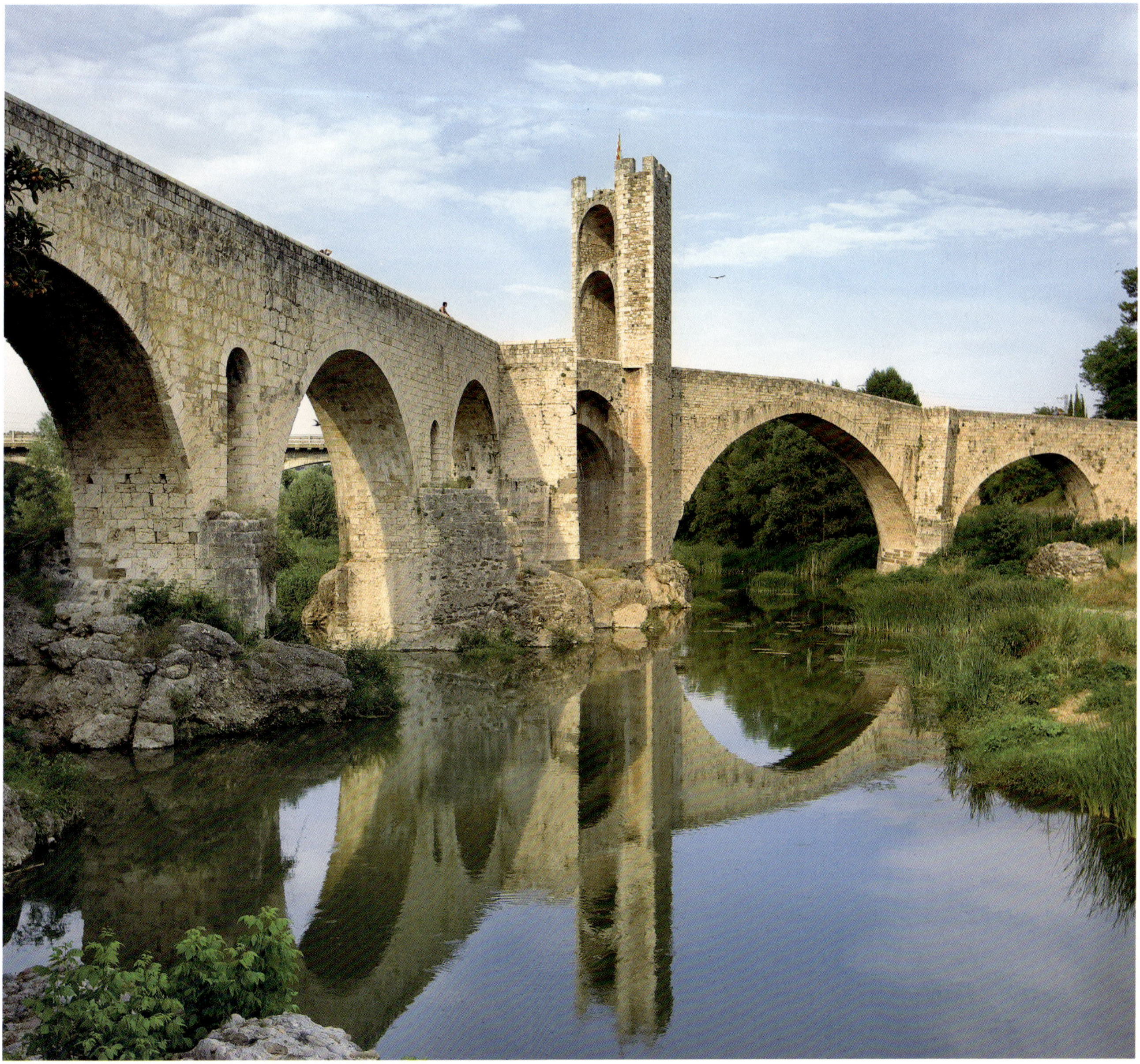

◂ (above) River walkway. (below) River Fluvià

The fortified bridge

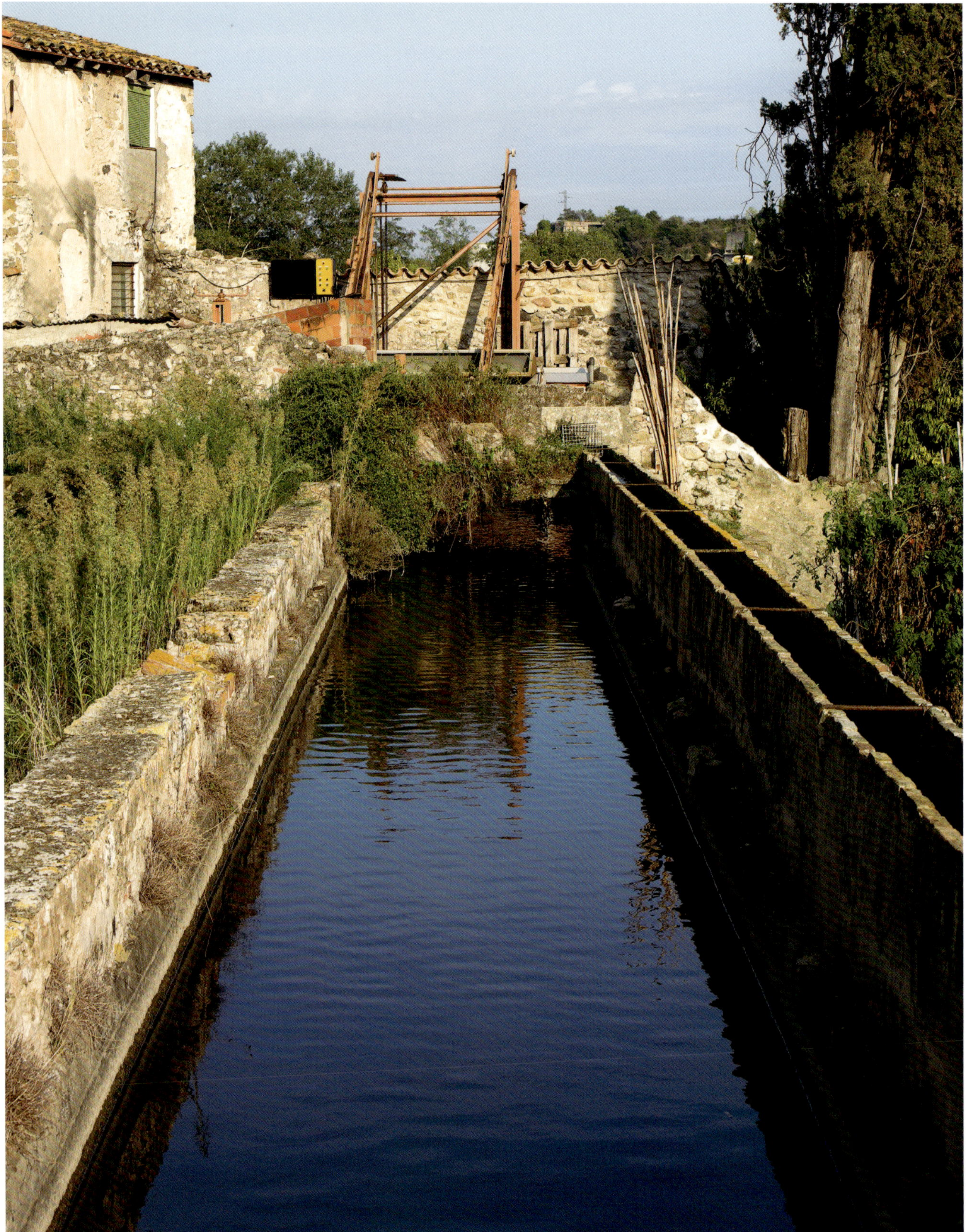

Molí d'en Subirós ▸

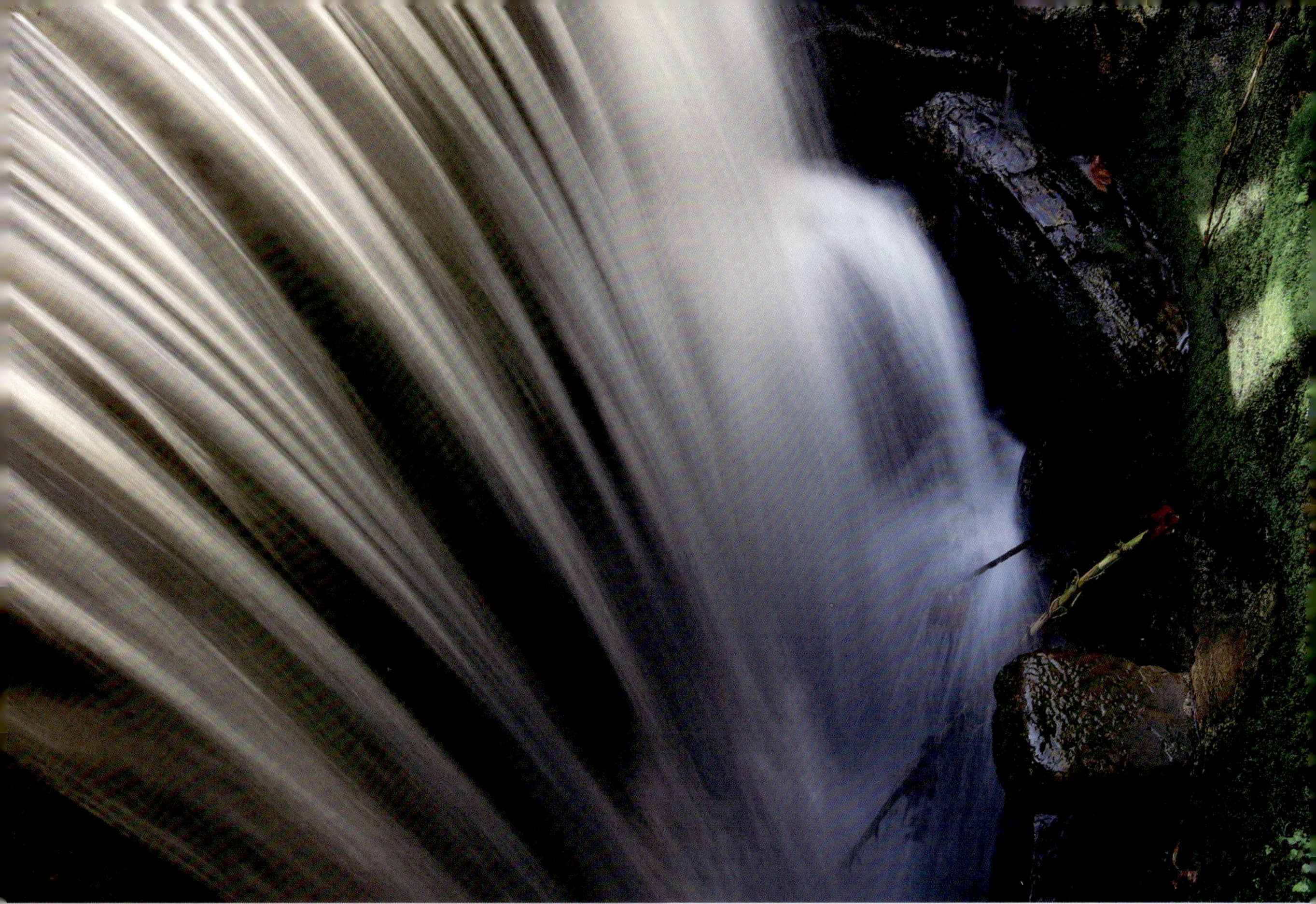

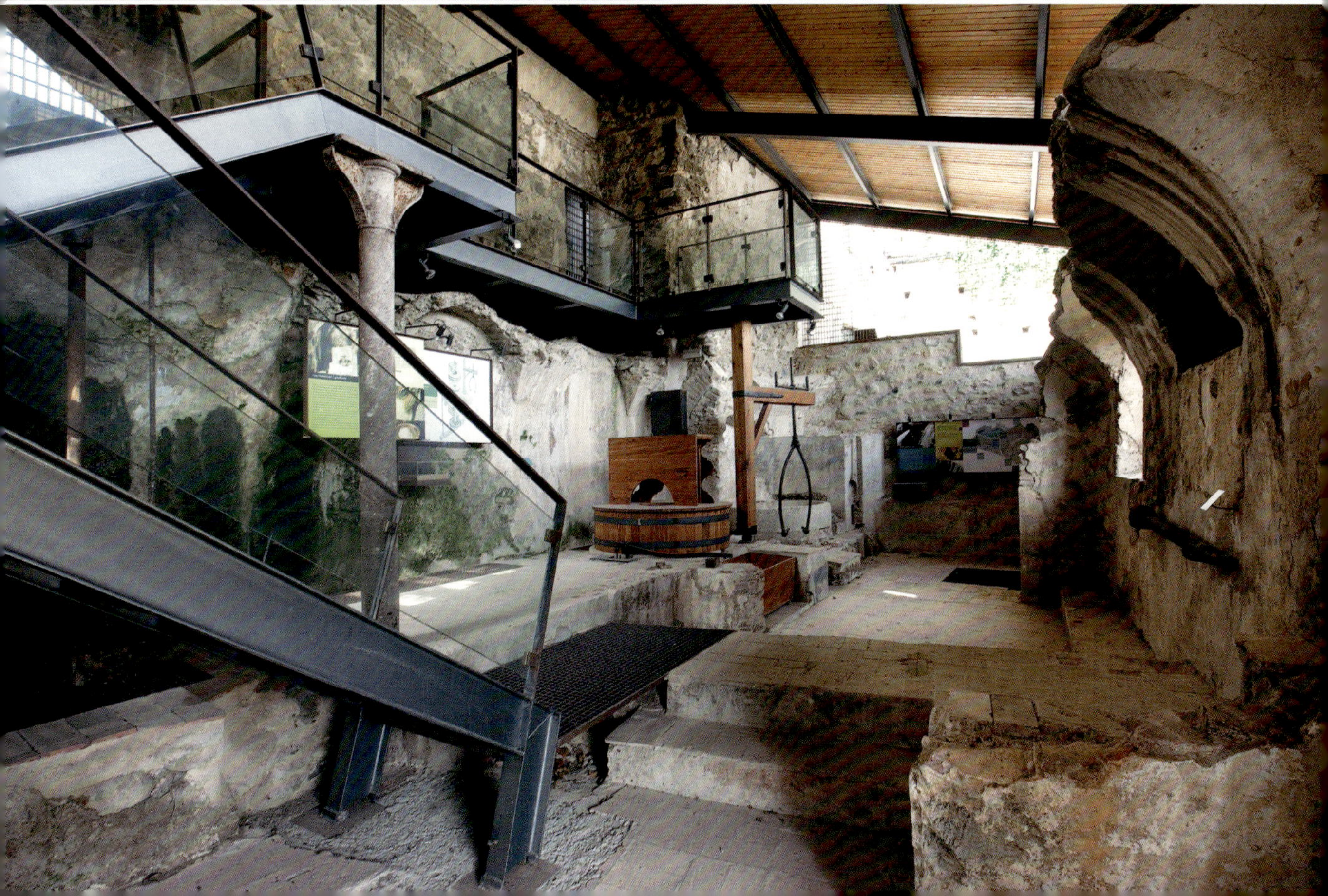

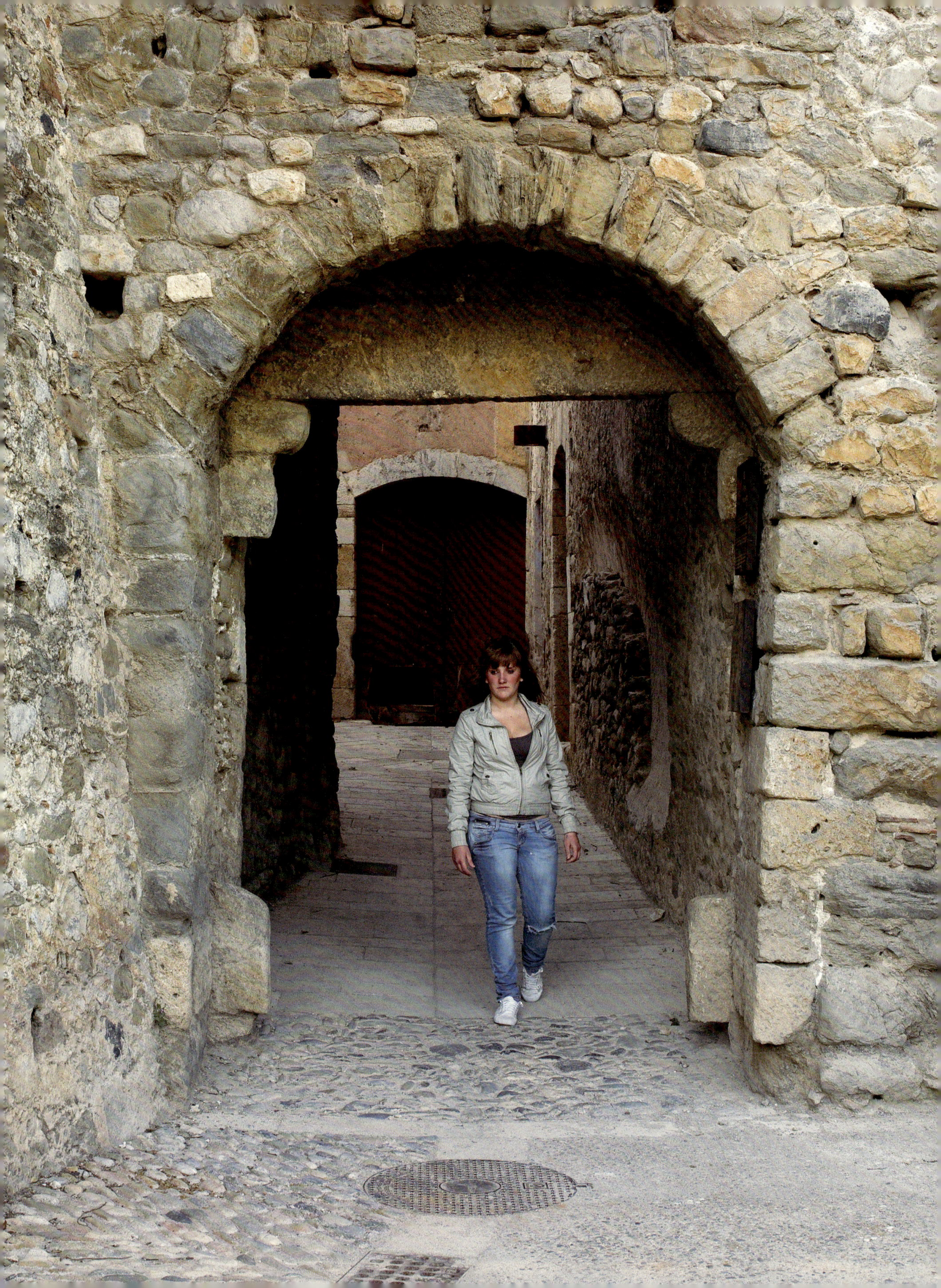

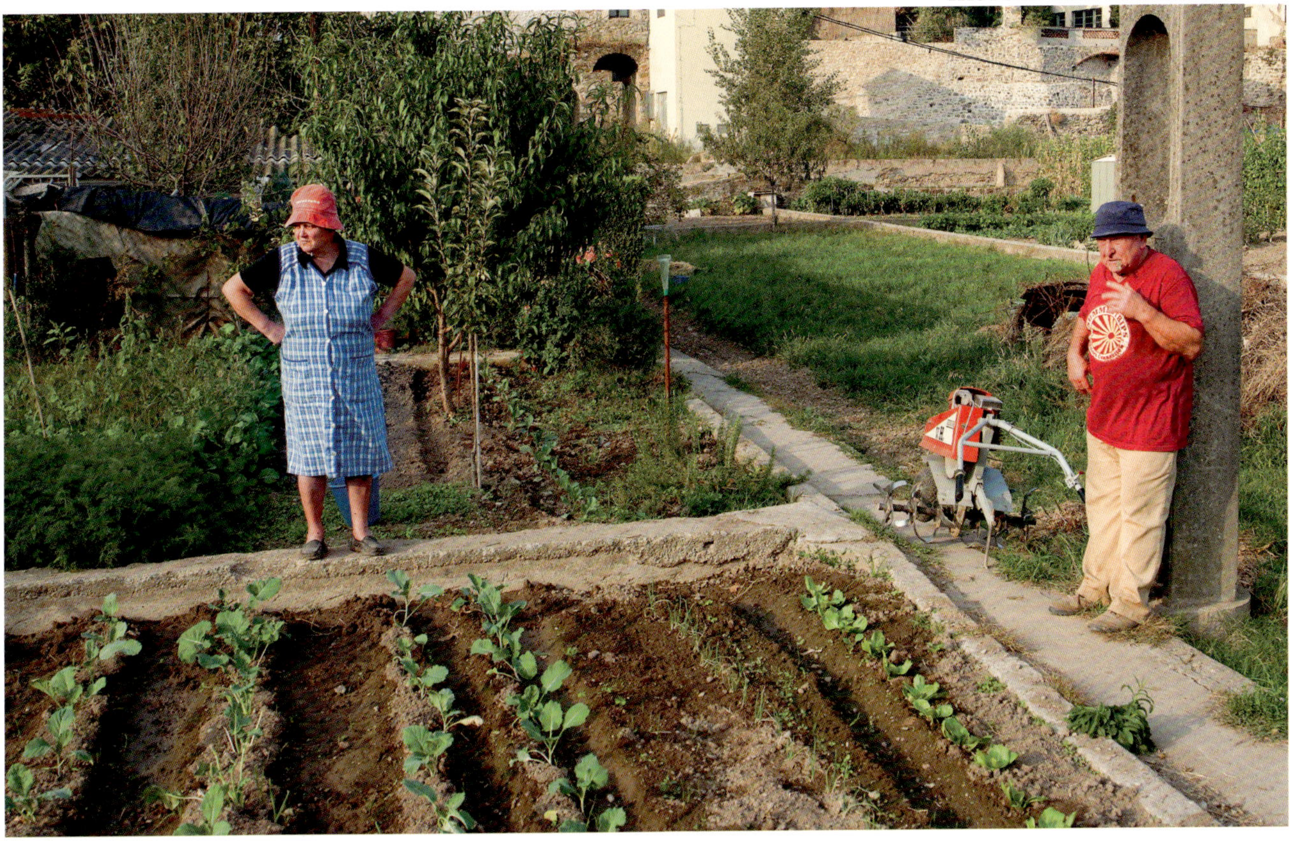

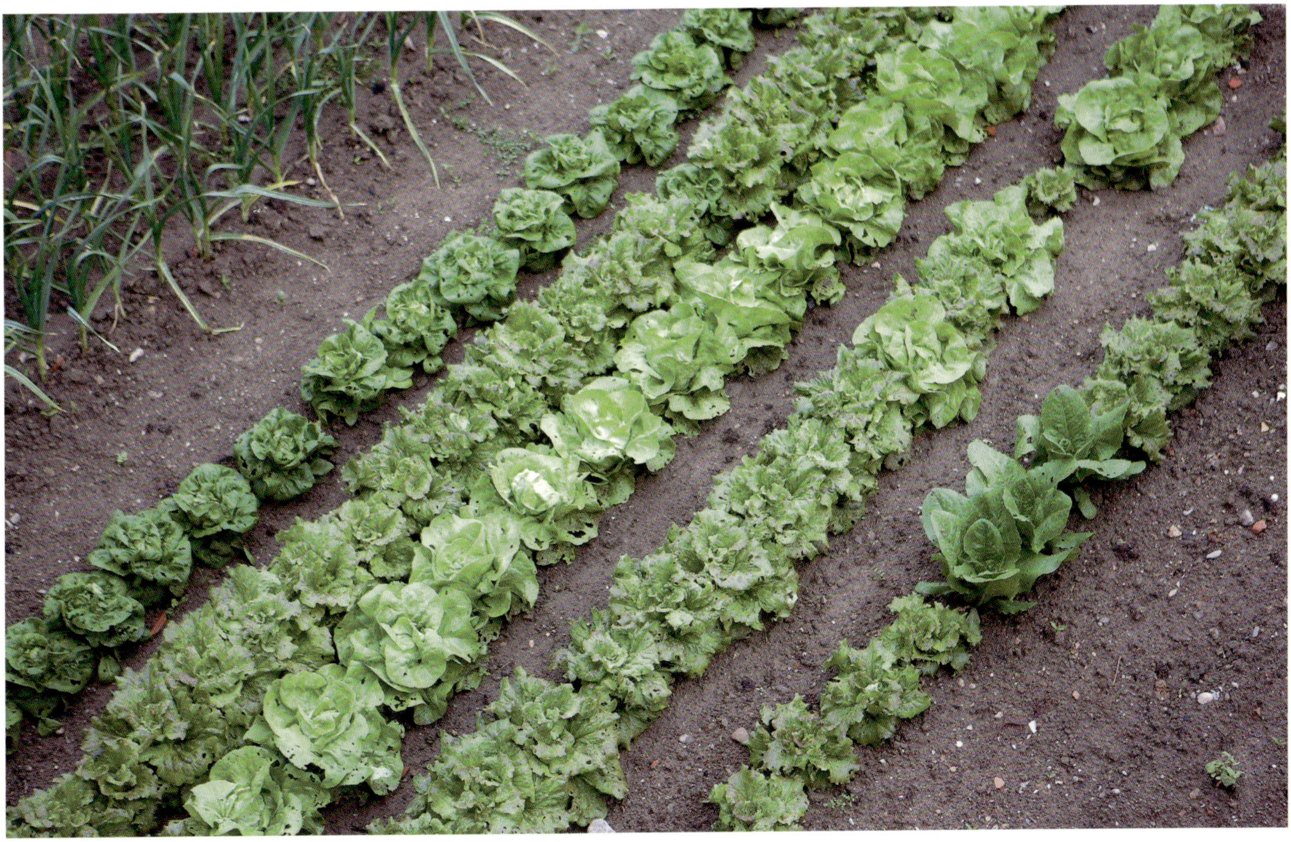

◂ Portal dels Horts

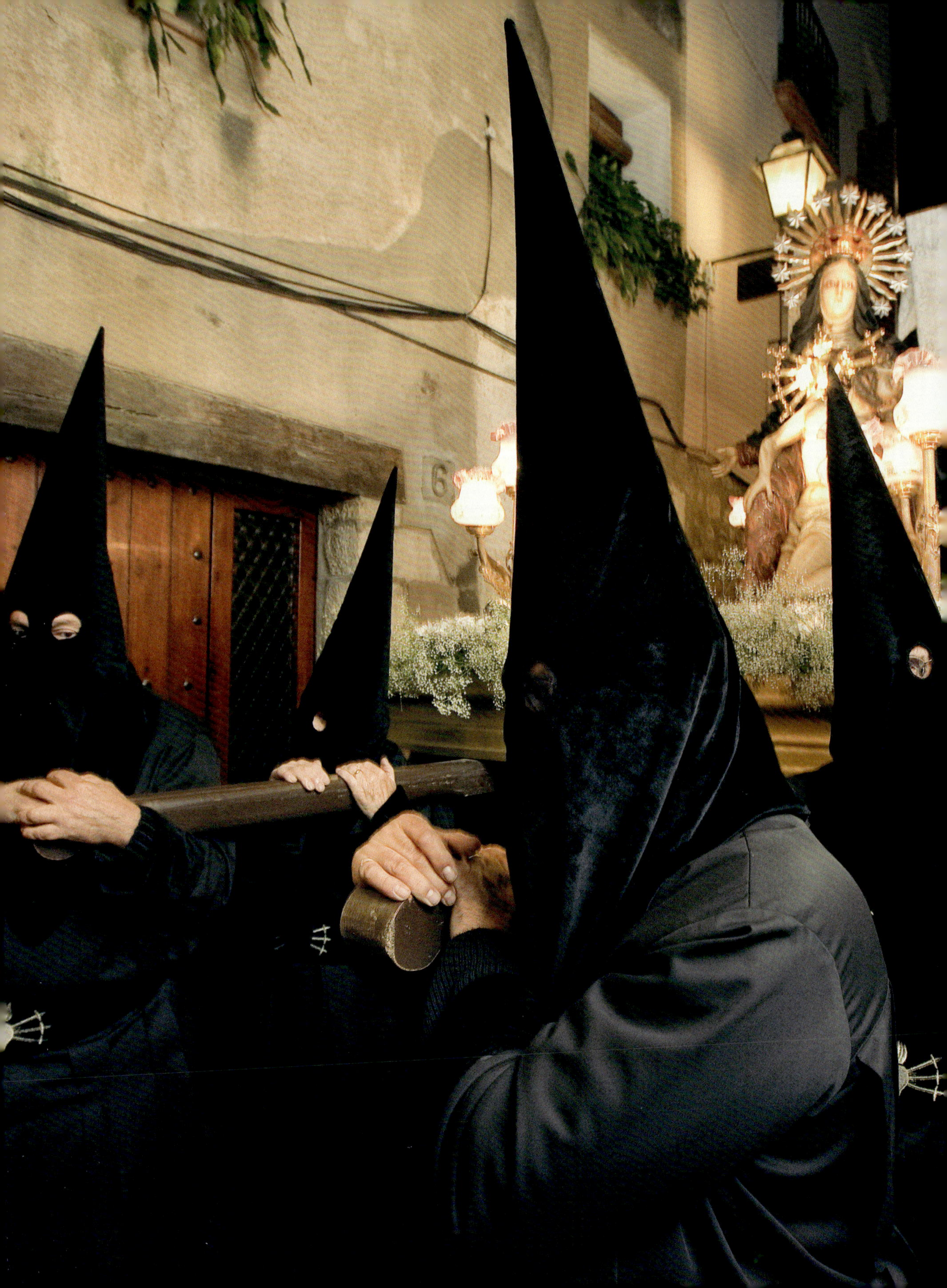

Festivals and traditions

The social, cultural and festive pulse of Besalú consists of the wise combination of old and new customs, of conserving rituals and celebrations that date back centuries, and consolidating festivities and fairs that, with time, will be a historical legacy that the future generations will receive. In essence tradition is this: transmitting —often orally— from fathers to sons, historical facts, beliefs, religious doctrines, in short, customs and habits that have sometimes become routine rituals that have survived generation after generation. The culinary tradition, for example, is one of these customs, a way of doing things, which has been passed from mothers to daughters over whole periods of time.

To measure the activity of a town, one of the indicators to take into account is the number of entities and associations, and in this Besalú is no exception, quite the contrary in fact. *Acunç recerca i divulgació* was introduced to the public in 1994 with a fair that has become a referent, a not-to-be-missed event when Easter approaches. I refer to the *Fira de la Forja i el Ferro* (*Forge and Iron Fair*) that, during some events, is also attended by wood and cabinet-making craftsmen. The sound of the hammer tapping on the anvil comes from the courtyard of Can Llaudes, the same melody that, for years now, for fifteen days accompanies artists and visitors, who look intently and with curiosity at tables, lamps, doors, hangers and other items, fruit of the talent and skill of the smiths, who work the untameable iron until giving it the most suggestive and kindest forms.

For sure, however, if we were to take a look at everything that been done and is still done in Besalú from the past until now, we would only find one event capable of really bringing together the whole town in a fraternal way. It is not exactly a new event, but quite the contrary: it is the oldest in living memory and perhaps for this reason, for the strength of tradition that has been maintained unaltered with the passing of time. If you are thinking about the annual festival, then you are mistaken. Those from Besalú, however, already know I am talking about the festival of the Virgin of the Dolors and, specifically, the procession, which each year is experienced and felt by each person. Following it devotedly barefoot around the streets holding a candle, tapping lances and beating drums in the handling of *manaies* or on the original quintains, lining up the participants wearing a tunic, singing the Salve in the square... But even the oldest of traditions evolve; the changes ensure its survival. And that is why 2009 will pass into history because an unusual event took place. For the first time in more than 300 years since the Venerable Congregation was founded, a woman had the honour of being appointed prioress and, therefore, of carrying the banner of the Dolors. A festival in with a capital 'F'; do not confuse it with the annual festival. The annual festival. I mentioned it before. We cannot ignore it. The annual festival is dedicated to the saints Prim and Felicia, but the latter has never had the prestige and dedication of the former. In my memory, she has always fallen from the pedestal, and when we speak about the festival we never mention her and always say, "For Saint Prim this and for Saint Prim that". "For Saint Prim it will be more than 50 years now that La Bisbal has come" or "For Saint Prim there will be another after-the-wedding-day party" or "For Saint Prim a river descent of homemade boats will be organised" or "For Saint Prim the square will be full of people dancing *sardanes*" or "For Saint Prim the festival's opening speech will be read by someone born in or related to Besalú" or "After Saint Prim winter will be coming"... In any case, a few days before Saint Prim, precisely during the first weekend of September, there is an authentic, original festival atmosphere to be felt; not in vain is Besalú medieval. Since its consolidation, now

◂ **Procession of the Dolors**

many years ago, for three days for everyone who enters by any of the old entrance gates to what had been the capital of the earldom, it is as if they had taken a voyage through time, as if they had landed in the middle of the 12th century, and were privileged witnesses of how people lived in that age of splendour, passionate and unique, where Count Tallaferro was owner and lord of these lands; dominions that were fought over as much as they were loved, where people prayed and traded. And in the business centre par excellence we go to the main square of Besalú.

The references to the weekly market are very, very old, before the medieval period. Documentary evidence dates as far back as 1027, and with time it established itself as the number one commercial centre of what would later be the county of La Garrotxa. Farmers, craftsmen, traders and business people came from all parts, but not only outsiders did business, but the Besalú locals too. Thus trade in the town prospered and, indirectly, everyone gained. Today, every Tuesday, traders set up their stalls between both squares, the two epicentres of the town, Plaça Major and Prat de Sant Pere, joined by the narrow Carrer del Canó.

The procession of the Mare de Déu del Mont does not arouse the devotion and passion of that of the Dolors, but the festival, the procession that has been made for time immemorial to the peak, has a special meaning for whoever takes part. That is why I recall a very special edition of the procession.

"From the peak of Rocapastora you could see the entourage of the procession climbing from which came a bunch of red dots, the barretina *hats that the pilgrims wore, the men who went ahead of the procession. In some sections of steep and narrow path, they looked to the stars to climb, but the procession of the Mare de Déu del Mont, every 8th of September, day of the found virgins, was obligatory for one reason or other, and nobody wanted to miss it. And the young men and women of courting age even less. This was a great opportunity to do some. Nobody ignored the procession of the Mont. All the people from the villages that grew on the sides of the imposing mountain of Mont —Lligordà, Beuda, Segueró, Maià, Crespià, Lladó and Besalú, and, sometimes, even the parish of Banyoles— climbed to worship the virgin that protected them throughout the year. The priest let the oldest man go at the front and thus ensured that the retinue went slowly, little by little, at quite a deliberate pace in order to pass the rosary. The youngsters, however, were unable to wait and were anxious to escape climbing a slope on a bend where the rector could not see them, and strayed off running and shouting. They stopped halfway and had a bite to eat and a swig of wine from the wineskin bottle. Once at the top they sang the couplets in honour of the Virgin and entrusted themselves to God to have a good harvest and so that there would not be any evil plague that would make the cattle sick. Today, what nobody missed was the festival outside the hermitage afterwards, on the area of level ground. They organised festivals that seemed more like those held in spring because they shared out blessed loaves of bread, celebrated the splendour of the vegetation, and the fullness and exaltation of life, of loves, and performed agricultural rites of protection and fertility with crosses of flowers, fires and smoke to keep away the evil spirits. Whatever you did was not enough to celebrate the procession of the Mare de Déu del Mont, a gathering that lasted all day and in which, once the spirit had been satiated and satisfied, the only thing left to do was feed the stomachs of the pilgrims".*

Obviously the passing of time has completely changed the procession of the Mare de Déu del Mont, but I like to think that that wild and rough mountain spirit still accompanies us.

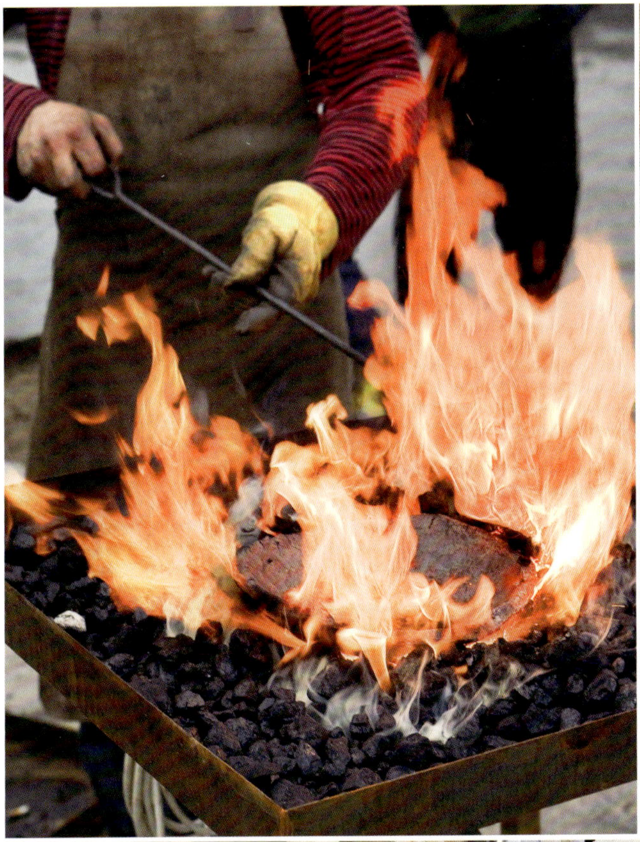

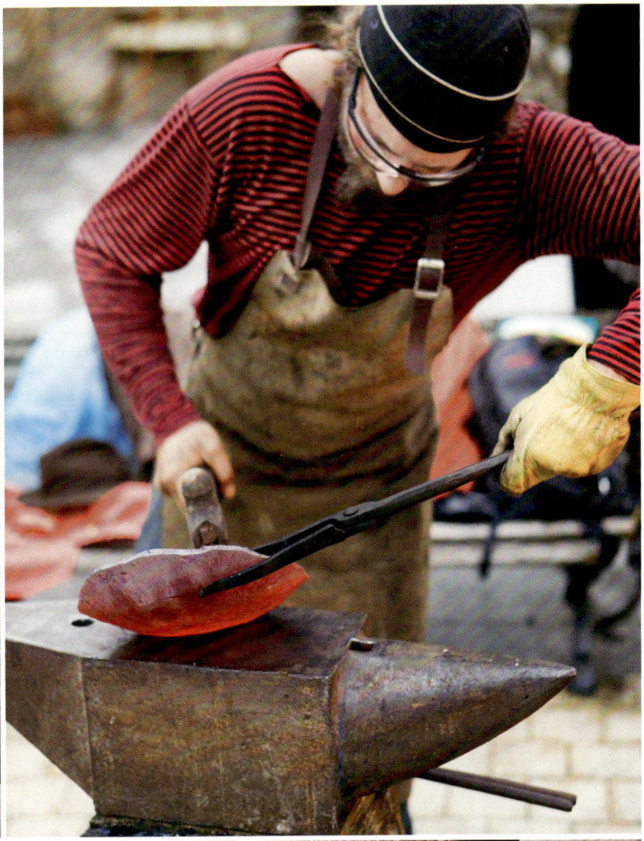

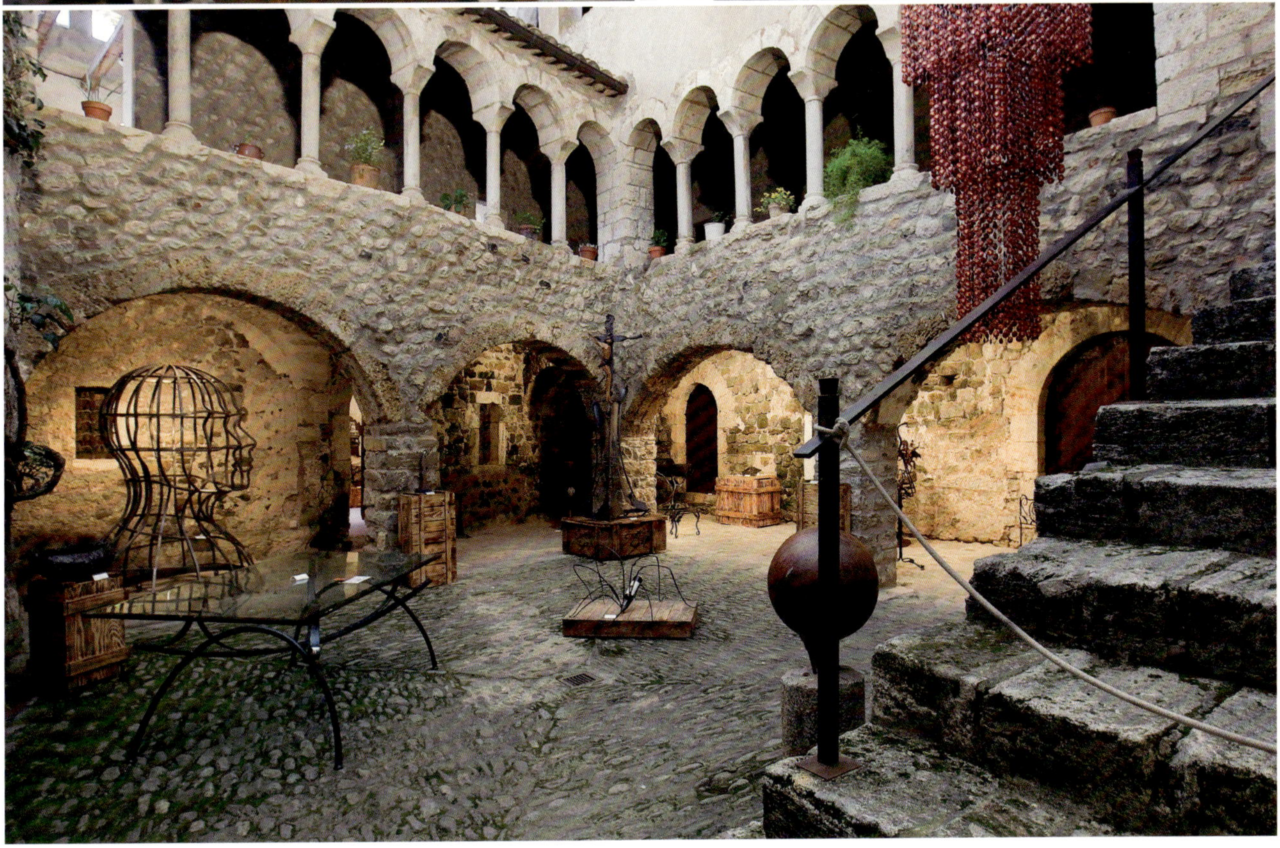

Forge and Iron Fair

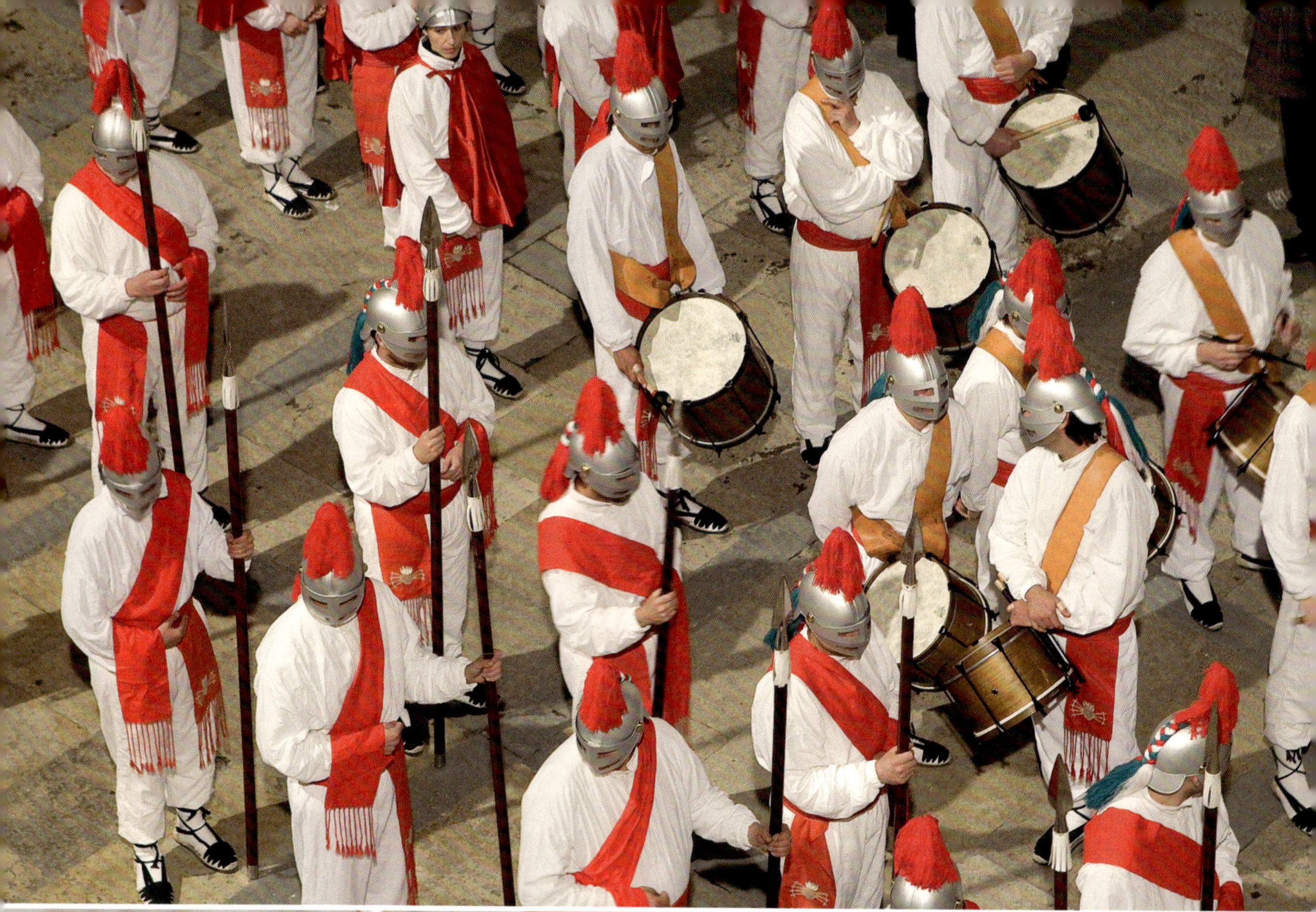

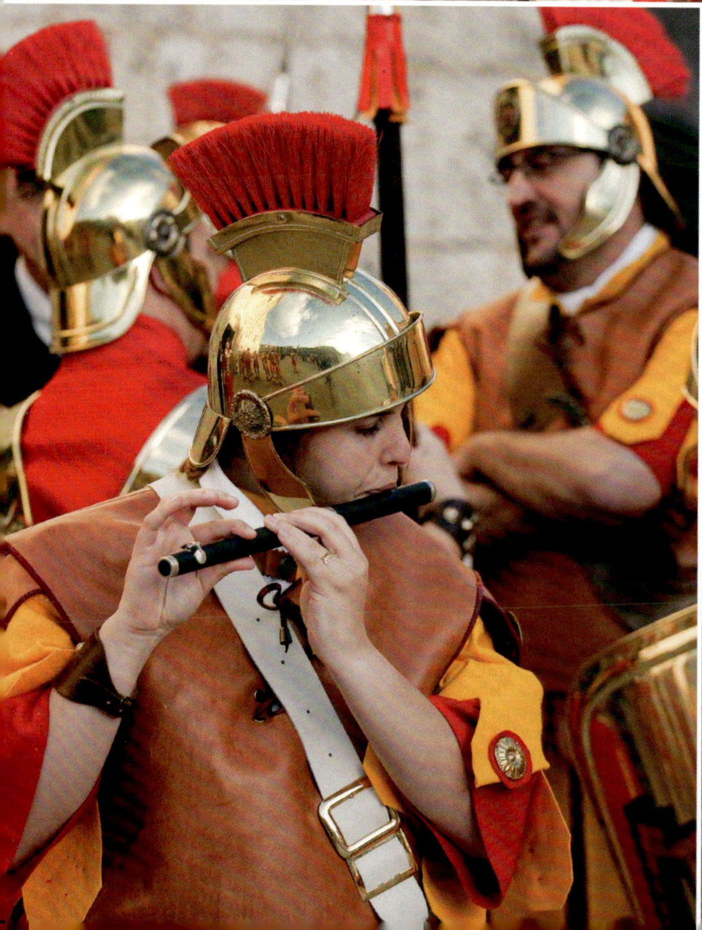

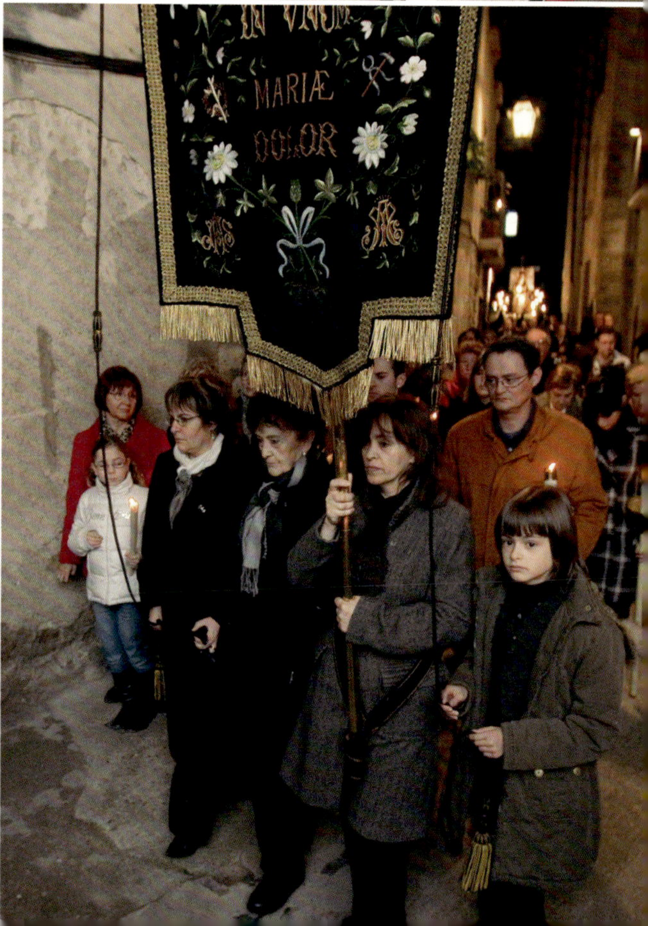
MARIÆ
DOLOR

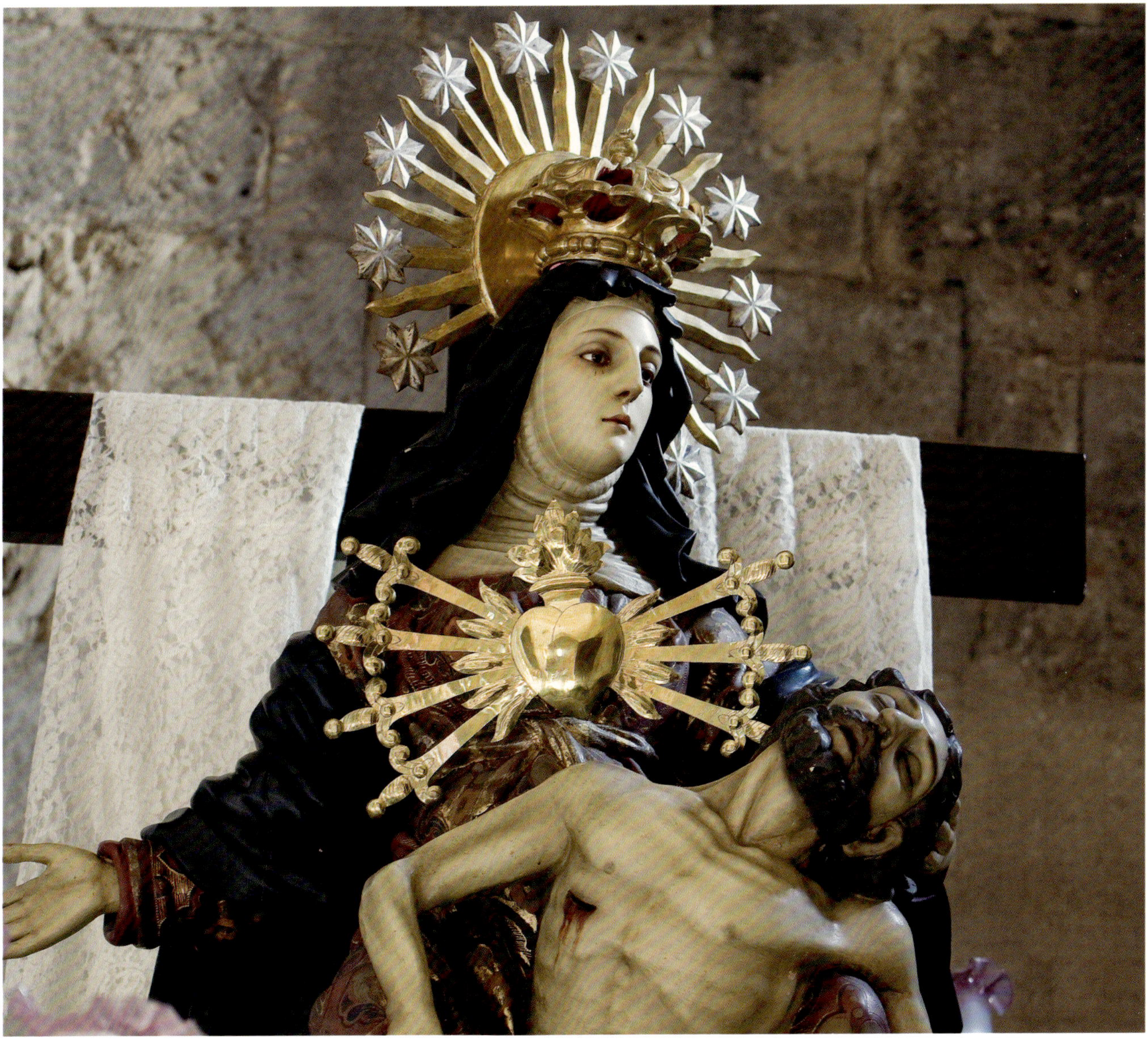

The Virgin of the Dolors

It is the image of the Pietà, Jesus coming down from the cross and in the arms of his Mother; it is in the church of Sant Vicenç. The congregation of the Virgin of the Dolors is at its busiest during the five-day period of devotion and the Day of the Dolors, Good Friday, which is held on the Friday before Palm Sunday. The festival of the Day of the Dolors in Besalú has been a local festival for many years now, and it would not be wrong to state that for many local people, it is the festival par excellence. During the first four days of the quinary period, cultural events are held and a daily mass, presided over by the prior and the organisers. On the fifth day, Good Friday, known as the Festivity, there are activities throughout the day, from 12 midday with the mass until 10 at night, when the procession ends, which is the most important activity held that day.

◂ (above) The Quintains. (below) The *Manaies* and the *Priora*

Song of the Salve ▸

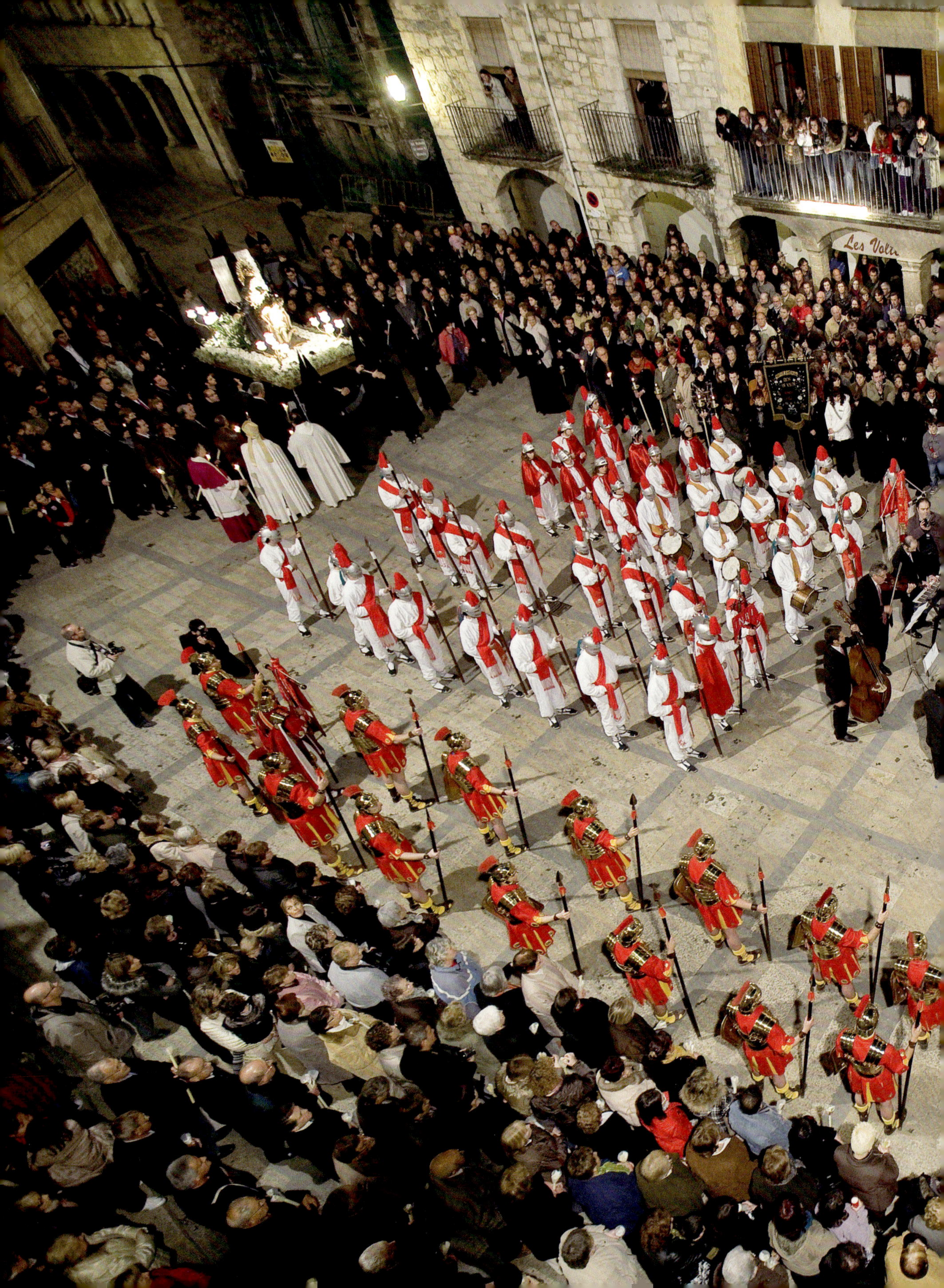

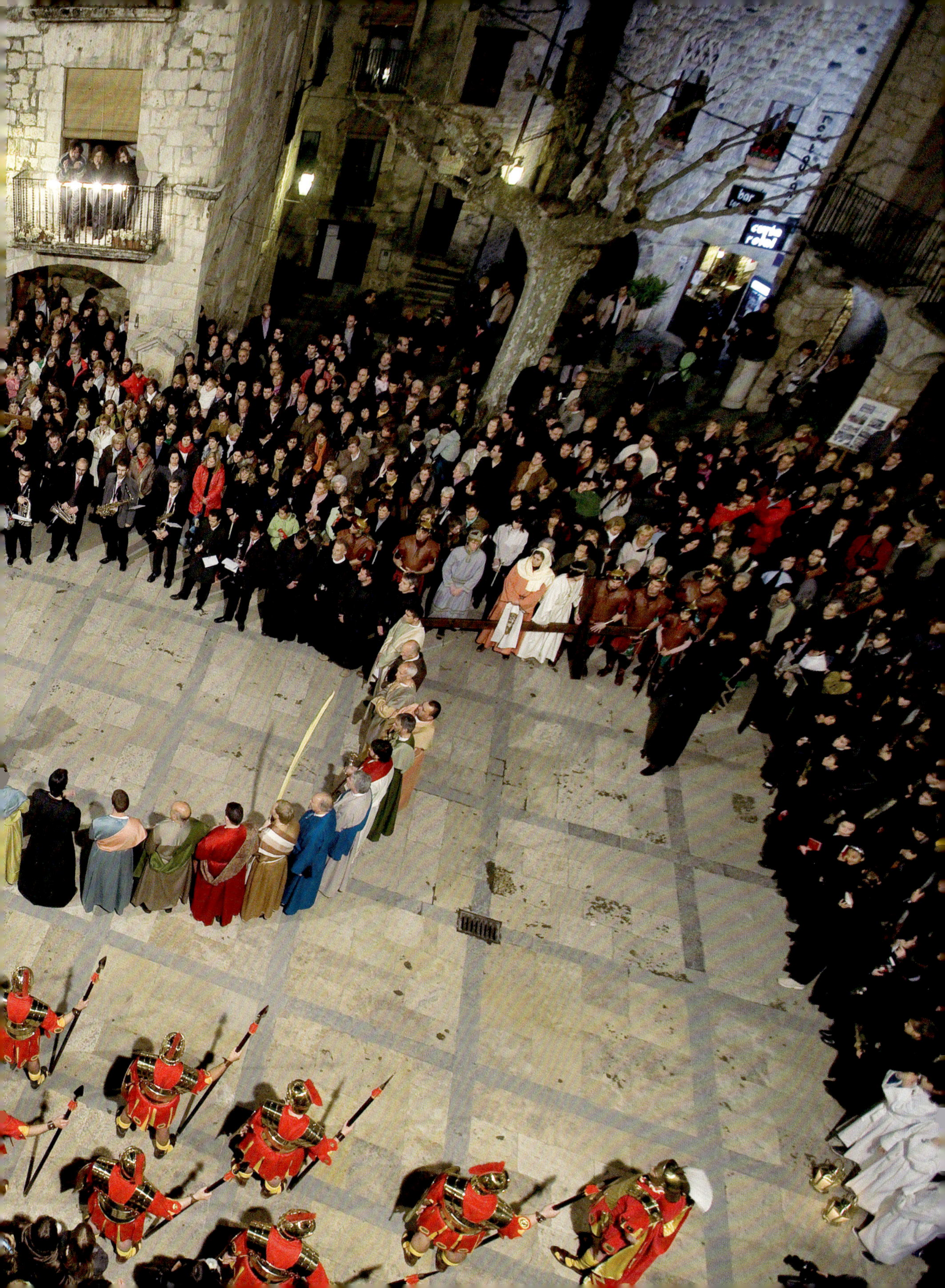
bar

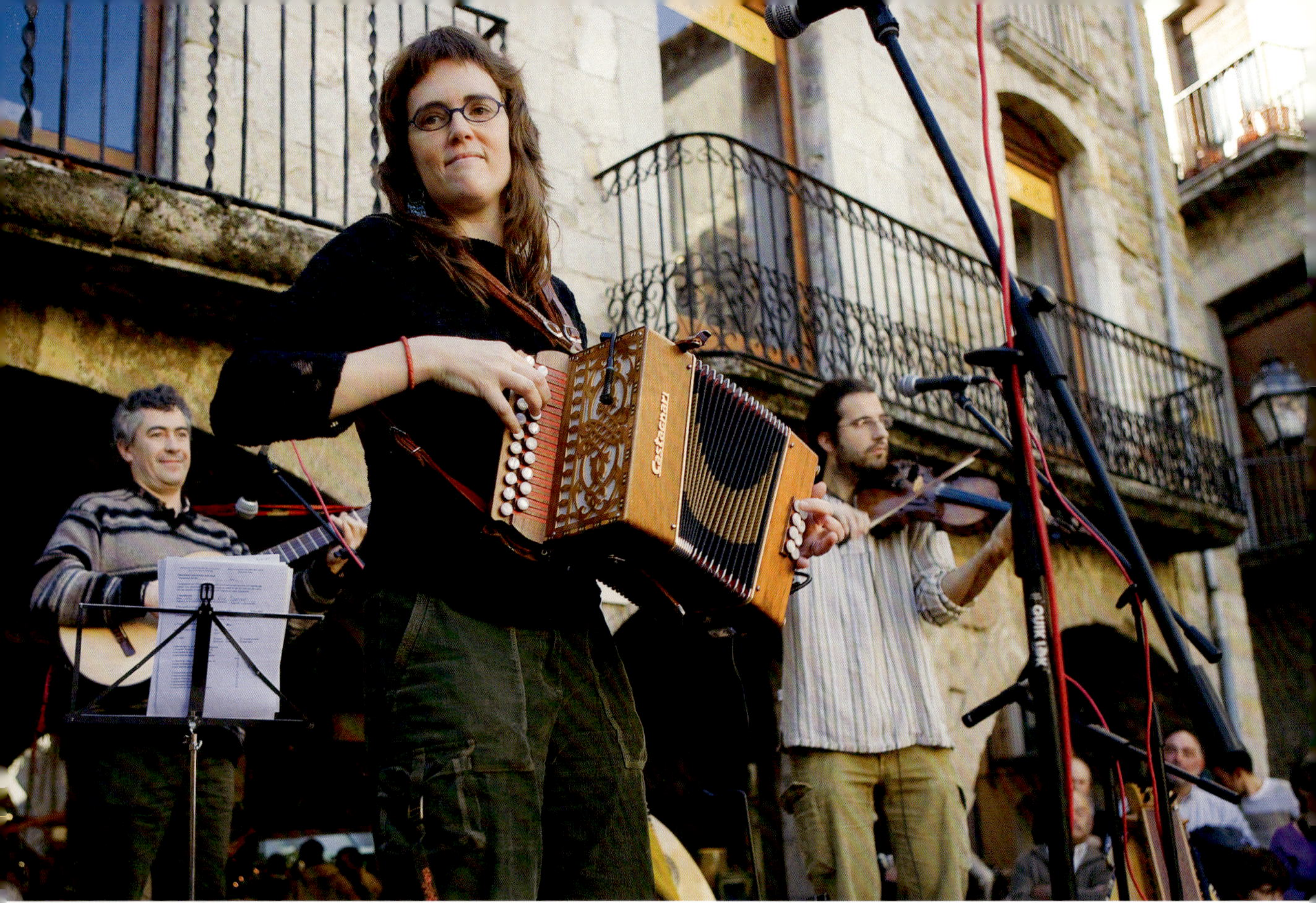

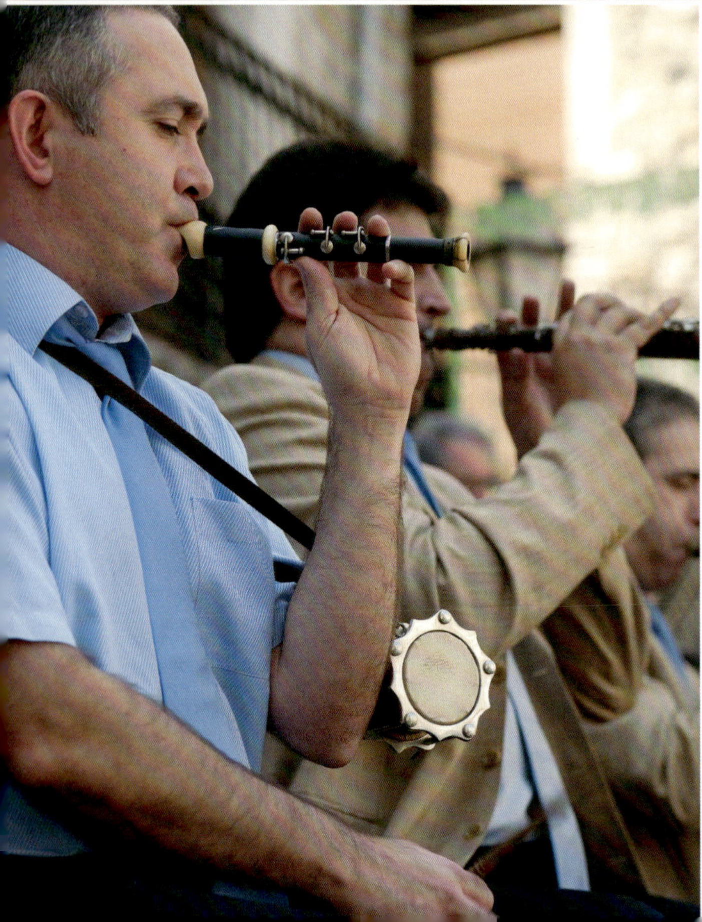

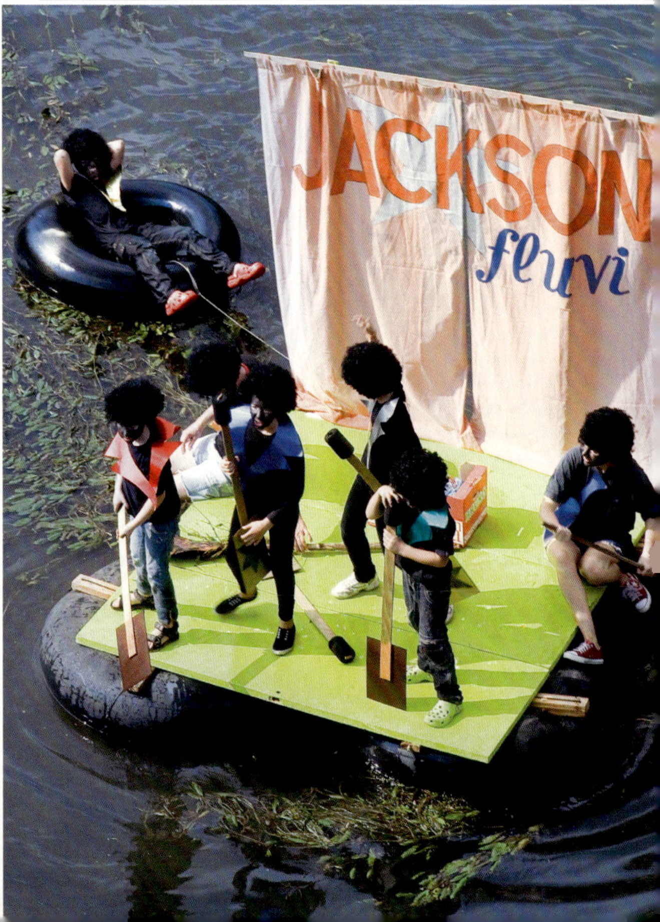
JACKSON
fluvi

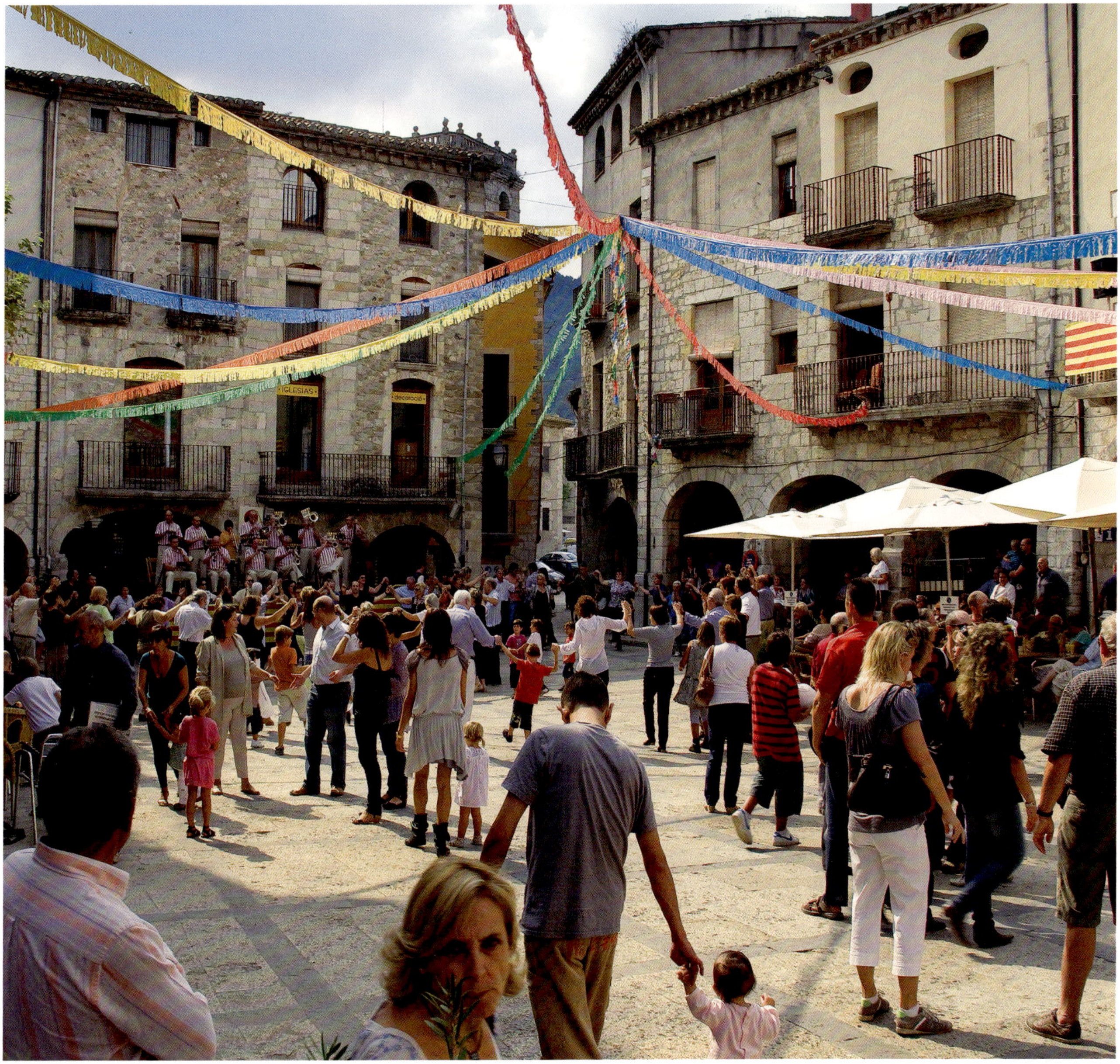

The annual festival

Sant Prim and Sant Felicià in Besalú, on the 24 September, is held on the closest weekend to the date. There are photography and lacework exhibitions, dances, concerts traditional *sardanes*, fishing and clay pigeon shooting competitions. On the Sunday of the annual festival, at 12 midday, the *Remigius Fluvii* or *River Regatta* is held, a popular river descent with home-made boats.

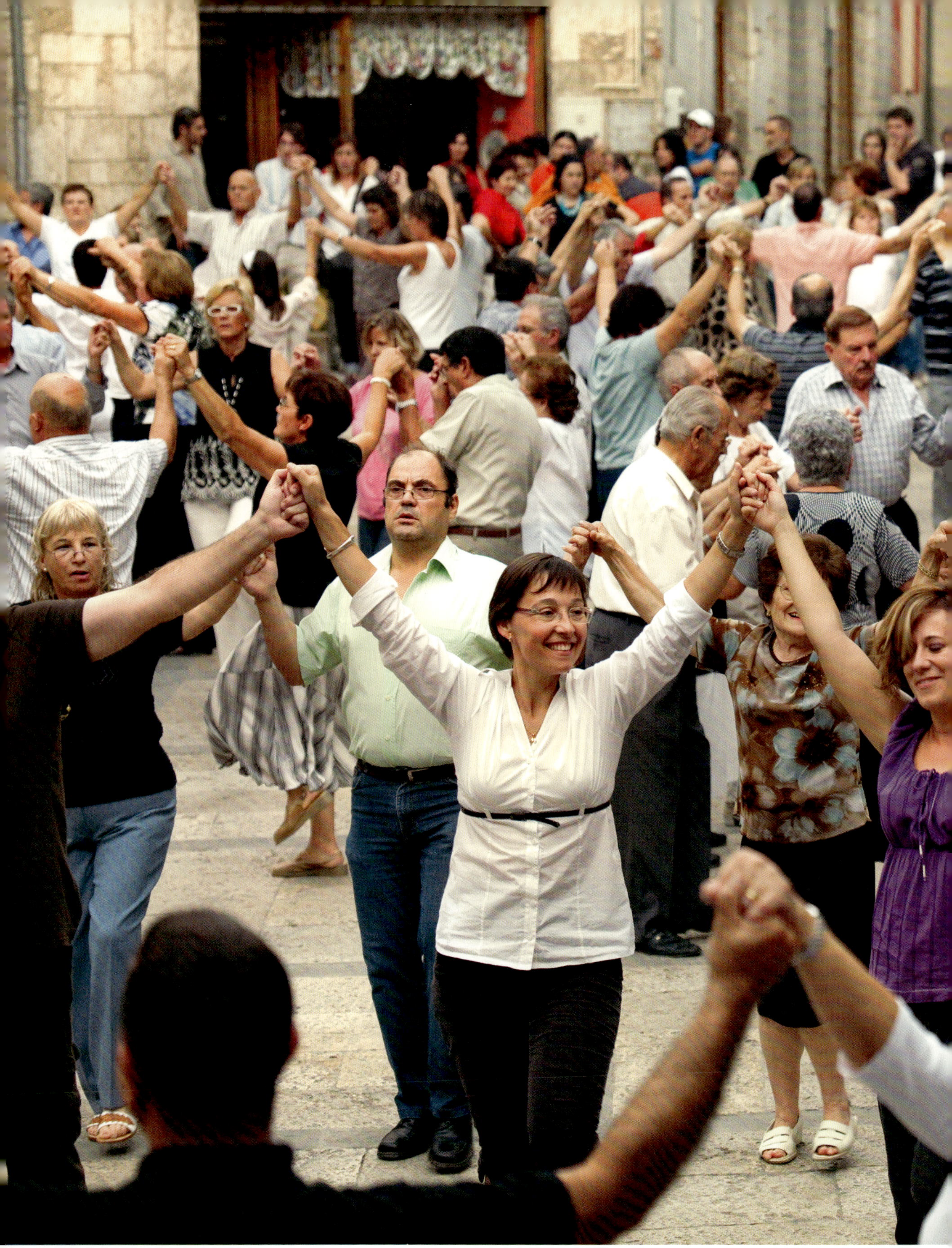

Sardana dances in Plaça de la Llibertat

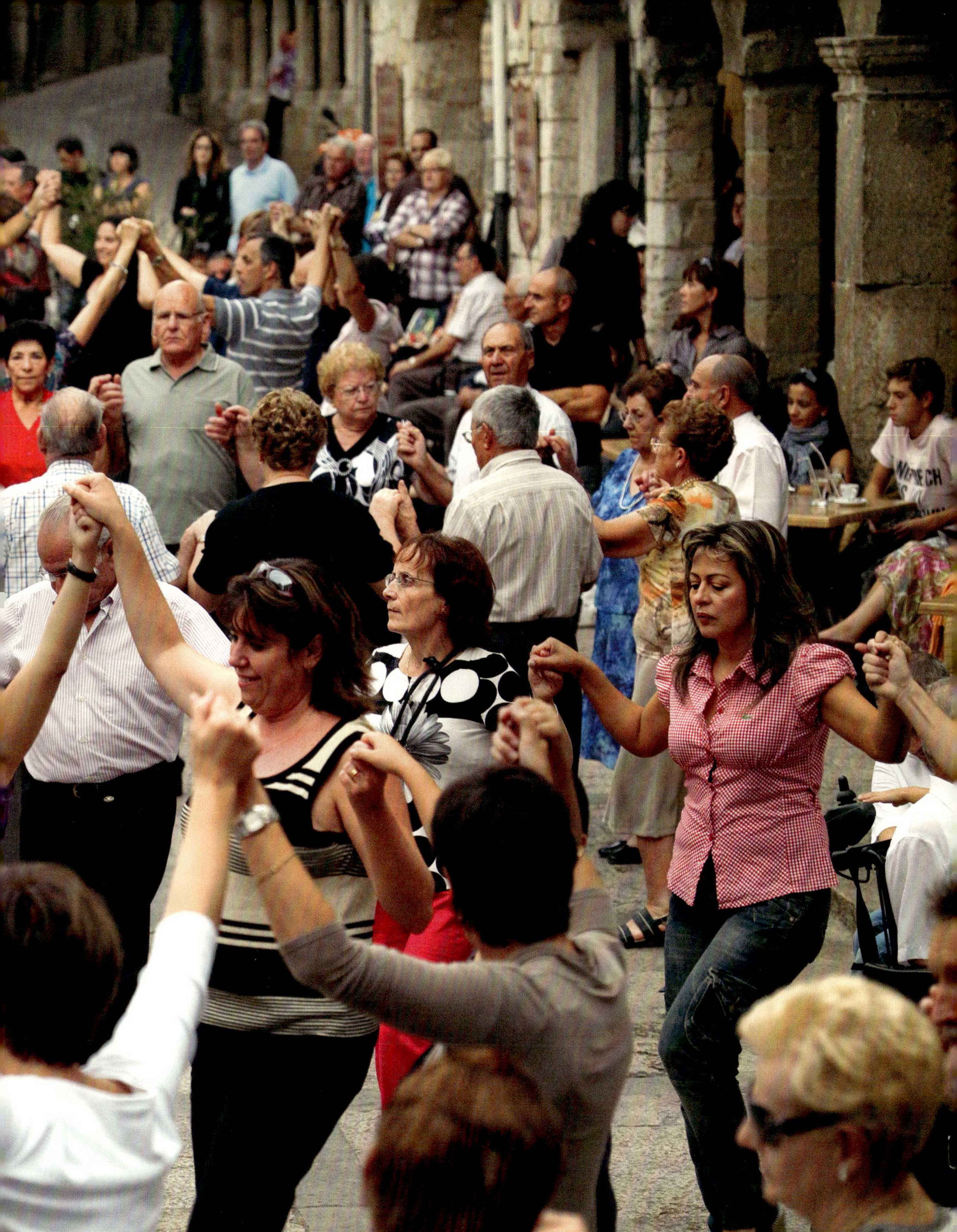

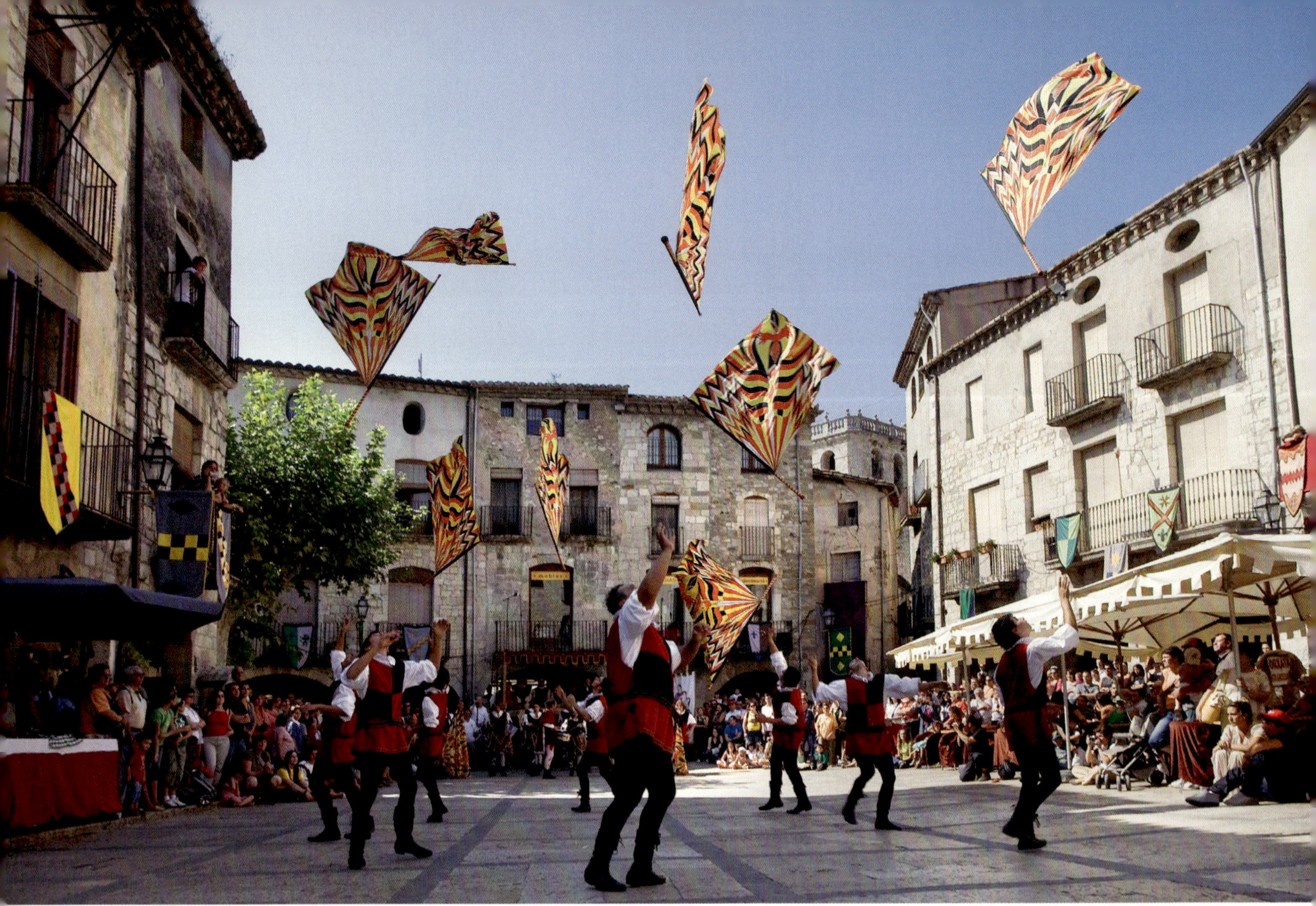

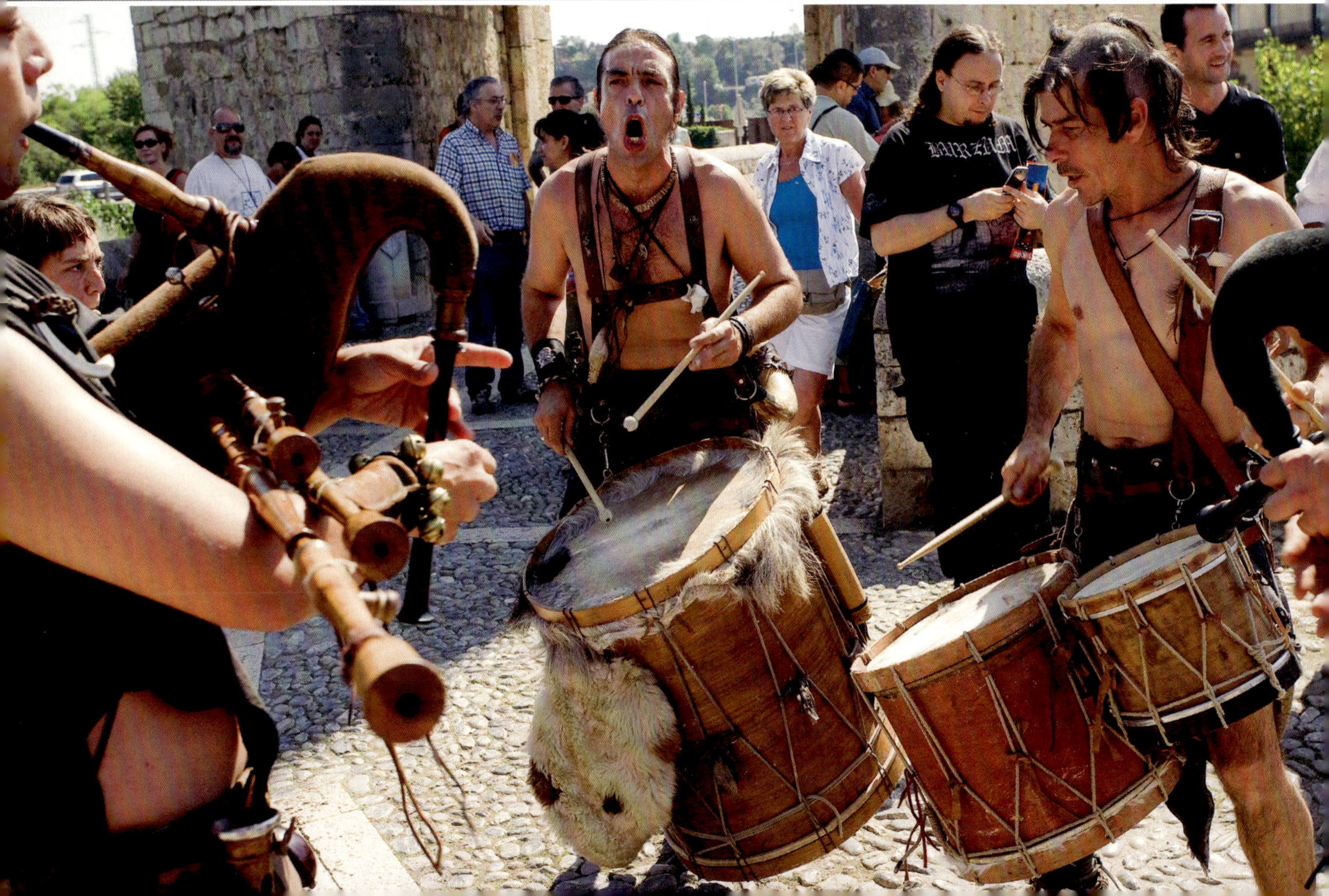

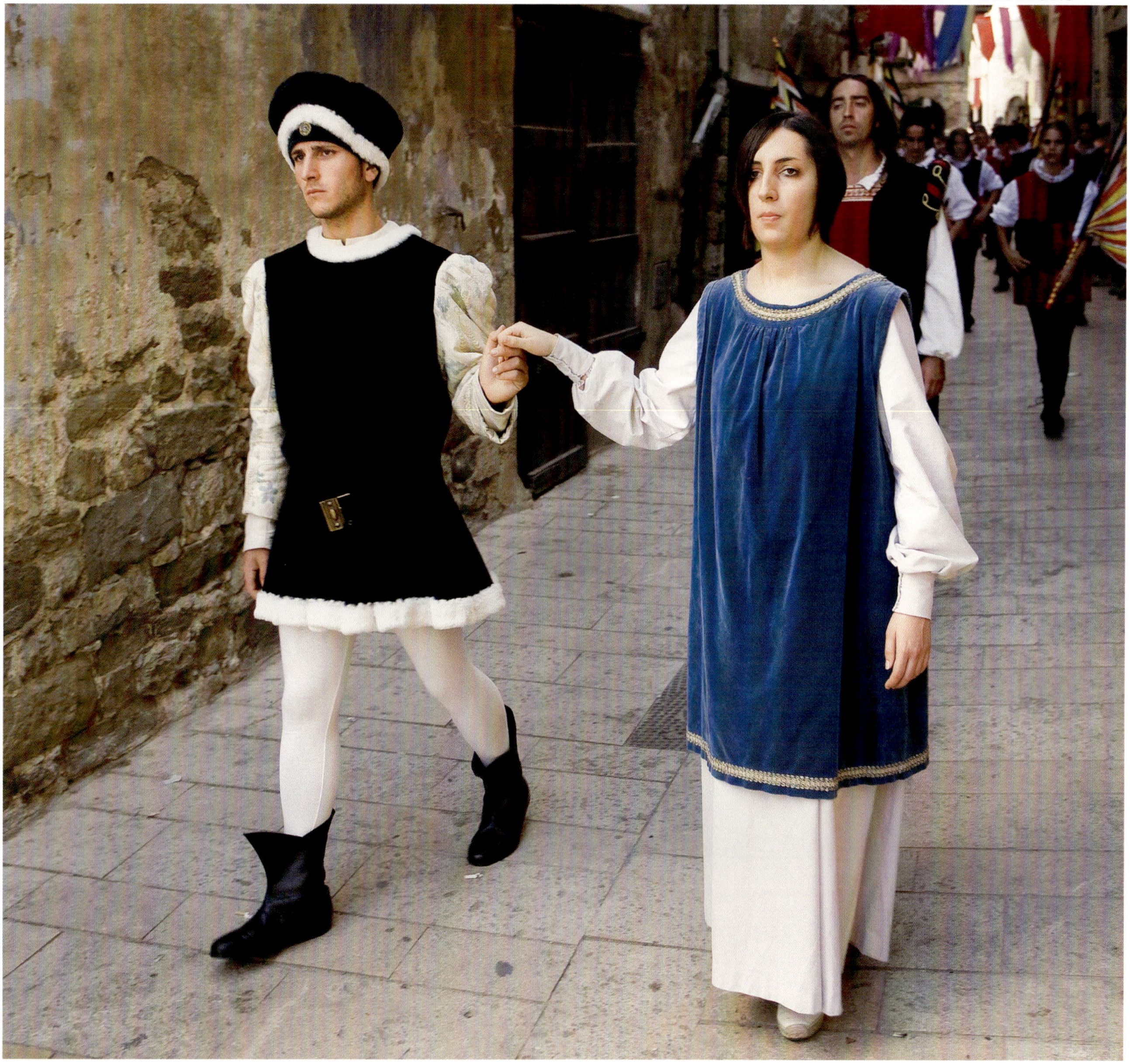

Medieval Besalú

Around the year 1000, at the end of Carolingian domination, Besalú was, without the slightest doubt, one of the most important Catalan counties, and in the 14th century continued to be the most important trade centre in the Garrotxa province. During the first weekend of September they want to recall this age of splendour, and this is why Besalú goes back a thousand years in time and the town centre becomes the old county offering a spectacle and historic memory. The streets are filled with characters that delight visitors with their tales and performances: troubadours, musicians, jugglers, court figures, craftsmen...

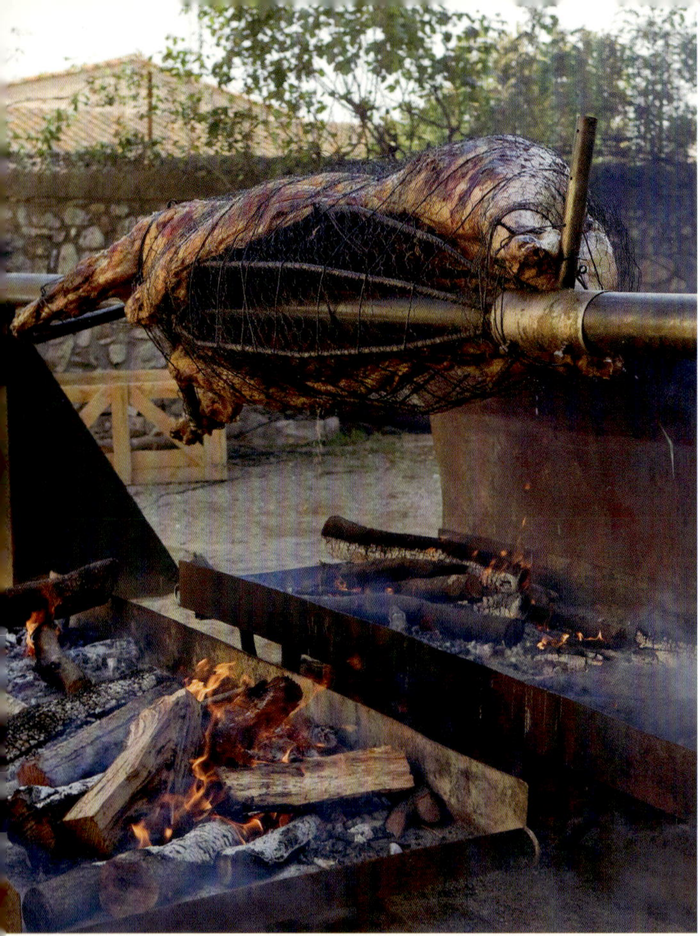
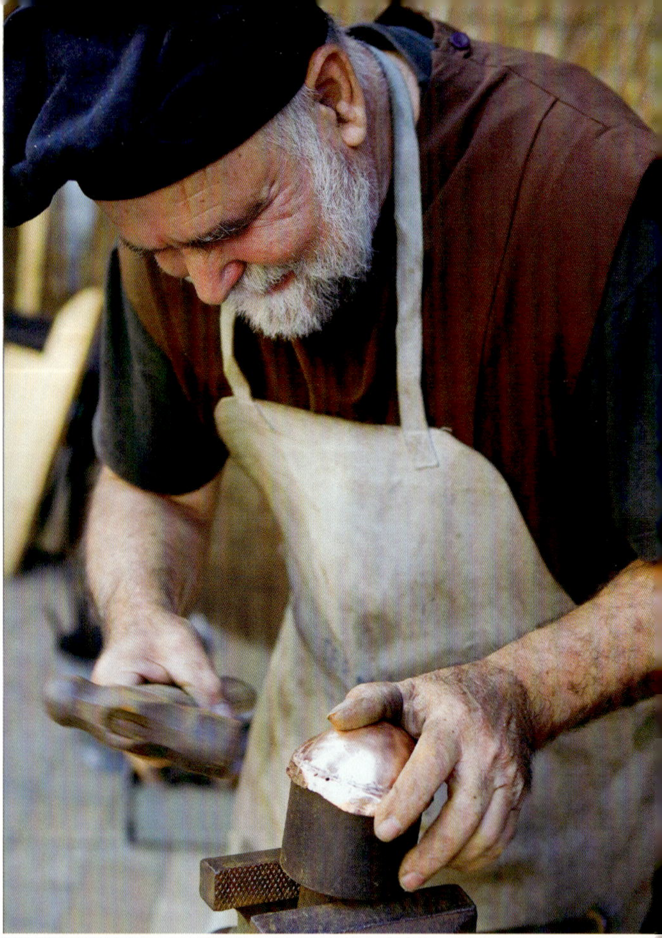
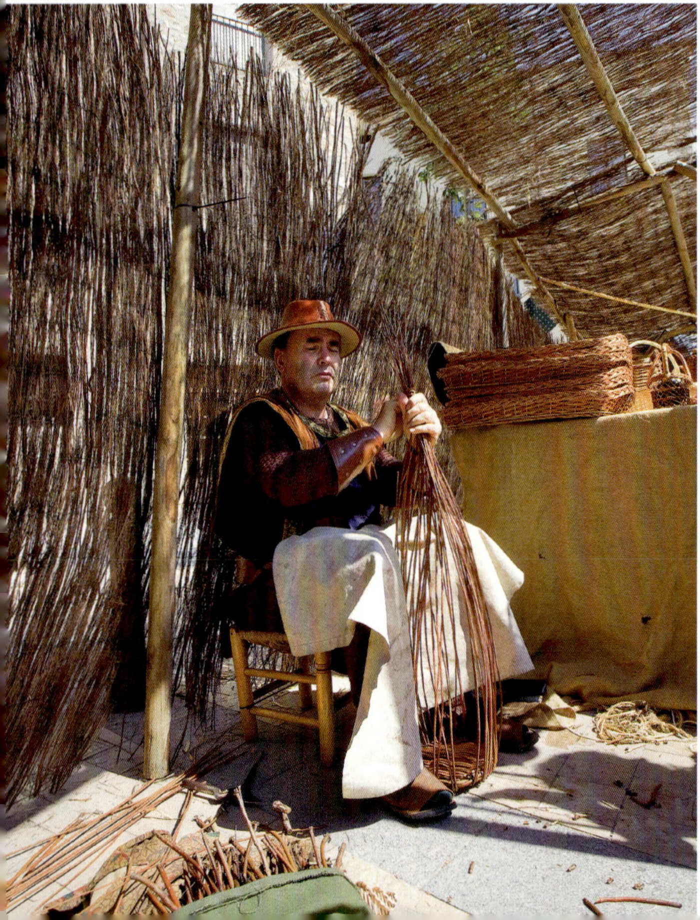
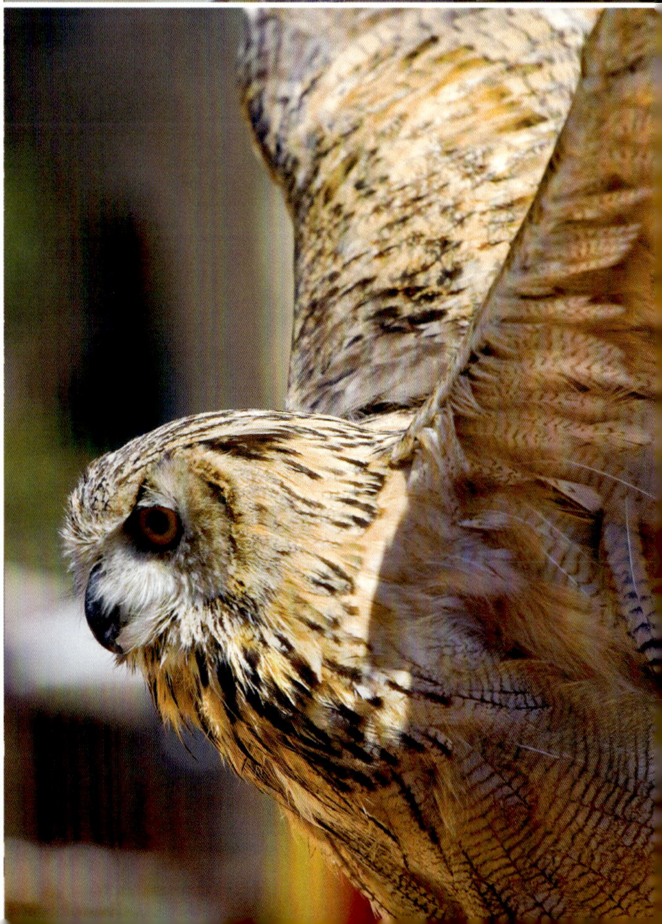

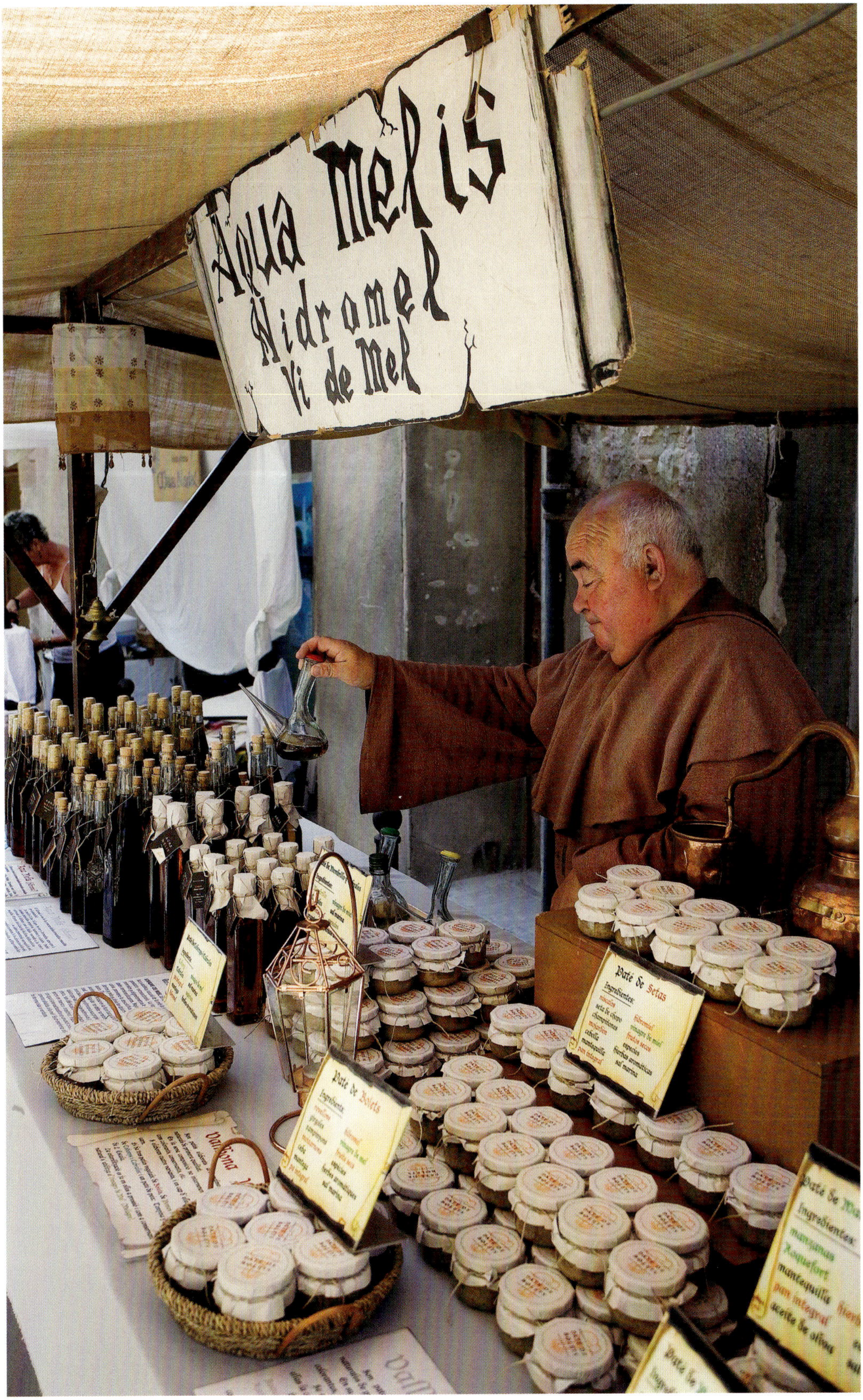

Medieval Fair

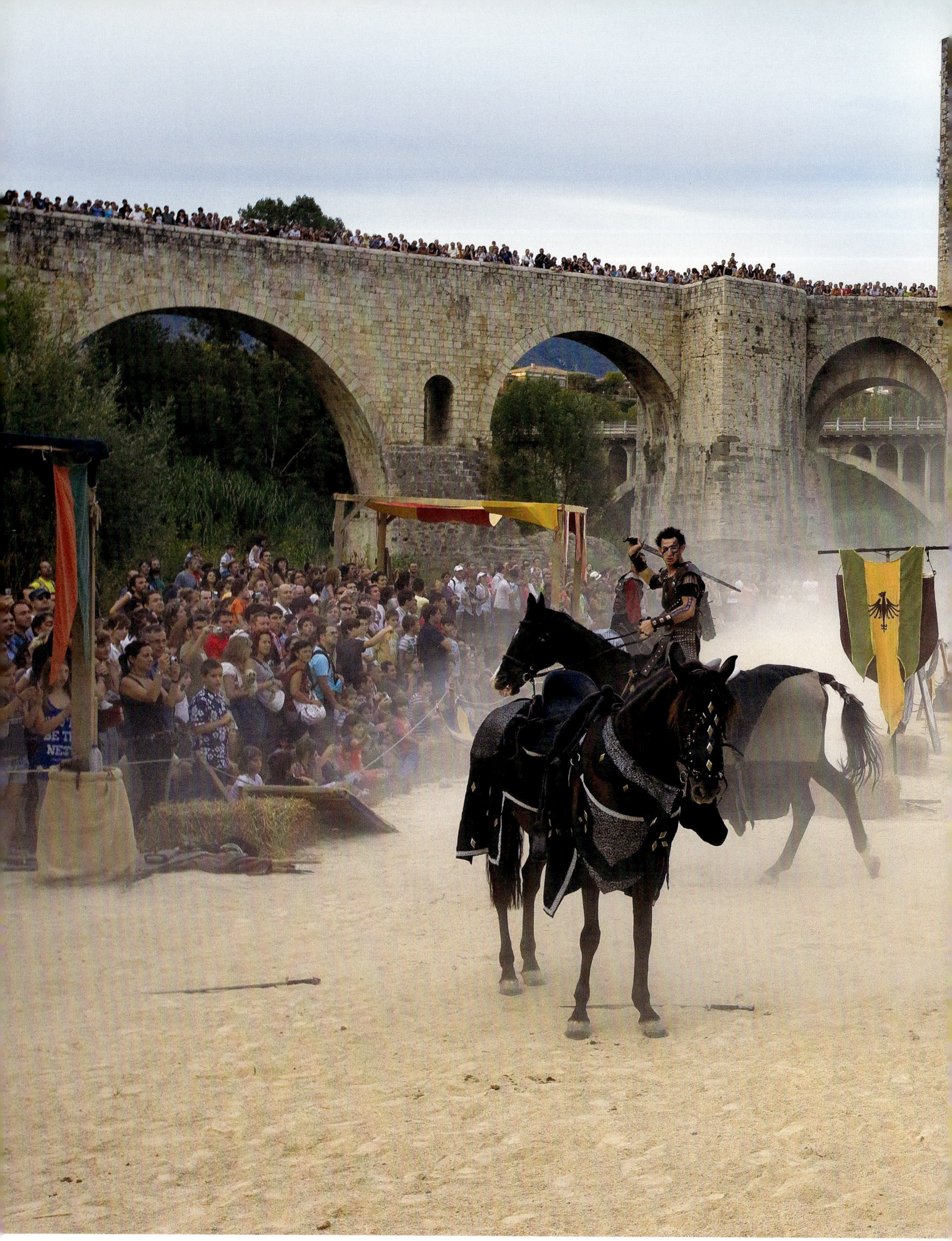

Jousting tournament

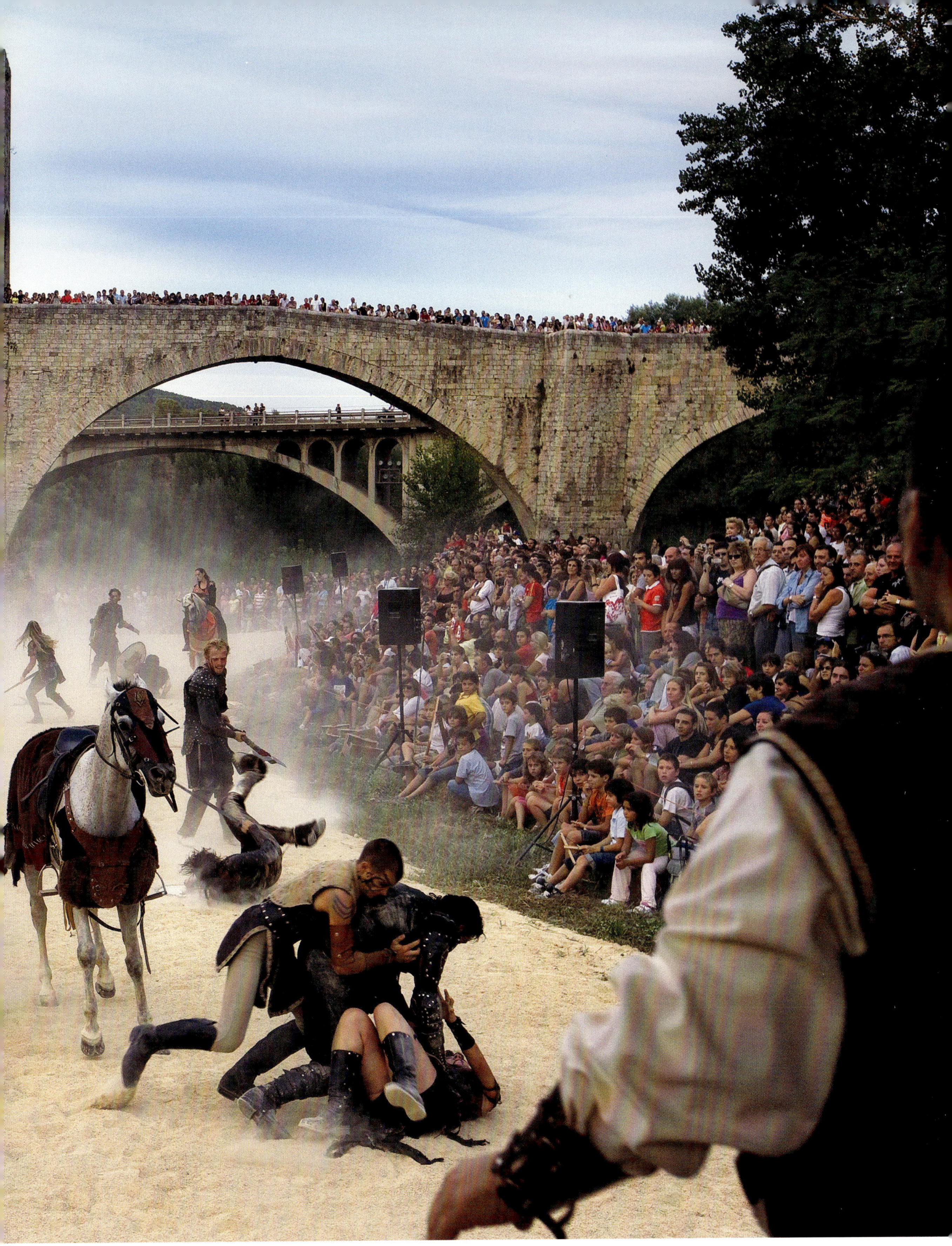

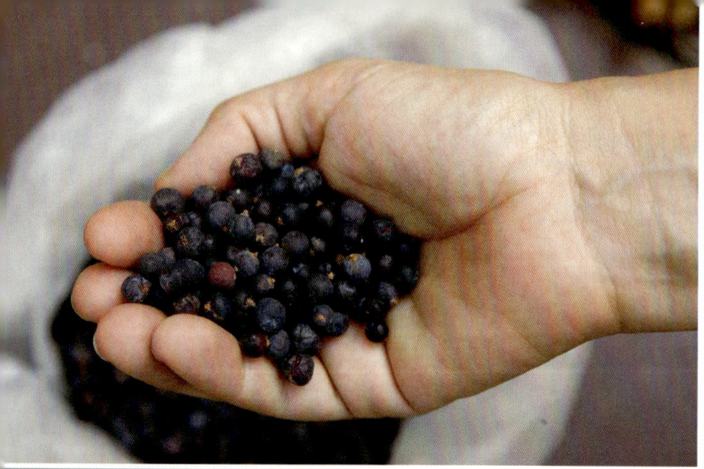
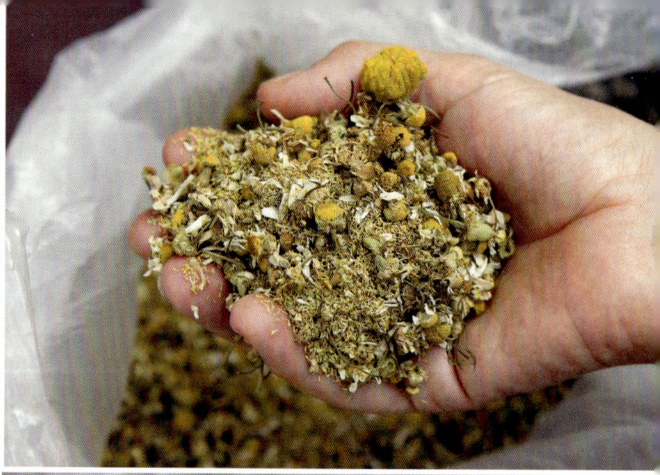
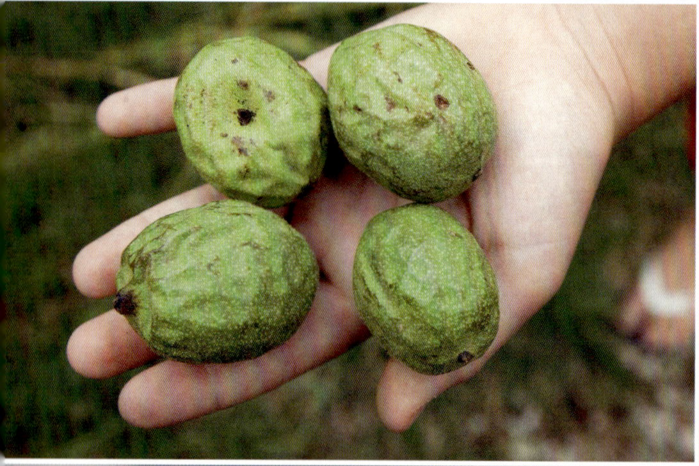
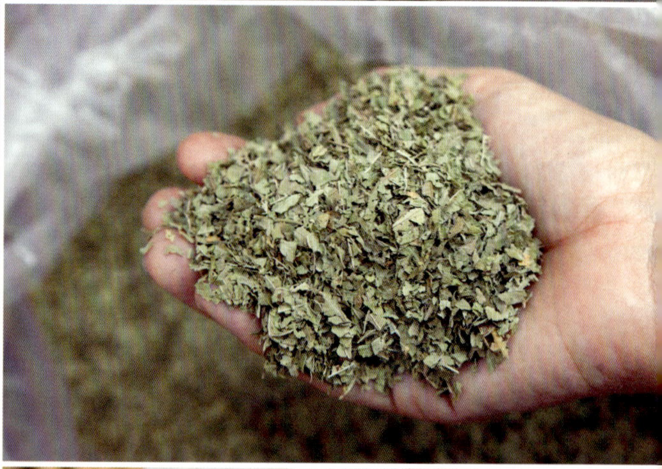
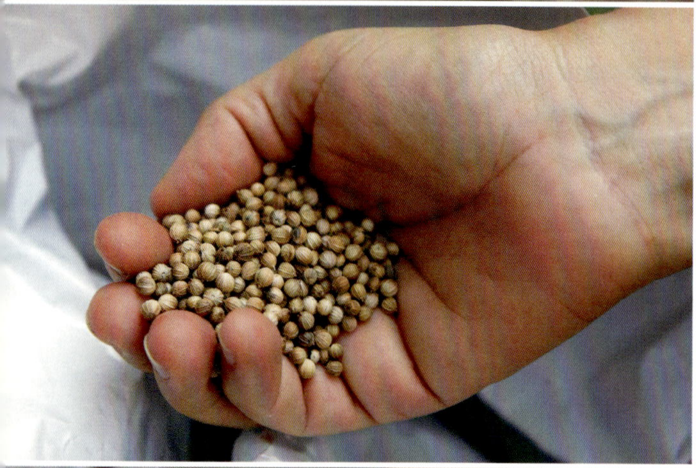
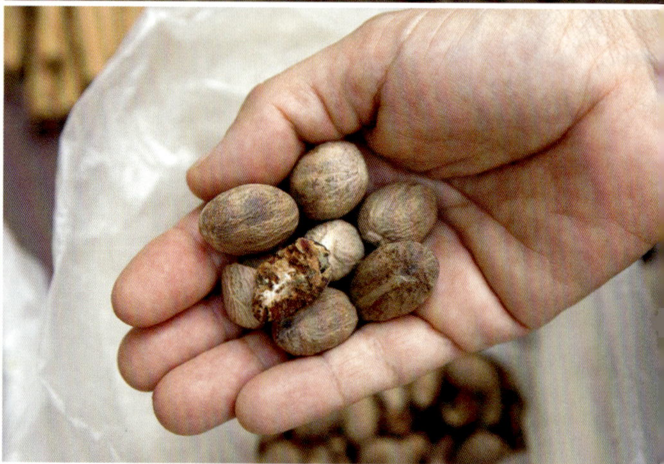
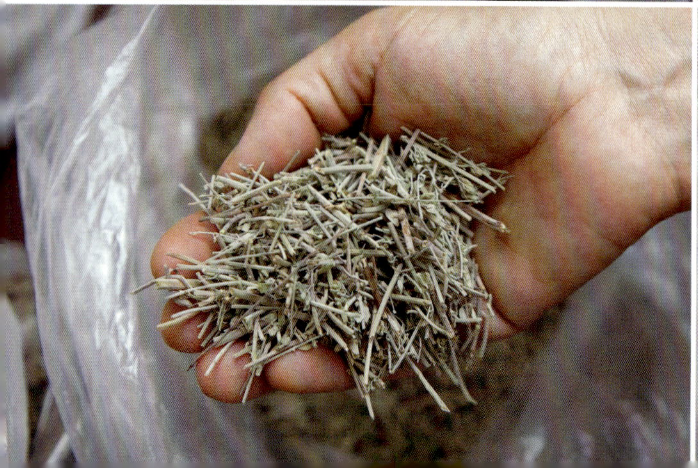
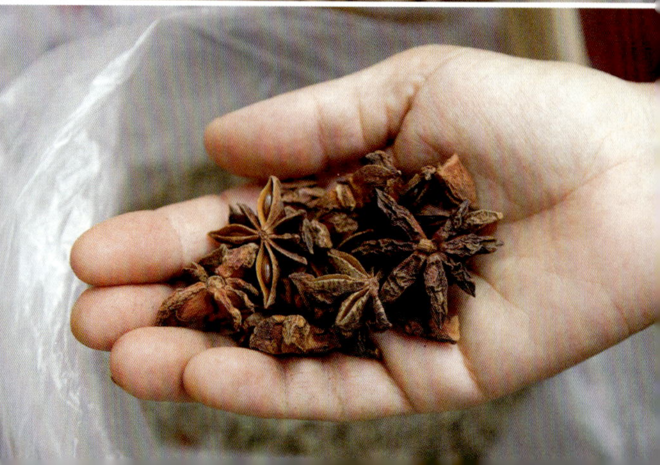

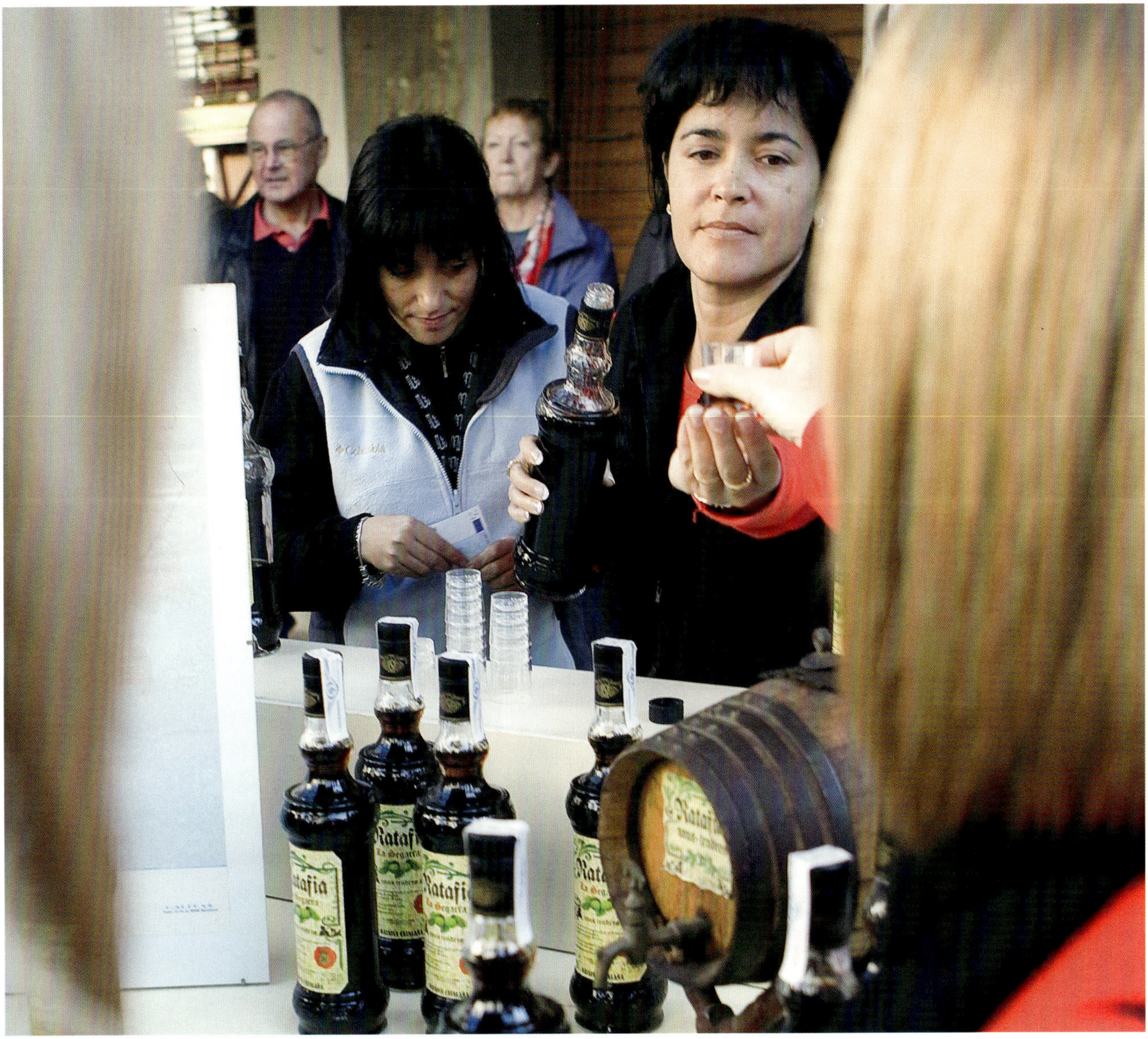

The *Ratafia* Fair

It is held on the first Sunday of December with an unmistakeable leading player: the *ratafia* liquor. It consists of the showing, tasting and selling of the *ratafia* liquors from Catalonia in the Plaça de la Llibertat, and, additionally, in El Prat de Sant Pere one can visit the craftsmen's market where they sell cured meats, clothes, *torrons* (almond nougats) and toys for the approaching Christmas period.

Ratafia is a traditionally-made liquor and, in many cases, homemade. That is why there is no standard recipe and each one is made in its own way, although they all have the same ingredients such as the unripe nuts picked before St John's day or aniseed. The different herbs or spices that each maker adds mark the character of each producer's liquor.

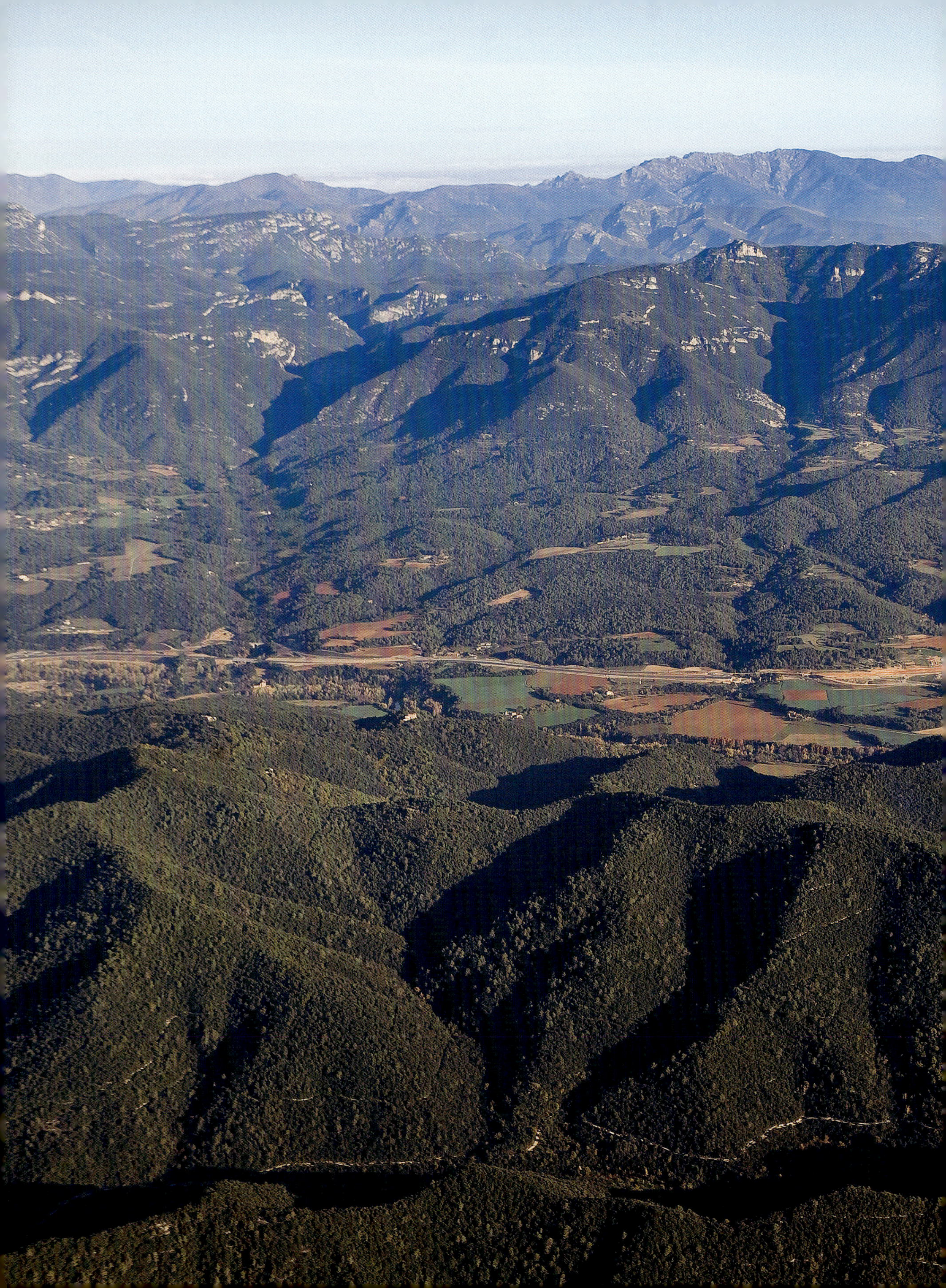

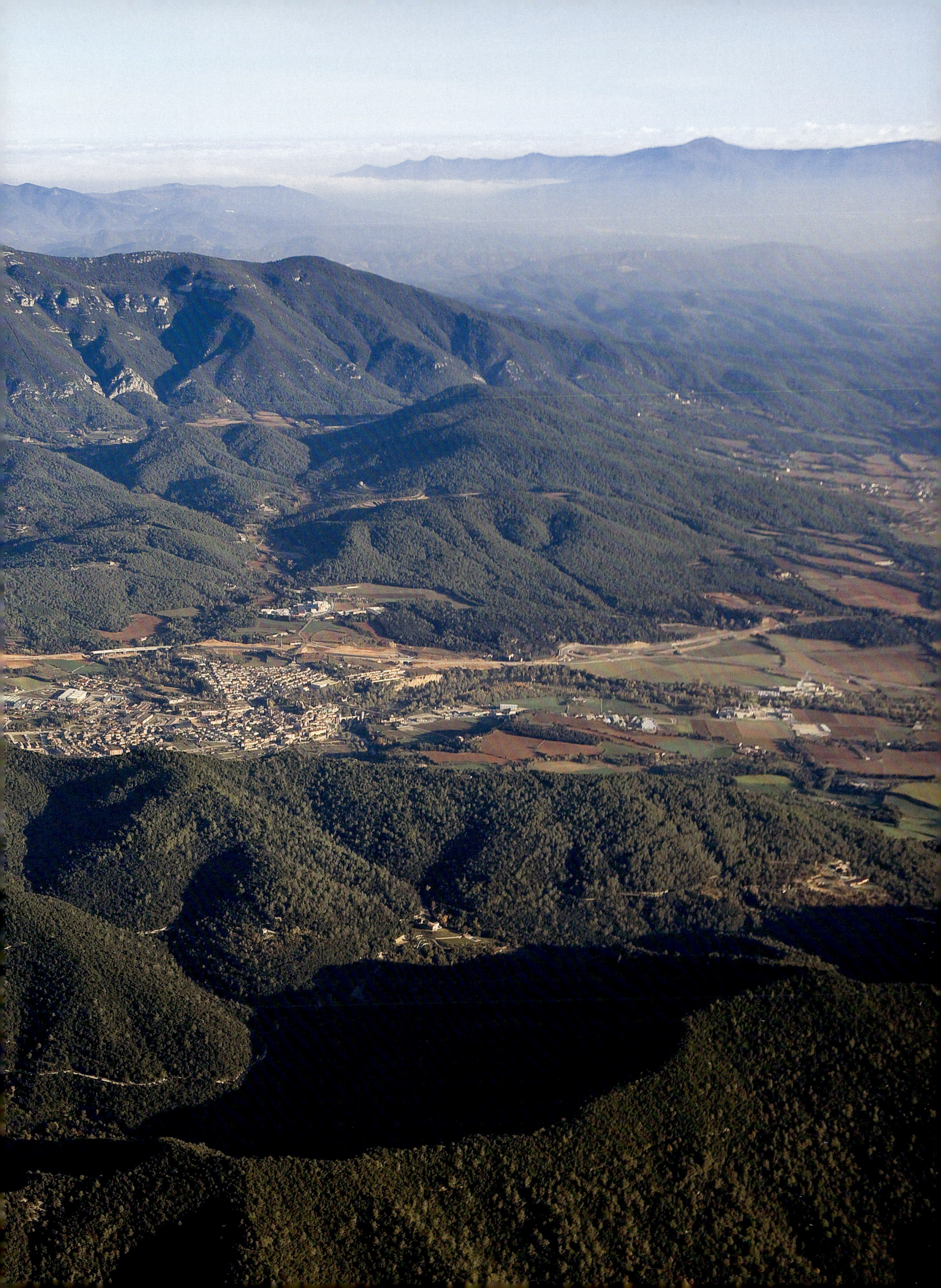

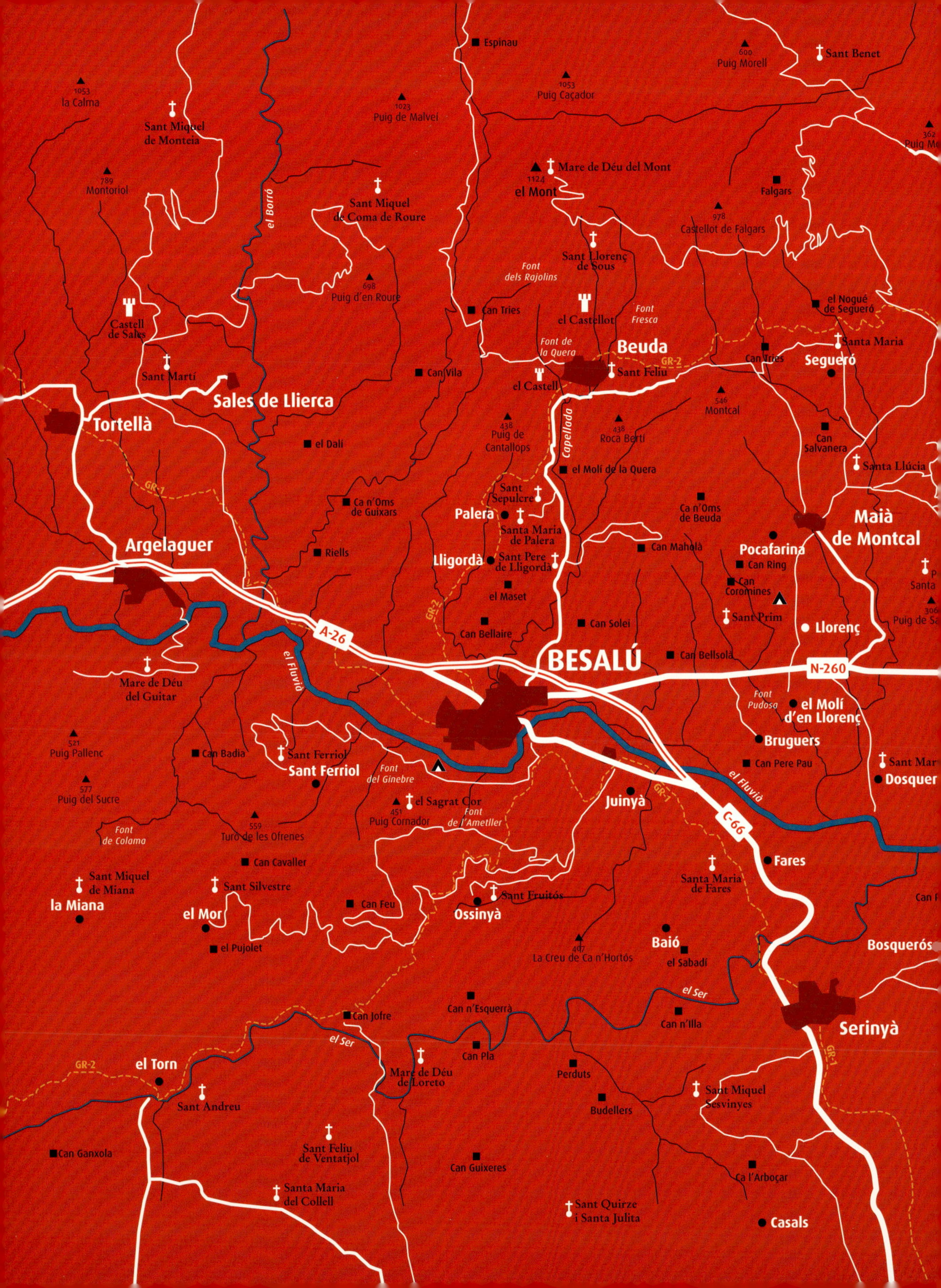

Espinau
600
Puig Morell
Sant Benet
1053
la Calma
Sant Miquel
de Monteia
1023
Puig de Malvei
1053
Puig Caçador
789
Montoriol
1124
el Mont
Mare de Déu del Mont
Sant Miquel
de Coma de Roure
el Borró
Falgars
978
Castellot de Falgars
Sant Llorenç
de Sous
Font
dels Rajolins
698
Puig d'en Roure
Castell
de Sales
Can Tries
el Castellot
Font
Fresca
el Nogué
de Segueró
Font de
la Quera
Beuda
Sant Feliu
GR-2
Can Tries
Santa Maria
Segueró
Sant Martí
Can Vila
el Castell
Sales de Llierca
Tortellà
546
Montcal
438
Puig de
Cantallops
Capellada
438
Roca Berti
Can
Salvanera
el Dalí
el Molí de la Quera
Santa Llúcia
GR-1
Sant
Sepulcre
Ca n'Oms
de Guixars
Ca n'Oms
de Beuda
Palera
Santa Maria
de Palera
Maià
de Montcal
Argelaguer
Riells
Can Mahalà
Pocafarina
Lligordà
Sant Pere
de Lligordà
Can Ring
Can
Coromines
el Maset
Sant Prim
Llorenç
GR-2
Can Bellaire
Can Solei
A-26
el Fluvià
BESALÚ
Can Bellsolà
N-260
Mare de Déu
del Guitar
Font
Pudosa
el Molí
d'en Llorenç
521
Puig Pallenc
Bruguers
Can Badia
Sant Ferriol
Sant Ferriol
Font
del Ginebre
Can Pere Pau
Dosquer
el Fluvià
577
Puig del Sucre
el Sagrat Cor
451
Puig Cornador
Font
de l'Ametller
Juinyà
GR-1
C-66
Font
de Colamo
559
Turó de les Ofrenes
Can Cavaller
Fares
Sant Miquel
de Miana
Sant Silvestre
Santa Maria
de Fares
la Miana
el Mor
Can Feu
Sant Fruitós
Ossinyà
Bosquerós
el Pujolet
407
La Creu de Ca n'Hortós
Baió
el Sabadí
el Ser
Can n'Esquerrà
Can Jofre
Can n'Illa
Serinyà
el Ser
Can Pla
GR-2
el Torn
Mare de Déu
de Loreto
Perduts
GR-1
Sant Andreu
Sant Miquel
Sesvinyes
Budellers
Sant Feliu
de Ventatjol
Can Ganxola
Can Guixeres
Ca l'Arboçar
Santa Maria
del Collell
Sant Quirze
i Santa Julita
Casals

The setting

The physical setting has marked the personality of Besalú, as can be noted in the original name of the town *bisuldunum*, fortress between two rivers, the Capellades and the Fluvià. The Fluvià, throughout its more than 97 kilometres, passes through twenty villages and towns; from Vall d'en Bas to Sant Pere Pescador it draws, outlines and shapes the idiosyncrasy of a people and lands between La Garrotxa and L'Empordà. Nor can we forget the influence that growing in the presence of the mountain of the Mont has had. A wild, rugged setting, with a broken relief and a great variety of vegetation: holm-oak woods mixed with pine woods and oaks, among other trees, which bring a great variety of shades to the mountain according to the season. You don't need any festival marked on the calendar to climb up to the Mare de Déu del Mont and visit the sanctuary, monastery and church. The origin of the sanctuary is closely linked to the monastery of Sant Llorenç, already documented since the 10th century, in the Pla de Sous. According to the legend, the Benedictine monks wanted to build a small church dedicated to the Virgin, a little higher up from the monastery. The very next day after starting the work on this point, some things happened that, a priori, the monks could not explain. The tools were found far from the site where they had decided to build the church; someone had moved them higher up, on the peak of the mountain. The same thing happened on several occasions. Finally, the monks understood that this was a sign from Heaven: the chapel had to be built at the top of the Mont... and that is what happened.

On the sanctuary side of the Mare de Déu del Mont, there are three villages perched on the mountain: Lligordà, Palera and Seguerό, the three forming part of the municipal district of Beuda.

Officially, the parish district of Lligordà has existed since 1079 and is within the municipal district of Beuda. This parish houses the church of Sant Sepulcre de Palera, the hermitage of the Mare de Déu de Palera and the church of Sant Pere de Lligordà. South of its walls is the cemetery where the heirs and heiresses of the outlying country houses rest; Can Barraca, Can Oms, Can Maholà, Can Bellsolà, Can Bellaire, Can Tries, Can Solei, Cal Maset...

Palera has always formed part of the district of Beuda but the first reference to its church of Sant Domènec appears in a testament of the Count-Bishop of Girona, Miró Bonfill, in 979. The lords of Palera, Arnau Gonfred and his wife Bruneguilda, had the basilica built in 1075 and it was consecrated as a Benedictine priory in 1085. The impossibility for Christians to go on pilgrimages to Jerusalem, occupied by the Turks, was the reason behind the construction of the basilica. And this is why it was established that making a pilgrimage to Holy Sepulchre of Palera conceded the same indulgences as doing it at the Holy Sepulchre of Jerusalem. When the Crusades re-conquered the city, the rule stayed valid and has thus been maintained until today; once a year, the Knights of the Brotherhood of the Holy Sepulchre still meet there. There is another curiosity. In the centre of the church there is a stone —different from the others, brighter– above which, according to the legend, during the summer solstice, around eleven in the morning, falls a ray of sunlight that enters by the large window of the apse, and which reflects on the flagstones on the ground the letter "Y". As you can imagine, this effect has given rise to all kinds of superstitions and legends that would deserve a separate volume. Not very far from *Sant Domingu*, which is how, in reality, the church-basilica of Palera has always been known, you must not miss the visit to a small church that might easily go unnoticed, hidden among the thick branches of the wood, although there are some signs that will lead you to Santa Maria de Palera. It is the minimum expression of a sacred spot open to worship. Any ceremony held there is done under the watchful eye of what is popularly known as the Virgin Riallera (the Smiling Virgin). A unique alabaster carving —dug from the quarries of Beuda— that has in her smile the charm of a church with the feel of a hermitage. However, it is essential that you come across another smile, that of Baldiri, who will open the door for you to enter this singular church that will take you to another time.

Segueró is, above all, its Romanesque church of Santa Maria. Of a single nave and built in the 11th century, it has an original looped apse and a fortification work over the entrance. If you go inside, you will find the image that has been conserved of the Virgin, a 14th-century carving in alabaster... but Segueró is also the ancestral home of the Nogué de Segueró family, a lineage that has lived since the early 13th century in what we could consider one of the best examples of what was a mansion of rich country landowners in Catalonia.

When I hear the name of Beuda many things and diverse references come into my head, but above all two names: Can Marcelinu and Cal Xelió. They are the names of two restaurants. The first one still exists, although in reality, it is called Restaurant Montserrat, although everyone knows it by the name of the owner. The second is no longer there, but it was a unique establishment that served some exceptional meat dishes. Beuda is the central point that brings together these villages. In Beuda, where my father who was born in Lligordà went to school, there is the Moorish castle and the church of Sant Feliu, a Romanesque church from the 11th century in which not only its interior is outstanding, but also the stone stairway that ascends along the façade to the bell tower. Inside is conserved a very valuable 12th-century baptismal font, decorated with figures in relief and some small blind arches. The church of Santa Llúcia de Beuda and Castellot, also known as the Moorish castle, are two more attractions of the village of Beuda. Before reaching the main square of Beuda. I would also recommend a stop at the fountain of the Quera.

Just a couple of kilometres from Besalú begins the extensive district of Sant Ferriol. Since 1922, the sanctuary that dates from the 18th century has given name to this place characterised by a wild but ordered landscape, of leafy woods and with several scattered chapels of Romanesque origin: Sant Miquel de la Miana, the church of the country house of Torn, Sant Andreu, Sant Silvestre del Mor, Sant Fruitós, the church of La Miana and Santa Maria de Fares.

Losing oneself in the outskirts of Besalú and enjoying the exceptional nature of this setting will make you feel really special, as if someone has given you a present.

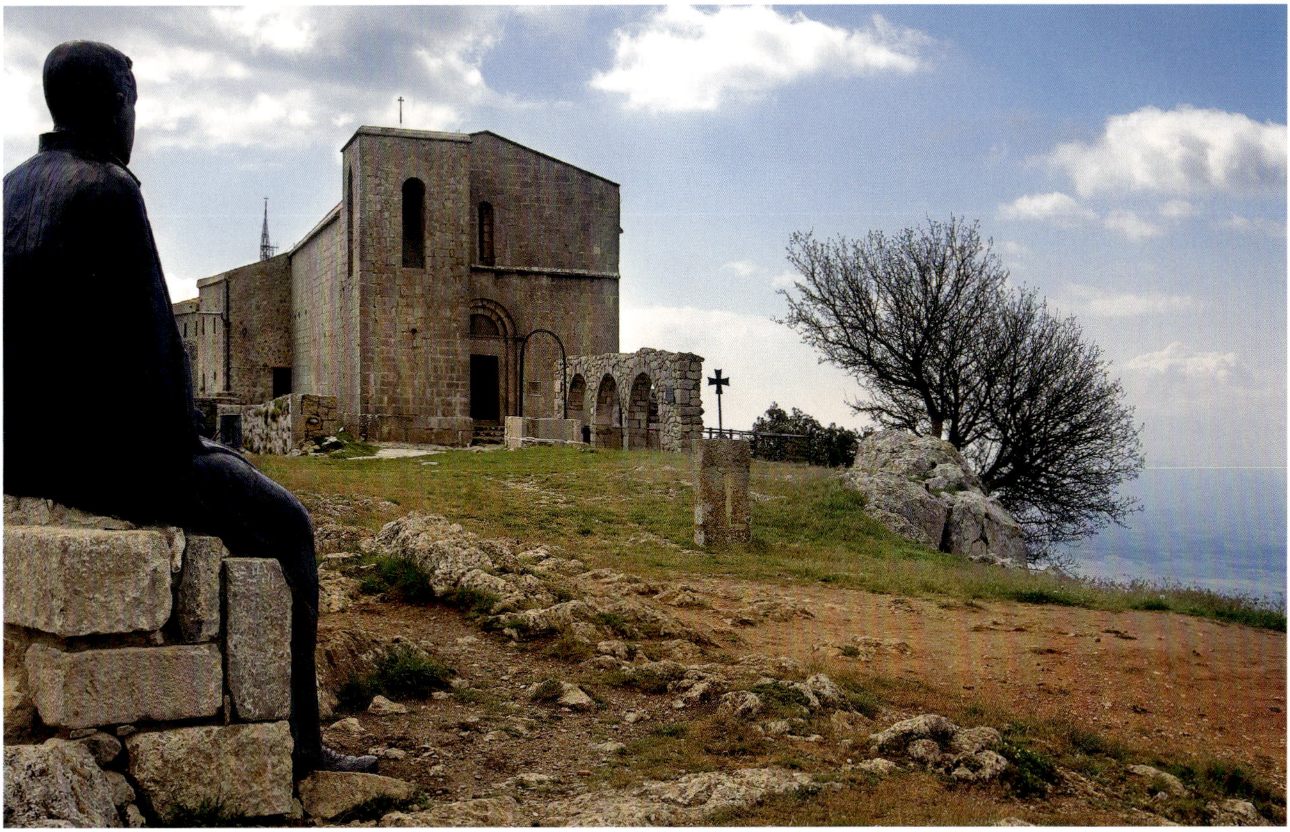

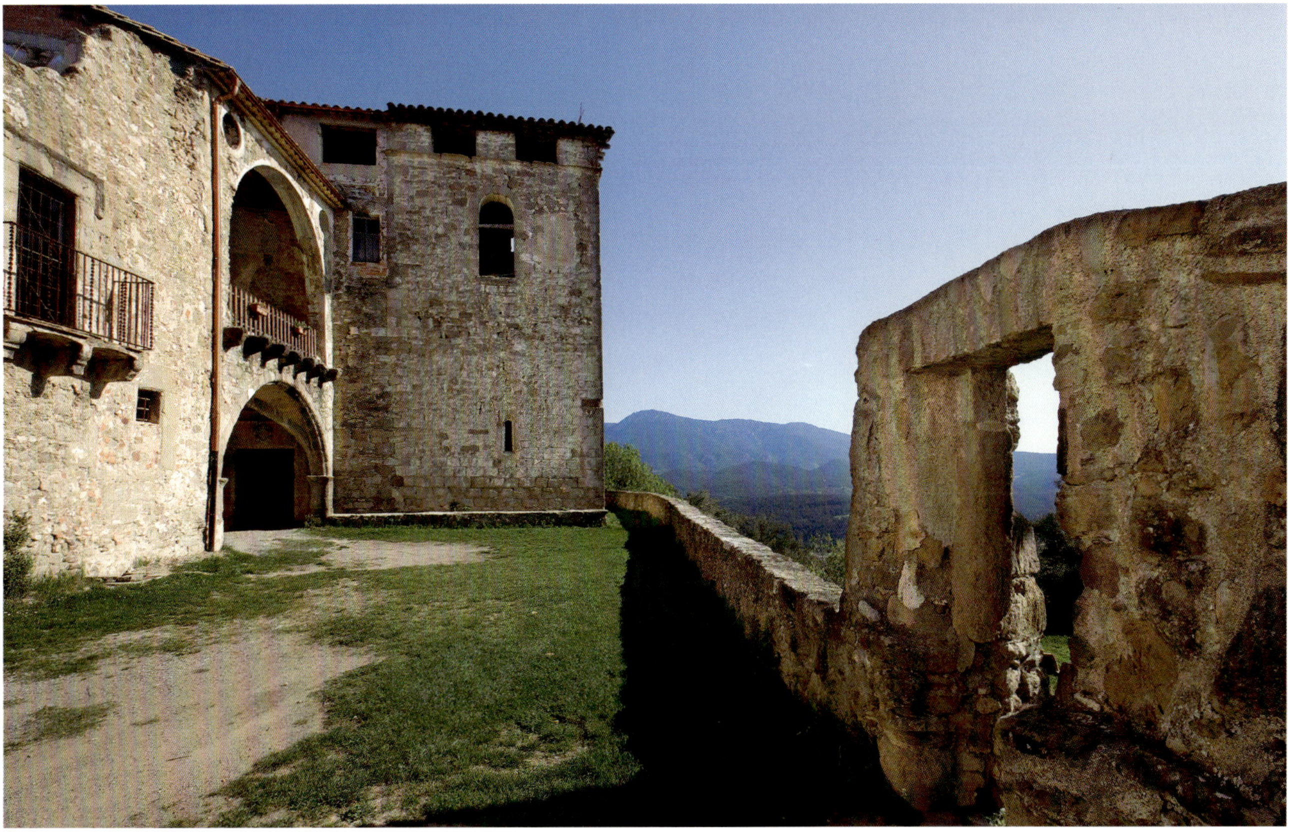

(above) Mare de Déu del Mont. (below) Sant Ferriol

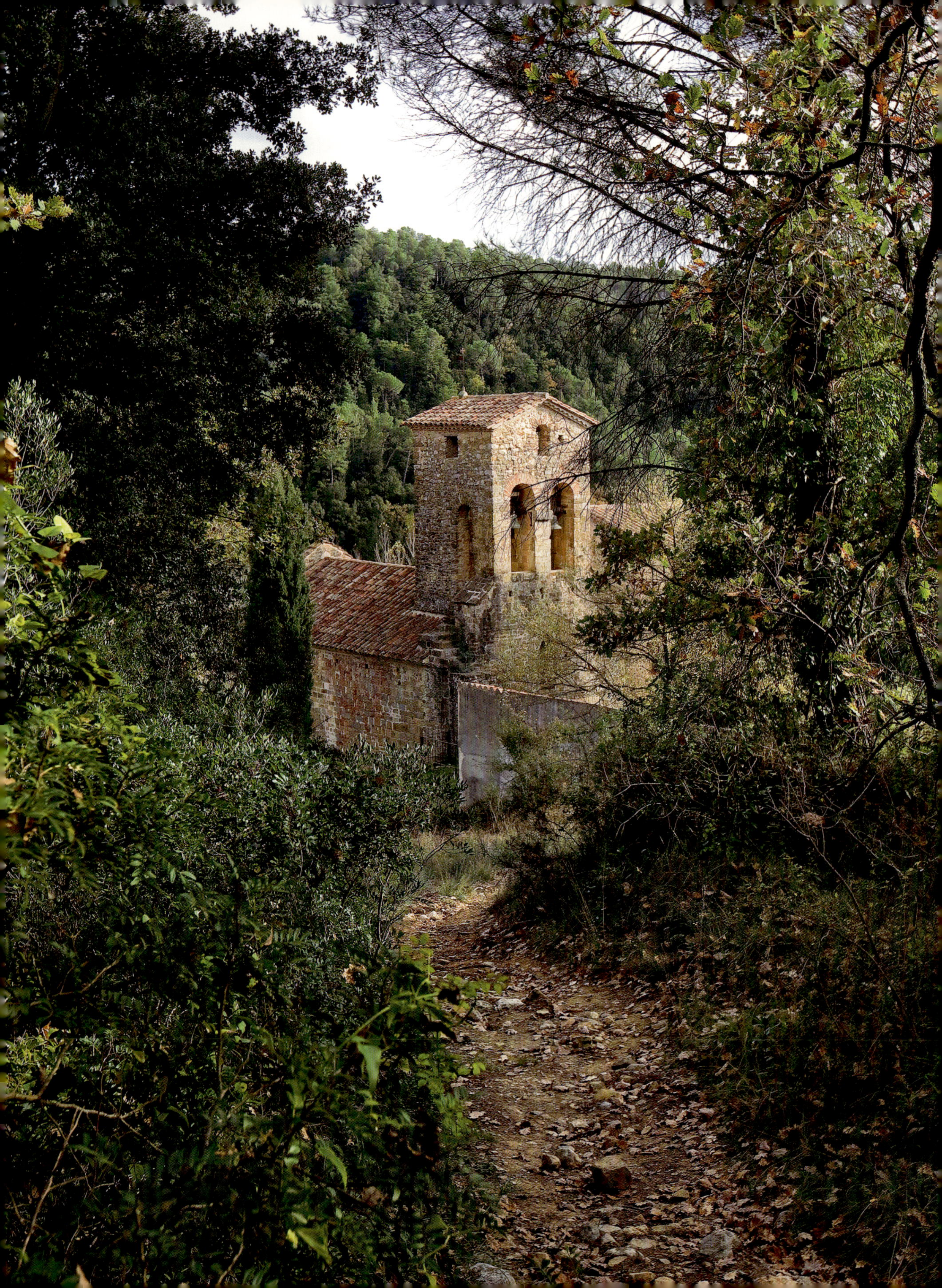

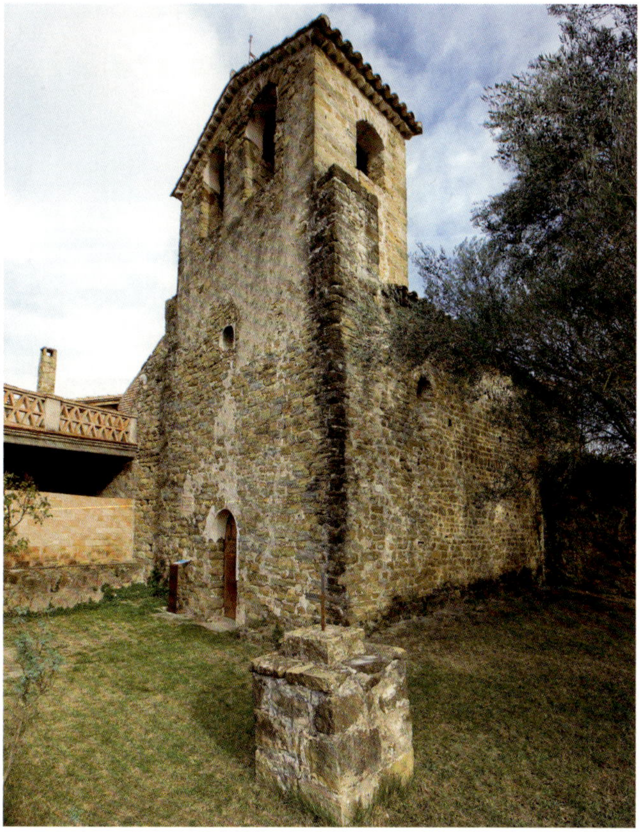

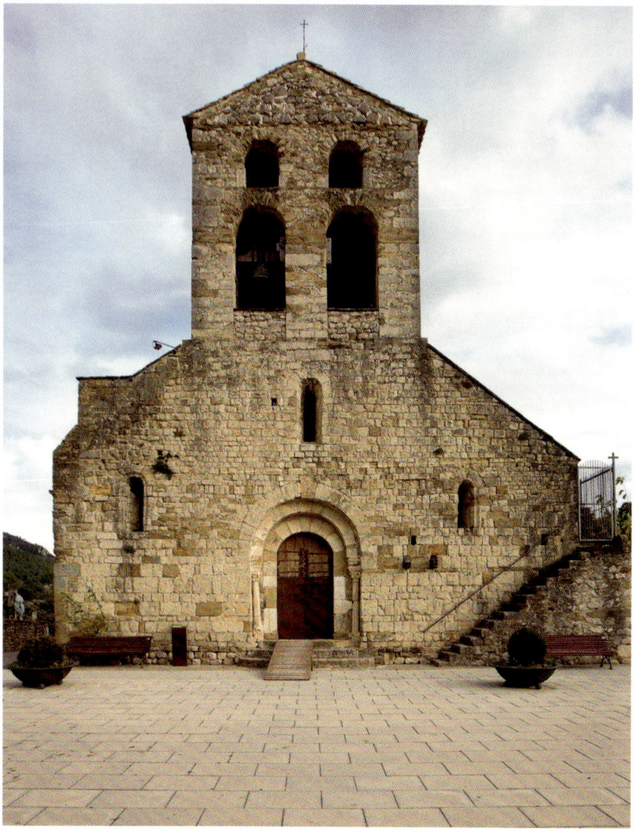

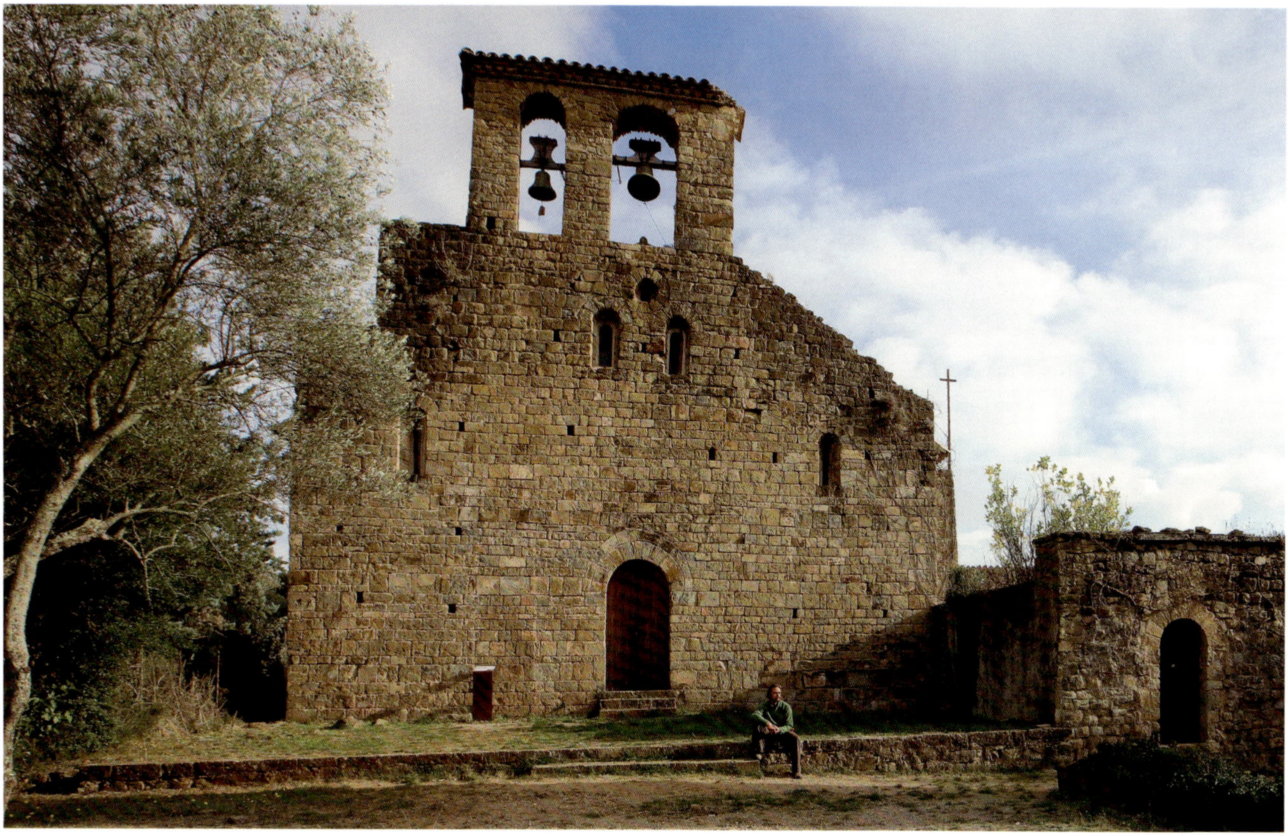

◂ Sant Pere de Lligordà. (above) Santa Maria de Palera and Sant Feliu de Beuda. (below) Sant Sepulcre de Palera

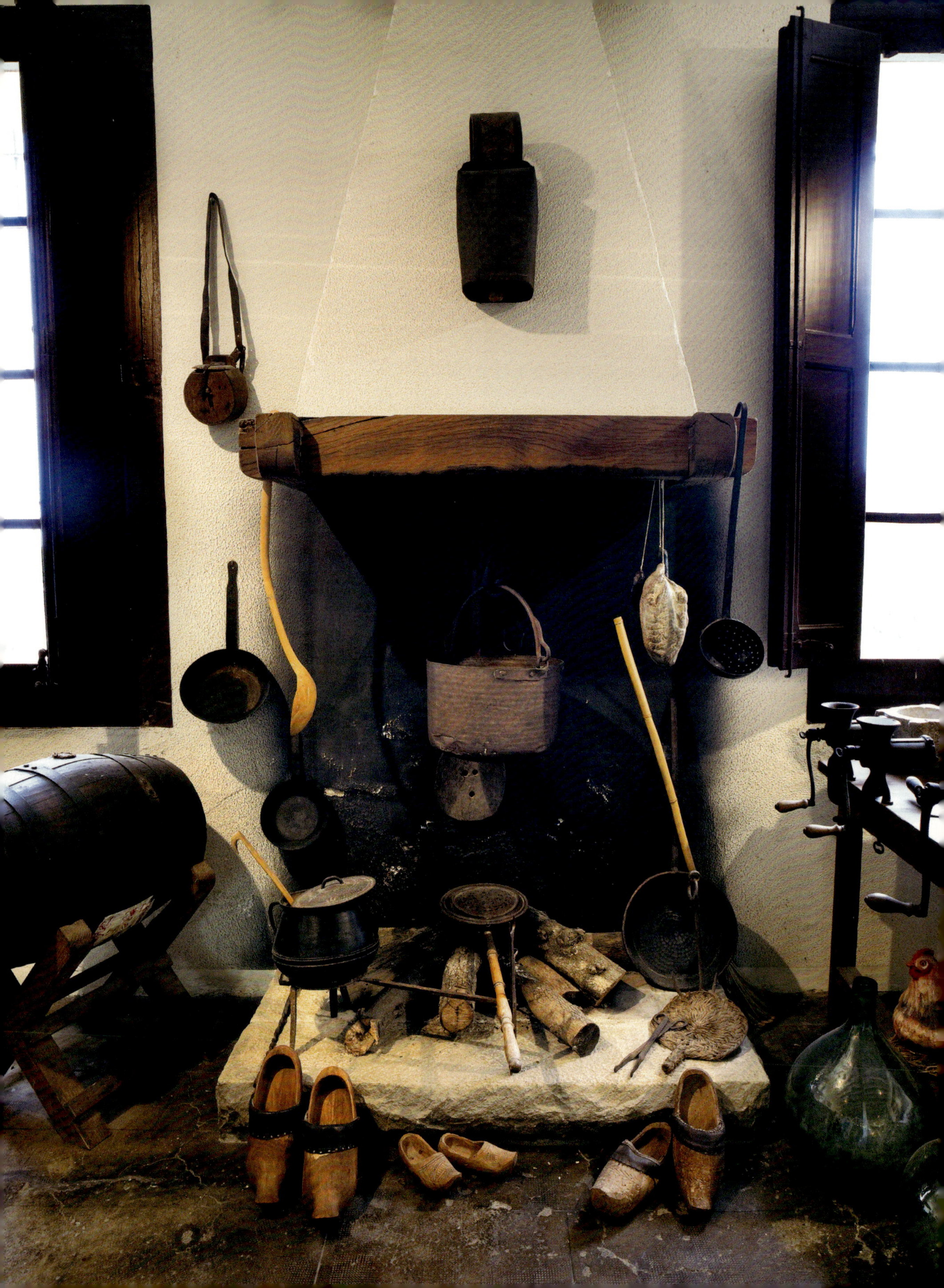

The cuisine of Besalú

Besalú is a crossroads open to all influences and it is no surprise that this is also reflected in the gastronomy, with a cuisine that is a compendium of medieval, Jewish and volcanic influences. They say that the cuisine of the whole world, however distinct it is, can always be cooked on the same stove. And in this corner of La Garrotxa the volcanic charcoal grills have maintained a gastronomy with personality, a loyal reflection of the landscape and the people, transferred onto the plate, the best letter of introduction for understanding what its inhabitants are like and what they enjoy eating. And seeing as we are now stopping for lunch, and talking about food and drink... Since 1993, around the end of November, early December, the town dedicates itself to the tasting, after the preparation, of the traditional spirit made with unripe walnuts: the popular *ratafia*. The one from Besalú is prepared, according to local tradition, with the plants and herbs that grow on the slopes of the Mare de Déu del Mont. The festival not only extols this drink of doubtful medieval origin. The *Rata fiat* —the Latin locution that meant *stay signed or agreed*— was used to ratify, sign and seal a deal after a litigation, and as a show of understanding, the undersigned took a couple of swigs of this spirit that had been macerated for 40 days in the open. Many of these spirits were digestive and invigorating, although in some cases they were also linked to the world of spells, magic potions and love-potions. However, another objective of the fair is to preserve the tradition and promote the responsible drinking of *ratafia* and, above all, its preparation. This desire is shown with the holding of a singular competition restricted to only the people of Besalú to discover which of them makes the best *ratafia*. Given the origin of the majority of winners of the competition, popular wisdom states that that of Besalú is the most Catalan of all the *ratafias*, because the locals who nearly always win are those that live in the Onze de Setembre district, the old *Cases Barates*.

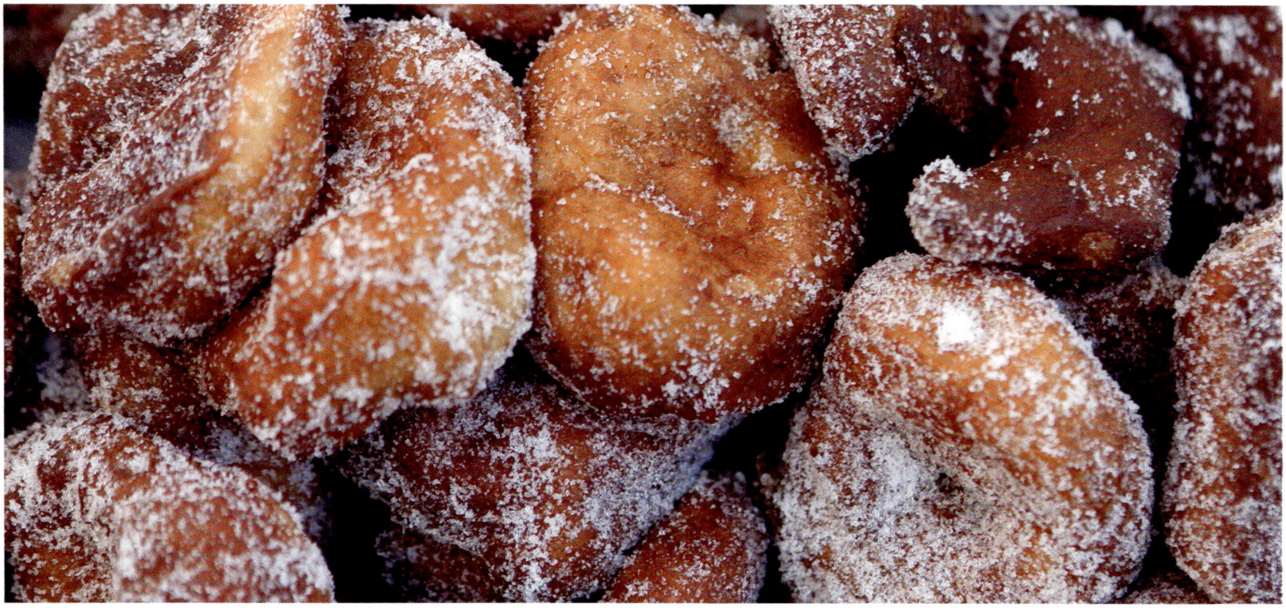

Ratafia

INGREDIENTS:

5 litres of liquor
1.500 g of brown sugar
15 tender walnuts (picked approximately around Saint John's day (June 23), which is when they are juicier and easier to squash)

Spices:
1 small cinnamon stick
2 soupspoons of aniseed
10 cloves
Chinese aniseed, five pieces
1 soupspoon of nutmeg

Aromatic plants:
1 bunch of camomile (dry, from the previous year)
5 stalks of fresh mint
10 stalks of lemon verbena, half dry and half fresh
1 stalk of elder flower
4 stalks of rosemary
4 stalks of thyme
4 handfuls of pennyroyal
2 small bunches of rue
4 or 5 leaves of bitter orange

Others:
4 teaspoons of ground coffee
2 tablets of dark chocolate
1 lemon peel
1 orange peel

PREPARATION:

This is the recipe of a *ratafiaire*, Irene Roura, who has had the privilege of winning the prize on more than one occasion.

Place the ingredients in a glass decanter to macerate for 40 days, and shake the recipient every day. After the forty days, filter the contents with sterile gauzes or with cheesecloth.

Irene, moreover, adds an innovation. "At home, it is now tradition, when friends come for supper, to accompany the coffee with a little glass of *ratafia*; that's why we wanted to invent something, and now there are always ice cubes of *ratafia* in the freezer, to combine with the coffee in summer".

According to her, the best prize is being able to see her *ratafia* bottled for the next year's competition, so that everyone can try it.

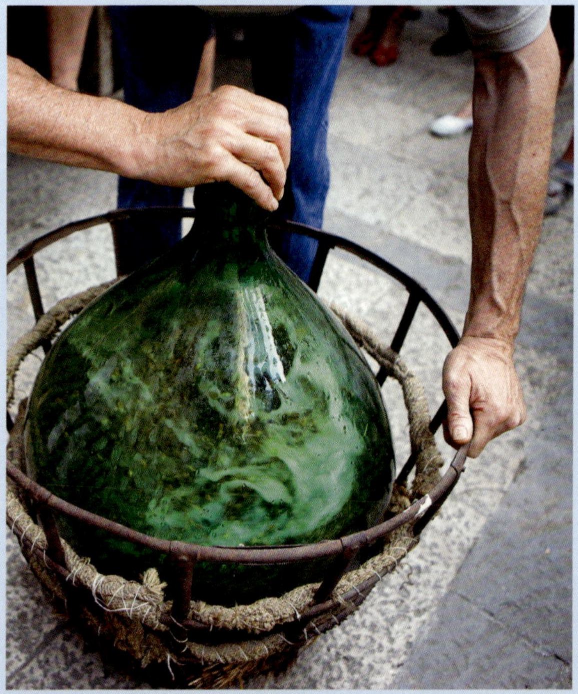

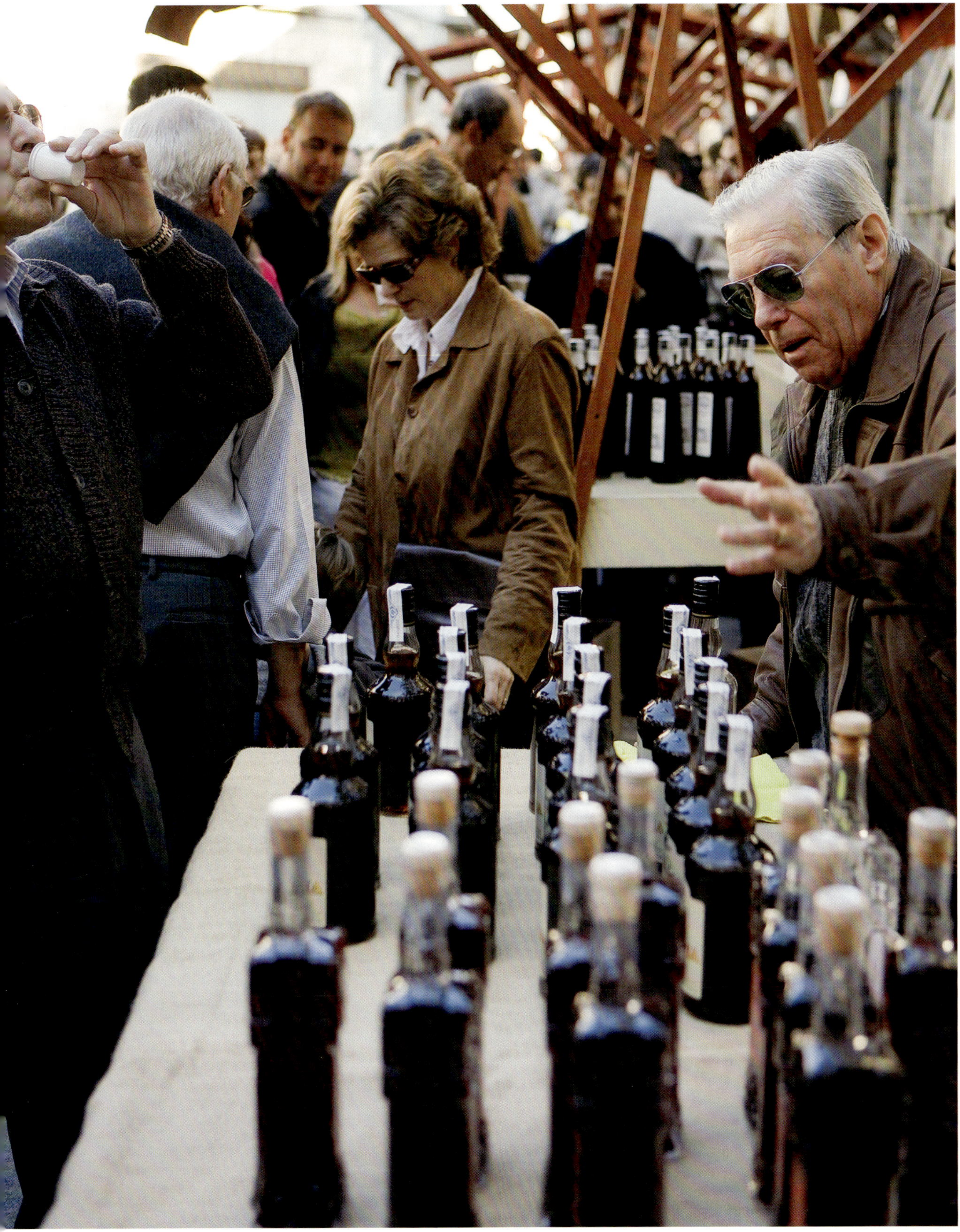

Sweet and sour rabbit, a medieval dish

INGREDIENTS FOR 4 PEOPLE:

1 rabbit weighing 1½ kg
100 g of dried prunes
100 g of smoked streaky bacon
½ dozen onions
White wine
100 g of sugar
4 spoonfuls of vinegar
Flour
Salt
Stock
Pork lard

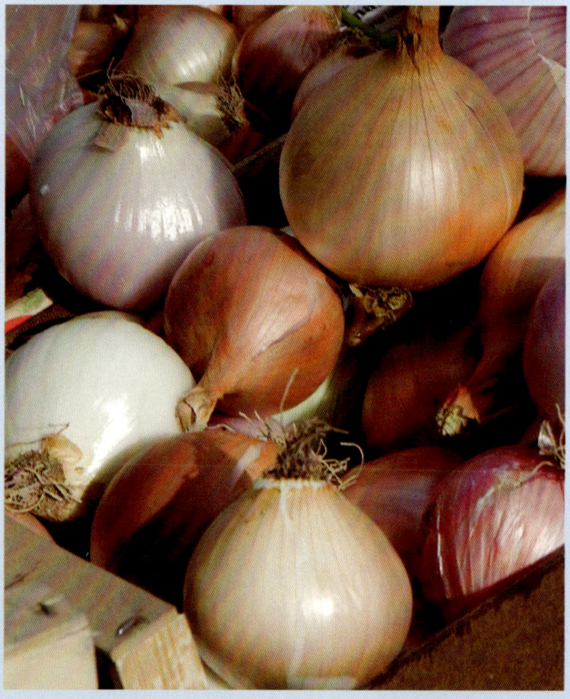

PREPARATION:

Soak the prunes in hot water for a couple of hours. Meanwhile, clean the rabbit and when dry, cut it into pieces and dip in flour. In a casserole pot, place the pork lard, a splash of oil and fry the streaky bacon. Immediately add the cut onions and leave it until it is browned. At this point, remove the onion and the streaky bacon from the pot and, with the remaining oil, fry the pieces of previously floured rabbit. Once fried, pour on a splash of wine and let it evaporate. Add salt and pepper generously and pour on a little stock. Cover it and leave on a low flame for a long hour. After this time, add the previously browned onions and streaky bacon and accompany it with the prunes that you have soaked two hours before. Let it cook for another half hour. If you see that the sauce thickens too much, you can add more stock. After half an hour, remove the pieces of rabbit, the streaky bacon, the prunes and the onion from the pot; put it all aside close to the stove, where it will keep hot. In the pot, all that will remain now is the sauce stuck after having roasted the meat; unstick it with a couple of spoonfuls of wine.

Meanwhile, in a pot, heat the sugar with half a spoonful of water, and when it is at the point of being caramel, add the vinegar and stir until the sugar has all dissolved. Now is the time to add it to the rabbit sauce, mixing it all and pouring it on top of the rabbit now placed on a plate, accompanied by the prunes and onion.

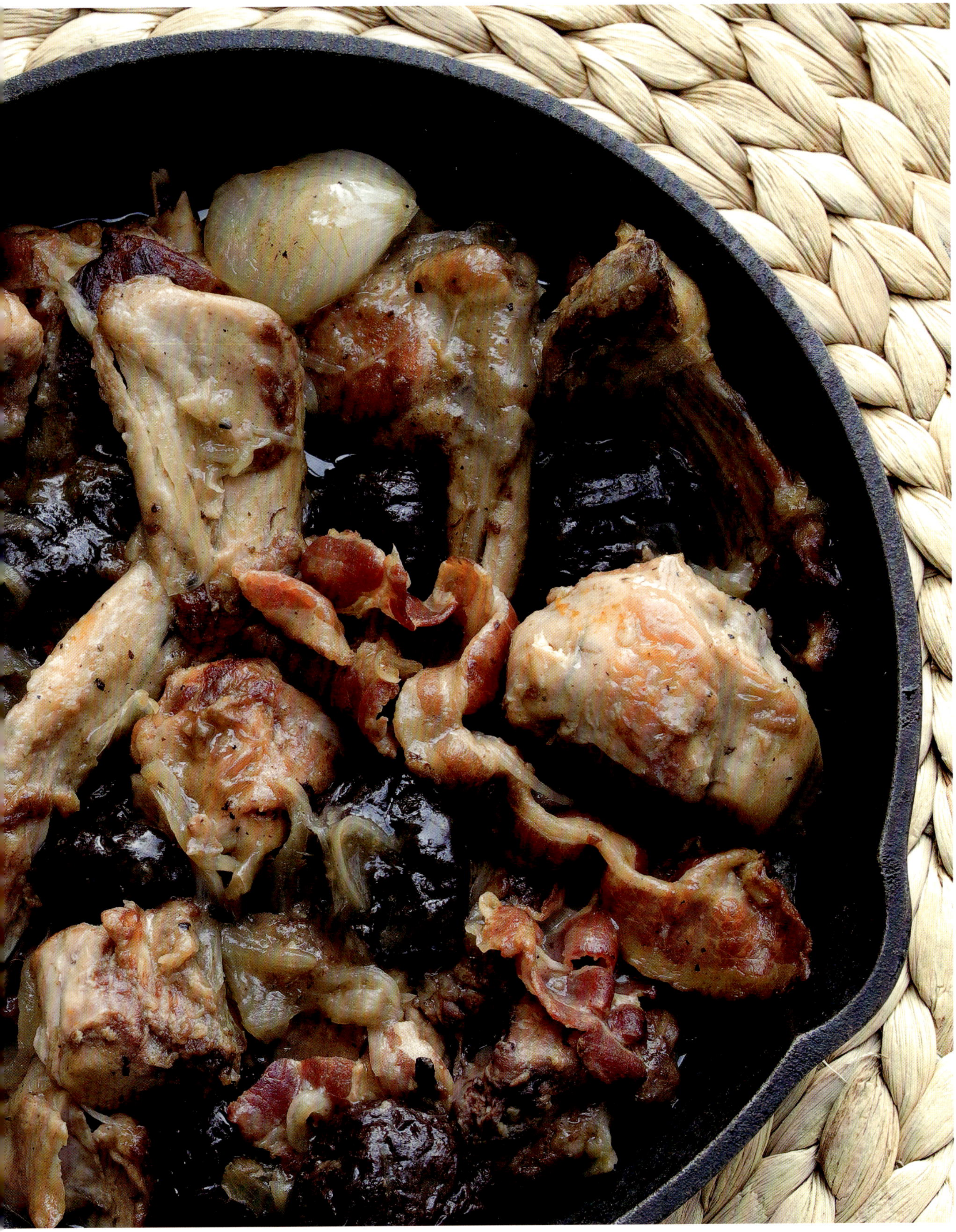

Adafina, the Jewish soup

INGREDIENTS FOR 4 PEOPLE:

5 chicken breasts, or beef
5 large onions
4 patatoes
4 eggs
2 whole garlic heads
½ kg hard wheat grain
300 g cooked dry beans
1 spoonful of cinnamon
2 or 3 spoonfuls of honey
2 spoonfuls of paprika
Salt

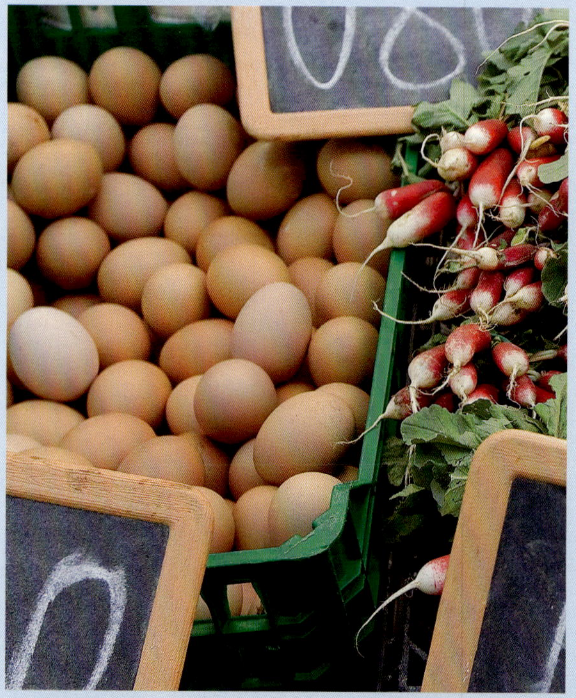

PREPARATION:

Chop up the onion and fry lightly in a covered saucepan, on a low flame, so that it lets out all the water very slowly. When you see that the onion is almost transparent, add the paprika. Stir continuously so that the paprika does not burn, let it cook for a couple of minutes and turn off the stove.

Separately, in a saucepan with water and lots of onion skins, boil the eggs. When you peel them, the white will have turned brown. Put them to one side.

Then, in a pot that fits in the oven, place the previously cut and boiled chicken, potatoes cut into large pieces, garlic, wheat and eggs. Cover it all with hot water and season it with the cinnamon and honey. Salt it all and leave it to cook covered, on a low flame. After about 15 minutes, add the cooked beans and lightly fried onion. It is very important not to stir the pot, so that all the ingredients are settled; some gentle movement will be enough. After 15 more minutes, you can place the pot in the pre-heated oven and leave it to cook for a few hours at a low temperature. Traditionally it is left to cook all night. If you see that it may be dry, you can add a little water. Serve hot. If it is eaten on the *Sabbath*, it can be accompanied with the typical plaited bread, the *challah*. Also, the *adafina* that is left over will be much richer the more it is cooked, since on reheating it, the flavours become more intense and concentrated.

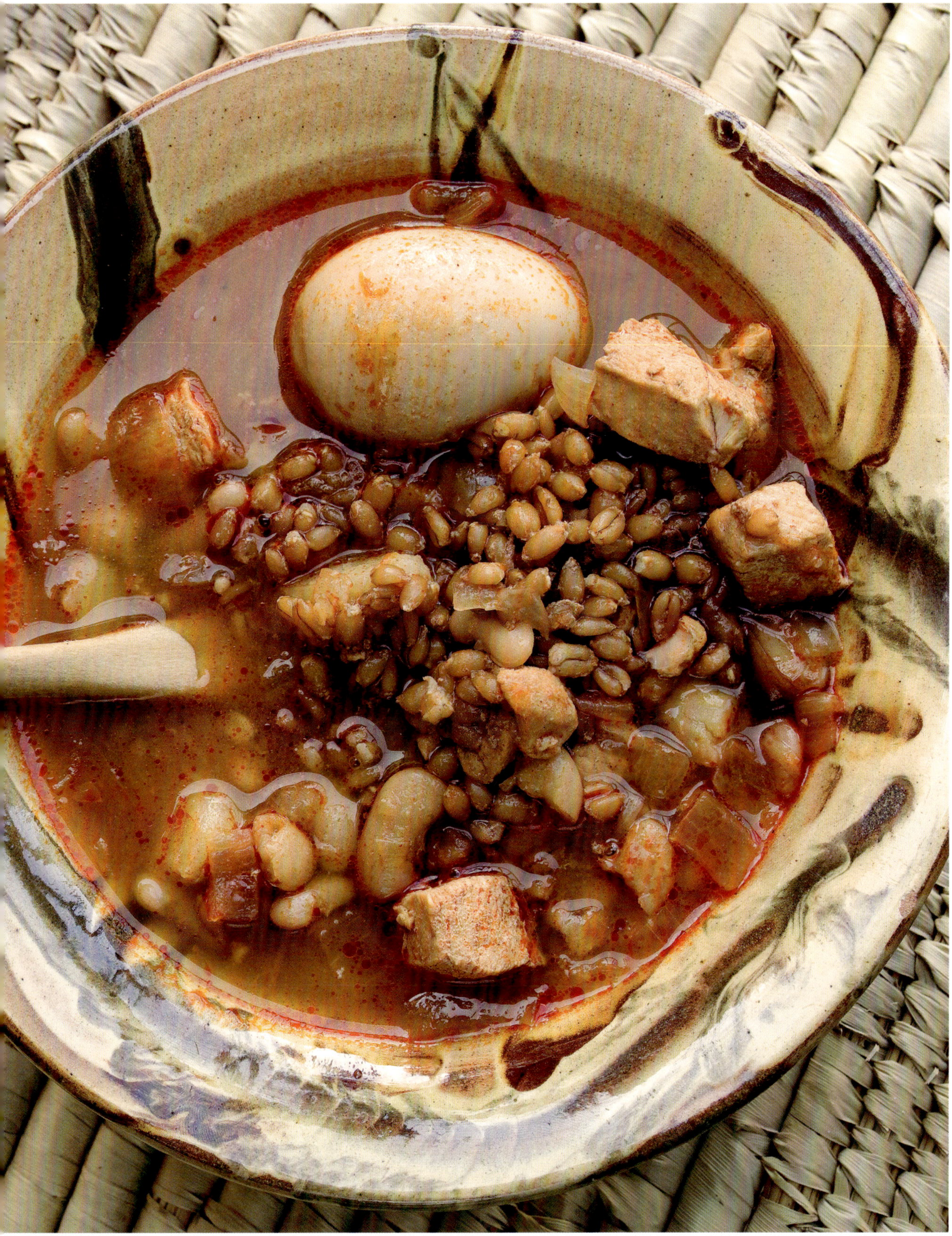

Saracen wheat porridge with reduction of *ratafia*, a volcanic dish

INGREDIENTS:

250 g of Saracen wheat flour
½ l of water
A splash of olive oil
A sprinkling of salt

TO DECORATE THE DISH:

1 dl of Russet *ratafia*
2 strawberries
A handful of pine nuts
Corinthian raisins
Pistachios
1 spoonful of sugar

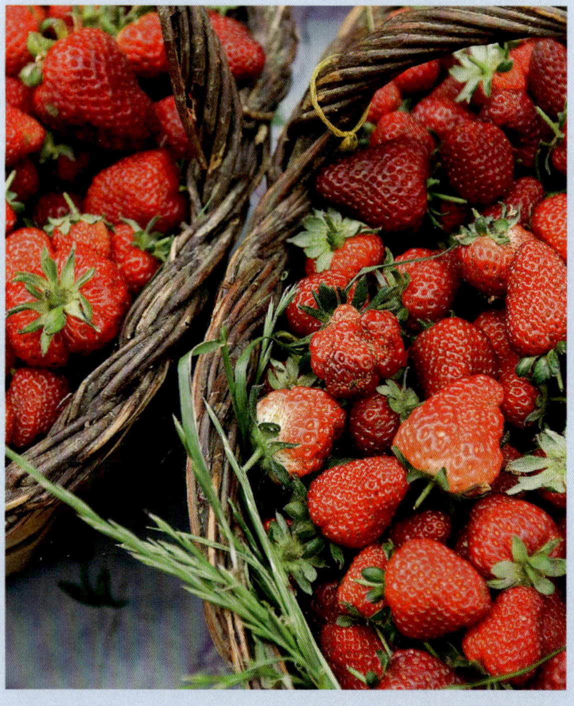

PREPARATION:

Boil the water and salt in a pot. When it starts to boil, pour in the Saracen wheat flour and wait until the water covers it. Just before it overflows, lower the flame and stick a wooden spoon in the middle to make a hole in the "ball" of flour. Cover the pot and leave it to steam cook for 20 minutes. With the pot off the stove, take out a little more than half of the water and work the mass with a fork until it is more or less consistent. When you have achieved a uniform mass, place it in a glass mould. Keep it in the fridge for 24 hours until it takes on body. Cut the mass into pieces of half a centimetre and put to one side. In a frying pan with little oil but very hot, fry the porridge slices until they brown, first on one side and then the other. When you remove them from the frying pan, place them on absorbent paper, and then on the plate. Decorate the plate with a little laminated strawberry, and chopped pistachios, pine nuts, Corinthian raisins, icing sugar and a strand of reduction of *ratafia*.

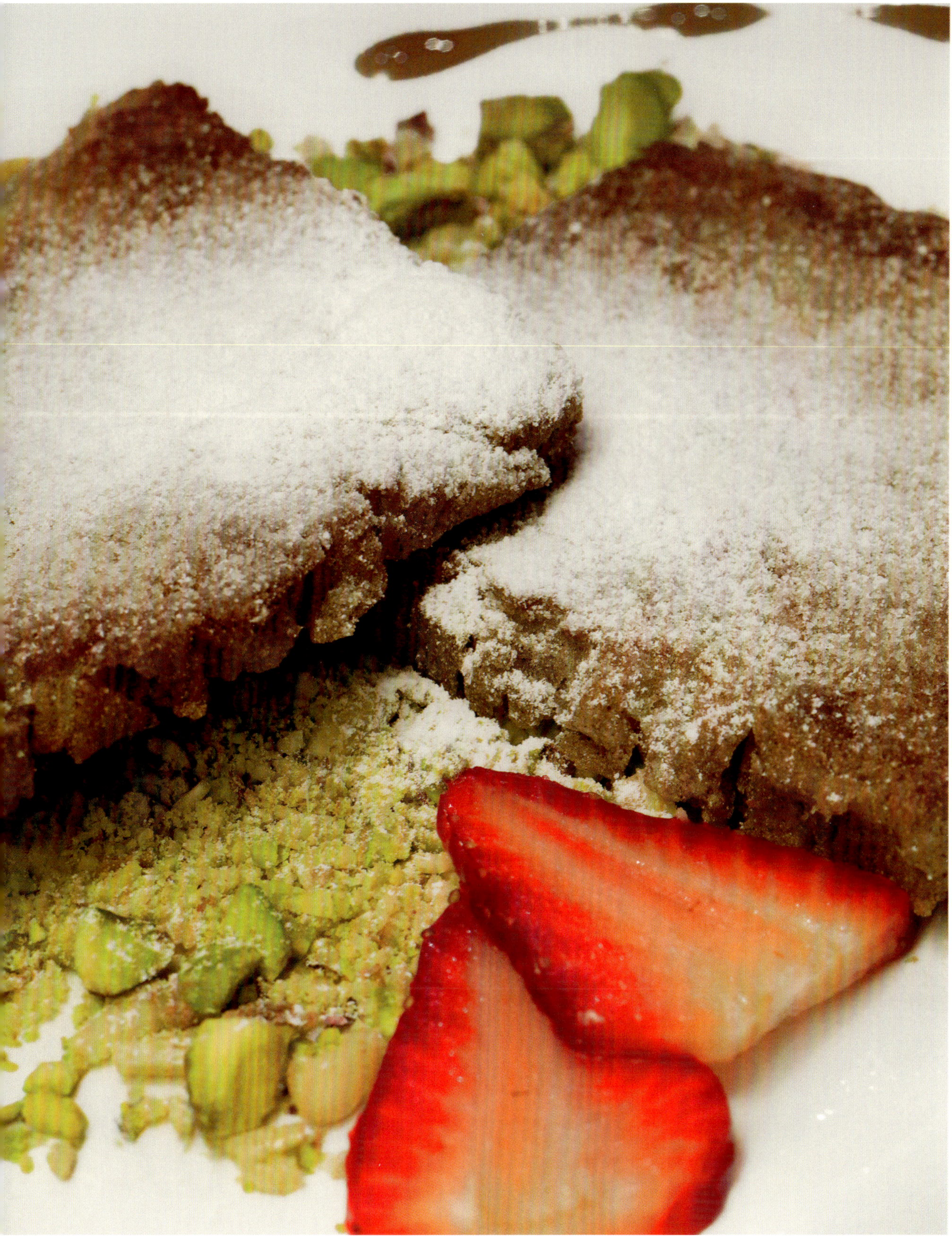

Besalú

Text
© Martí Gironell

Photography
© Jordi Puig
© Vador Minobis, pages 73, 76, 98(3), 99, 115

Graphic design
Joan Colomer

Layout and maps
Vador Minobis

Translation
Steve Cedar

Printed by
Tallers gràfics Soler

Acknowledgements
Besalú Town Council
Girona Provincial Council
Valvi Supermarkets
Besalú Tourist Office
El Rebost de Besalú
Faustina de Solà-Morales Dou
Miniatures Museum of Besalú

Registration number
B-24547-2010

ISBN
978-84-8478-444-9

TRIANGLE POSTALS, SL
Sant Lluís
Menorca
Tel. +34 971 15 04 51
Fax +34 971 15 18 36
www.triangle.cat